Computers in Mathematics Teaching

Spreadsheets: Exploring their Potential in Secondary Mathematics

David Green, Peter Armstrong
and Richard Bridges

	A	B	C	D	E	F
1	t years	p=population				
2	0.0	1000		dt=	0.1	years
3	0.1	1150		Init p=	1000	members
4	0.2	1319		Init t=	0	years
5	0.3	1508		b=	0.0002	members/year
6	0.4	1719		d=	0.1	members/year
7	0.5	1953		M=	9000	members
8	0.6	2208				
36	3.4	8333				

The Mathematical Association

© The Mathematical Association 1993

Published by

The Mathematical Association

259 London Road, Leicester LE2 3BE

England.

ISBN 0 906588 29 4

Bona fide owners of this book are granted permission

to photocopy any of the Worksheets in Chapter 4.

Copyright is reserved.

Printing by Audio Visual Services
Loughborough University of Technology

(Tel. 0509-222190).

Computers in Mathematics Teaching Series

Spreadsheets: Exploring their Potential in Secondary Mathematics

David Green, Peter Armstrong
Loughborough University of Technology

and

Richard Bridges
King Edward's School, Birmingham

The Mathematical Association

Computers in Mathematics Teaching Series
There are three books in this series, which are the product of work carried out during 1990-1993 by the *Microcomputers in Secondary Mathematics* sub-committee of the Mathematical Association's *Teaching Committee* under the chairmanship of David Green.

The other two books in the series are:

- *Numerator in the Mathematics Classroom*

- *Graphic Calculators in the Mathematics Classroom*

The Writing Team for this book
The material in this book was written by Richard Bridges, Peter Armstrong and David Green. Several worksheets were contributed by John Higgo, and much valuable advice and assistance was provided by Alun Green and Doug French.

Others who contributed significantly at meetings or by correspondence were:
Peter Akister, Peter Butt, R E Burke, Allan Carrott, Noel Dornan, Tandy Murphy, Paul Marshall, Malcolm Petts, Mark Twells and Tom Walsh.

Preparation for publication
The book was prepared for publication at Loughborough University of Technology with the support of the Department of Mathematical Sciences, for which the authors and the Mathematical Association are grateful.

Computer Discs and Worksheet Packs
The computer discs of prepared spreadsheets and the loose-leaf worksheet packs which may be purchased to accompany this book (see page vi) were prepared by Peter Armstrong, Richard Bridges, Alun Green and David Green.

Invitation to comment
Comments, criticisms, corrections and any other feedback relating to the spreadsheet discs, the worksheets or any part of this book are most welcome.
Please send your comments to:

Richard Bridges, King Edward's School, Birmingham, B15 2UA.

CONTENTS

Notes on Support Materials — vi

Foreword — vii

Chapter 1 What is a Spreadsheet? — 1

Chapter 2 Spreadsheets in Mathematics Teaching — 11
    2.1 Information Technology and Mathematics
    2.2 Spreadsheets and Mathematics
    2.3 Fundamental Spreadsheet Concepts and Terminology
    2.4 More Advanced Spreadsheet Features
    2.5 Availability of Spreadsheets
    2.6 Spreadsheets versus Programming Languages
    2.7 Adapting Mathematics for Spreadsheets
    2.8 Spreadsheet Reference Material

Chapter 3 Example Spreadsheets — 29
    3.1 Domestic Arithmetic
    3.2 Properties of Numbers
    3.3 Sequences and Number Patterns
    3.4 Geometrical Transformations and Matrices
    3.5 Solution of Equations
    3.6 Function Plotting
    3.7 Numerical Methods
    3.8 Series Expansions and Limits
    3.9 Data Handling and Statistics

Chapter 4 Example Worksheets — 61
    4.1 Worksheet lists
    4.2 Lower Secondary
    4.3 Upper Secondary
    4.4 Sixth Form/College

Chapter 5 Iteration — 111
    5.1 Using Fill Down
    5.2 Using the Calculation Iteration option
    5.3 Using IF
    5.4 Using relational operators
    5.5 Using Goal Seek
    5.6 Using Solver

Chapter 6 Dynamic Modelling and Simulation — 135

Indexes – Spreadsheet Terms, Mathematical Topics, Worksheets — 152

SUPPORT MATERIALS

Computer Discs

Many of the spreadsheets described in Chapters 3 to 5 have been prepared on disc for the following formats:

Excel – for PC compatible including RM Nimbus (version 2.1 onwards)
Excel – for Apple Macintosh (version 2 onwards)
Eureka! – for Acorn Archimedes (version 1 onwards)

N.B. Not all facilities are supported by earlier versions of the software.

Copies are available priced £2.00 (address below).

Please supply full details of your computer and of the spreadsheet software and version which you are using. It may be helpful to send a ready-formatted disc.

Worksheet Packs

The worksheets described in Chapter 4 are being made available in loose-leaf form for the following systems:

Excel
Eureka!

If the purchaser also supplies a formatted disc an electronic version (to the best of our ability!) will be supplied at no extra charge, in Microsoft Word and ASCII formats (please supply details of computer).

Worksheet packs are available priced £3.50 (address below).

Address

> Dr David Green
> Department of Mathematical Sciences
> Loughborough University of Technology
> Loughborough
> LE11 3TU

Spreadsheet Disc – £2.00
Worksheet Pack – £3.50
Please make cheques payable to D. R. Green.

Foreword

The purpose of this book is to collate and disseminate ideas about uses of spreadsheet software in the mathematics curriculum. These ideas have resulted from meetings of the *Microcomputers in Secondary Mathematics* sub-committee of the Mathematical Association's *Teaching Committee*, and also from correspondence and discussions with other interested teachers.

Although the authors have in the main referred to the *Excel* spreadsheet, and many of the Worksheets in Chapter 4 are designed with that particular package in mind, much of the material and most of the ideas will be easily translated to other packages such as *Eureka!*.

Spreadsheets already play an important and valuable role in many mathematics classrooms. However, much current use reflects the origins of the software and many spreadsheets look like the traditional data tables of commercial enterprise, with cell entries such as "costs", "price", "premium", "goods", "units" and "interest rate". Others bear similarities to those one would have expected to find in school science laboratory books over the last few decades. Where classroom spreadsheets do manage to hide their ancestry and emphasise *mathematics* rather than *commercial arithmetic* they often remain basically number grids, which in many other classrooms are the subject of pencil and paper exercises. Undoubtedly, the spreadsheet enables such grids to be processed more rapidly and relieves the tedium of arithmetic and hand-produced recording, so that investigations and conjectural approaches to learning are enhanced. But it could be argued that it does not extend the boundaries of the classroom as far as it might. The graphics facilities of spreadsheets are often limited in classrooms to the representation of mathematical functions on x–y axes or numerical data on bar charts, pie charts and scatter diagrams. These are fairly familiar graphical techniques, which were common in schools before spreadsheets were thought of as a classroom resource.

It must be emphasised that all of the modes of use described in the previous paragraph have much to recommend them, and their use should be widespread and prominent. They undoubtedly enhance learning and encourage valuable and enriching applications of spreadsheets to mathematics. Nevertheless, the aim of this publication is to provide examples and suggestions to encourage the reader to explore the potential of the spreadsheet in the mathematics classroom much further and in a manner which moves the spreadsheet away from its commercial origins. It is our hope that the examples will be the source of new classroom practice rather than an improvement on activities which have long been tried and tested.

The essence of the examples described in this book is that they utilise the *dynamics* of spreadsheets to the full. Examples are provided of spreadsheets which use facilities such as user macros, add-in macros, advanced functions and graphics. These are applied to iteration, optimisation, simulation and modelling and to explore mathematical theory.

This does not mean that the learner's 'entry fee' to spreadsheets is increased prohibitively, for two main reasons. First, quite complex spreadsheets supplied by the teacher may be very simple to use (and a disc with many of those described in this book is available). Second, many of the Examples described employ only simple spreadsheet techniques and functions. Where advanced techniques *are* used, the customising facilities of the software are employed to hide difficult aspects or to present them gently to the learner. At the same time, the Examples and Worksheets are designed to encourage the learner to develop expertise in spreadsheet usage and to lead to awareness of the possibilities of the extensive range of facilities which a spreadsheet provides. Indeed, the learner may be encouraged to look upon a spreadsheet as a fourth generation programming language, which may be easier to learn and to use than more traditional languages. The possibilities of the spreadsheet are many and varied. The reader will find a variety of uses (and styles of use) in the different chapters of this book, which is a direct reflection of the wide variety of possible applications of spreadsheets in mathematical education.

There are several good *introductory* books on spreadsheets available to teachers but a shortage of books which take things a stage further. The main purpose of this book is to take such forward, exploratory steps. If spreadsheets are applied to mathematical topics, – both traditional and novel – in ways such as those described in this book, then the mathematics curriculum could develop in diverse, exciting and significant directions.

Chapter 1 has been included to provide a very short introduction to spreadsheets, which, combined with some practical work on a computer, should provide an adequate basis for profitably studying and using the rest of the book. However, this book is primarily targeted at teachers of mathematics who already have some basic knowledge of and experience with spreadsheets.

Chapter 2 begins with some thoughts on the reasons for using Information Technology generally in the teaching of mathematics. There follows an introduction to spreadsheet software in particular and its relevance to various topics in mathematics, after which is a more detailed explanation of the concepts and terminology common to all spreadsheets, and a brief discussion of some available software (at the time of writing). For those already familiar with the idea of using a programming language such as BASIC, Pascal or Logo to solve mathematical problems a comparison is made between that and the spreadsheet approach. The next section covers some of the common techniques used in framing a problem for spreadsheet solution. The chapter ends with notes and references on published material on using spreadsheets.

Chapter 3 describes Example Spreadsheets which have been set up to illustrate a range of different mathematical topics. These are available on disc – details on the next page. In many cases the description of the sheets should be sufficiently detailed to allow them to be re-created by the teacher from the information given.

Chapter 4 contains a large number of Example Worksheets for the secondary age range. They are nominally divided into three age bands: Lower secondary, Upper secondary, Sixth Form/College but these are only a rough guide, reflecting the ages of pupils on which they have be tried successfully rather than an indication of exclusivity.

Chapter 5 provides an in-depth look at using *Excel* to solve iteration problems, utilising a number of important spreadsheet techniques, including the built-in optimisation facilities.

Chapter 6 deals with more advanced techniques for dynamic modelling and simulation.

The Index at the back includes references to the mathematical topics covered by the Worksheets, as well as the key words in the book.

There is no substitute for practical experience, and the reader is urged to use this material in conjunction with a spreadsheet program.

Peter Armstrong
Richard Bridges
David Green.

CHAPTER 1

What is a Spreadsheet?

It may be a surprise to computer buffs that many teachers and students still ask, "What is a Spreadsheet?". Most questioners, of course, do have a vague idea that a spreadsheet is some sort of computer software but they are not sure what that software looks like or what it does. The easiest way to answer their question is to adopt the 'hands-on' approach and allow the questioner to **use** a spreadsheet. They will soon realise that the idea of a spreadsheet is not new. Like the 'electronic blackboard' of the 1980's it is an established idea transferred to a computer.

About 30 years ago, before computers were widely available in the worlds of commerce and industry, spreadsheets (although these were not commonly referred to by that name) could be found in many offices. They had often been introduced in an attempt to improve efficiency and to modernise production processes and management techniques. These spreadsheets consisted of grids (i.e. rows and columns) drawn on sheets specially coated to allow users to write and erase information with special pens. They were large and they might occupy a complete desk top, or possibly a complete wall of a reasonably sized office. The numbers of rows and columns were limited by wall space and because the *cells*, into which these rows and columns divided the spreadsheet, needed to be big enough for the user to write information legibly. Each week (or at other convenient intervals) the user would receive information from departments, offices and shop-floors giving production figures, costs etc. This information would be written into appropriate cells of the spreadsheet. A formula book would then be consulted and other numbers would be calculated based on the information in the spreadsheet. These numbers would be written in other cells as indicated by the formula book. The results from designated cells would be collated and included in reports sent to management. The next week the entries in the cells would be erased (or, if data were to be stored as records, a new sheet would be used) and the whole process would be repeated. One may well imagine how limited, tedious, error prone and time consuming the procedure was in practice.

Today, of course, computers are widely available in commerce and industry and they may be used to produce and display the rows, columns and cells of a spreadsheet.[1] This means that the use of a spreadsheet is no longer as limited, tedious and time consuming as it once was. Although a computer screen can only display a limited number of cells at one time the capability of *scrolling* gives rapid access to the cells of a spreadsheet consisting of hundreds of columns and thousands of rows (e.g. the Microsoft *Excel* spreadsheet can have up to 256 columns and 16384 rows). Using a keyboard and a mouse, data and formulae may be entered into cells quickly and, usually, quite easily. The computer can perform the necessary calculations with considerable speed. Hence, the spreadsheet has become a far more useful and viable commercial tool.

Fortunately the properties which the computer has brought to the spreadsheet also make it an attractive resource for schools and in particular for the mathematics classroom. A number of spreadsheets have been designed specifically for school use (e.g. *Grasshopper*, *Spread* and *PSS – A Primary Spreadsheet*). These are available at low cost but they are sometimes criticised for behaving quite differently from commercial spreadsheets. Some critics refer to them as pseudo-spreadsheets. Another criticism is that some spreadsheets designed specifically for classrooms are more difficult to use than some commercial spreadsheets. However, this should not be accepted as a generally valid criticism, since commercial spreadsheets vary enormously and some are easier to use than others. Be that as it may, it is certainly true that commercial spreadsheets such as Microsoft *Excel*, which are designed to take advantage of the intuition of users, are quite easy to use and would be most suitable for classroom use, as long as pupils were not expected to become skilful in using all their wonderful and inviting facilities.

Fortunately many temptations may be hidden from users (i.e. pupils), since the teacher should be able to customise most commercial spreadsheets fairly easily. Thus the initial 'entry fee' in terms of learning to use a spreadsheet can become very small. Other facilities available on a given spreadsheet may then be introduced to, or used, by a class of mathematics students in stages. It is usually quite easy for the teacher to *customise* a commercial spreadsheet, before the pupils use it, so that cell sizes (i.e. column widths and row heights), cell reference style, number format (e.g. decimal places), fonts (type, size, style), text alignment etc. are pre-set in a manner suitable for the age and ability of the class and the activity. Also, menus can sometimes be altered and facilities can be

---

[1] A note concerning nomenclature is worth making here. The word spreadsheet is commonly used as the name for the *software package* **and** for the *grid of cells*. Some manuals differentiate the two: for example Microsoft use the term *worksheet* for *Excel*'s grid. This would be good except that in common educational usage *worksheet* has another well-known meaning and this could lead to confusion! Here we shall use the term spreadsheet for both the software package and for the grid.

renamed, re-ordered or disabled and hidden.

A spreadsheet may be used like a simple calculator, a scientific calculator, a programmable calculator, a graphic calculator, a database, a computer assisted learning device (e.g. by using *macros*) or a modelling/simulation/statistical package if the teacher judiciously customises its facilities.

Because facilities may be selected and introduced in stages it is possible to use commercial spreadsheets at most age ranges in schools. However, despite its ancestry, it is perhaps not a good idea to introduce spreadsheets to school classrooms through commercial and management examples, although these abound in user's guides and manuals and, hence may be very tempting. The concepts and processes involved in such applications may be appealing to adults but they are unlikely to be familiar to school children or to be very motivating. More importantly they do not often illustrate the power of a spreadsheet, unless they are extremely sophisticated commercial applications. Fortunately, many other fields furnish more suitable vehicles with which to introduce spreadsheets.

Fig. 1 shows an example of a typical customised spreadsheet as it would appear on a user's computer screen. The example, which uses commercial software, has been customised to present larger cells than normal, to use bold and centrally aligned text and to suppress some of the spreadsheet facilities, so that it would be suitable for classroom use. It is common practice to use headings to label columns and rows, so these have not been suppressed, although it would be easy to do so.

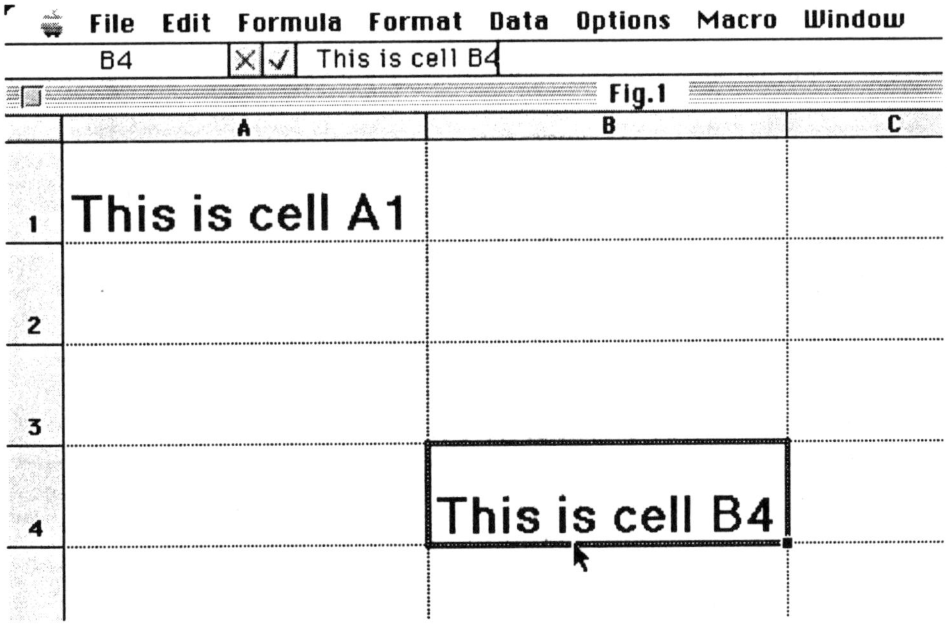

Figure 1

In Fig. 1 the cell in the fourth row and second column is referenced as B4.[2] This cell has been *highlighted*, as indicated by its border and the fact that the reference B4 appears in the *reference box* (immediately below **File**). When a cell is *highlighted* it is called the *active* cell. Notice that a piece of text (i.e. 'This is cell B4') has been entered into B4. This entry is shown in the *formula bar* (immediately to the right of the *enter box* which contains the *tick* symbol ✔).

An alternative style of referencing cells is shown in Fig. 2, where the active (highlighted) cell is referenced as R4C2. Some spreadsheets allow the user to choose the reference style preferred.

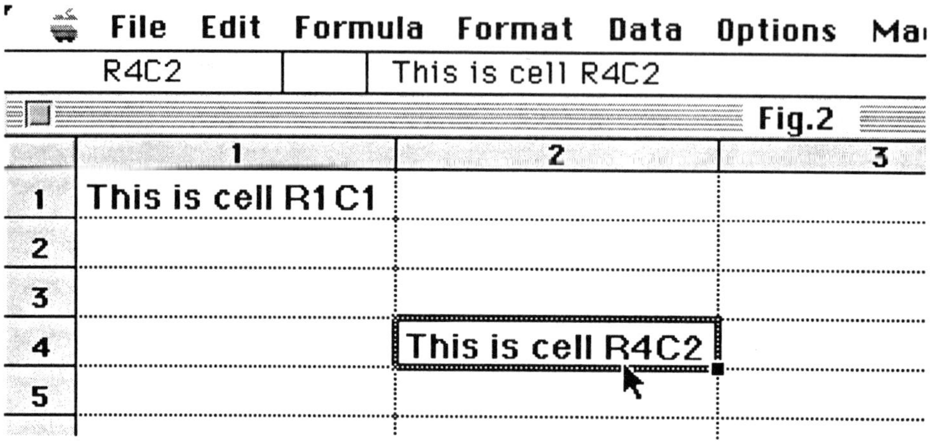

Figure 2

If a cell is the active cell then a user may choose to enter into it (i) *a constant value* or (ii) *a formula*. A constant value may be a number (including a date and/or time) or some text. A formula calculates a new value from values already entered into other cells. The manner in which active cells are selected varies according to the hardware and software but the information is usually entered by using the computer keyboard or a mouse. Fortunately these processes are quite easy to learn and master, especially if the spreadsheet uses an intuitive entry style.[3]

At an early stage children should quickly master the techniques of selecting an active cell

---

[2] In *Excel* column headings are either labelled using letters of the English alphabet supplemented by Roman numerals (e.g. *Excel* uses the column labels A, B, ..., Z; AA, AB, ...; ...., IV) or by counting numbers (e.g. 1, 2, ..., 256). Rows are almost always identified by counting numbers (e.g. 1, 2, ..., 16384).

[3] Certain spreadsheets require the user to "tell the computer" if the cell entry is to be a number, a piece of text or a formula. These spreadsheets include some designed for commerce and some designed for classrooms. This may cause difficulties for the novice user, especially in a school classroom. Fortunately other spreadsheets (such as *Excel*) take a more intuitive approach so that numbers are recognised as numbers, text as text and, if an entry begins with an "=" sign, a formula is recognised as a formula.

and entering either text or a number. If they use a mouse (or arrow keys) this may not even involve cell references, which they could discover and explore later. This facility may assist pupils in the National Curriculum Attainment Target 5: Handling Data, for example, to progress from Level 2a (where the example suggests they could "*collect data on those children who walk to school and those who travel by bus or car*" and "*illustrate with a block graph and draw simple conclusions*") to Level 3b (which has a statement of attainment "*construct and interpret statistical diagrams*"). If, at Level 2, the pupils have designed a data collection sheet and have constructed a block graph (i.e. a pictogram using a square for each pupil) using pencil and paper, it should not then be too difficult for them to design and construct the following spreadsheet on a computer (see Fig. 3). Only text and number entries are involved (no formulae).

	A	B	C
1	Transport	Pupils	
2	Car	2	
3	Bus	4	
4	Taxi	3	
5	Walk	5	

Figure 3

The pupils may then check their own graphs with those produced by a spreadsheet. In spreadsheets such as *Excel* graphs may be produced quite easily and embedded in the spreadsheet (see Fig. 4). These graphs can easily be resized and repositioned using the mouse.

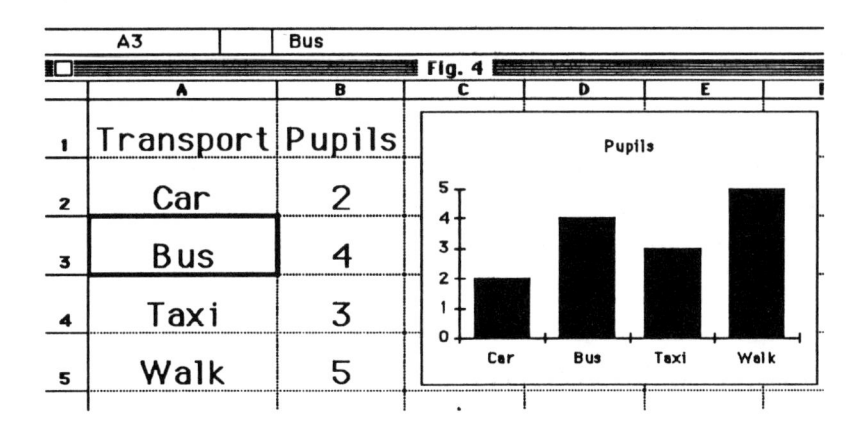

Figure 4

It will be seen that the graph of Fig. 4 is compatible with the programme of study of AT5 Level 3b which suggests pupil activity *which involves constructing and interpreting bar charts and graphs (pictograms) where the symbol represents a group of units*.

The power of a spreadsheet, of course, lies in its ability to use a formula in a cell which calculates a new value from values already entered into other cells. This facility may be introduced at a fairly early age (perhaps by using the spreadsheet as simple calculator with addition, subtraction, multiplication and division). In the example below (see Fig. 5) the numbers 74 and 25 are entered into cells B1 and B2 respectively. Then the formula '=B1-B2' is entered into cell B3. Thus, the result '49' is shown in B3. (Note: text has been entered into the cells of column A to describe the subtraction but this is not necessary and it may be preferable not to do this until pupils have some understanding of algebra).

	A	B
1	a =	74
2	b =	25
3	a – b =	49

Figure 5

The powerful facilities of *relative* cell references and *fill-down* and *fill-right* are extremely useful and, with care, these might be introduced to pupils soon after they have mastered the procedures of entering a number into a cell and a formula into a cell. For example, to construct a multiplication table pupils might enter the number 7 in cell A1 and the number 1 in cell B1. Following this the formula '=A1*B1' could be entered in cell C1 (giving 7 × 1 = 7) and then the formula '=B1+1' could be entered into cell B2. The pupils could then highlight the range of cells from A1 through A12 so that the fill-down facility could be used to copy the contents of A1 (i.e. the number 7) into the other highlighted cells of column A. The sequence 1, 2, 3,......, 12 may now be entered in column B by highlighting the range of cells from B2 through to B12 and filling down. The multiplication table would then be completed by highlighting the range of cells from C1 through C12 and filling down (see Fig.6). Of course, there are other ways of performing the same task, which might be chosen to meet the pupils' skills and abilities.

	C6		=A6*B6

	A	B	C
1	7	1	7
2	7	2	14
3	7	3	21
4	7	4	28
5	7	5	35
6	7	6	42
7	7	7	49
8	7	8	56
9	7	9	63
10	7	10	70
11	7	11	77
12	7	12	84
13			

Figure 6

In this way the idea of a *relative* reference may be introduced, especially if the spreadsheet allows formulae to be displayed as text. Fig. 7 is equivalent to Fig. 6 but it shows the formulae rather than the numerical entries and results.

	C5		=A5*B5

	A	B	C
1	7	1	=A1*B1
2	7	=B1+1	=A2*B2
3	7	=B2+1	=A3*B3
4	7	=B3+1	=A4*B4
5	7	=B4+1	=A5*B5
6	7	=B5+1	=A6*B6
7	7	=B6+1	=A7*B7
8	7	=B7+1	=A8*B8
9	7	=B8+1	=A9*B9
10	7	=B9+1	=A10*B10
11	7	=B10+1	=A11*B11
12	7	=B11+1	=A12*B12
13			

Figure 7

At early ages the idea of *absolute* cell reference is, perhaps best avoided, but it may be introduced later by taking another example from the National Curriculum (AT3 Algebra, Level 8b). This refers to the formula $v = u + at$ which might be discussed in terms of a stone falling a short distance under gravity without air resistance. In this case v and t may be taken as dependent and independent variables respectively and u and a as constants. A spreadsheet may then be useful to graph the change of velocity with time (see Fig. 8)

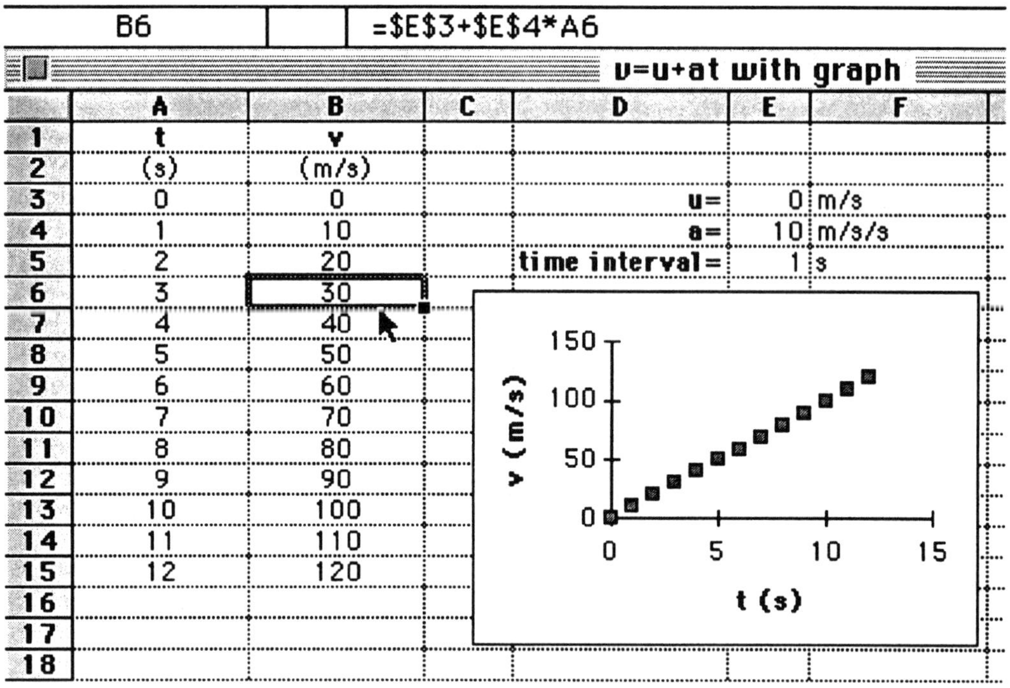

Figure 8

Using Fig. 8 the difference between a *relative reference* and an *absolute reference* may be explained. In Fig. 8 the values in the column of cells from A3 down to A15 (which contain the changing values of the variable *t*) were entered as follows. Firstly, the number 0 was entered into cell A3. The formula '=A3+$E$5' was then entered into cell A4. Using *fill-down* the contents of cell A4 were then copied into the cells A5 to A15.

The variable *v* was entered into cells B3 to B15 as follows. The formula '=$E$3+$E$4*A3' was entered into cell B3. Using *fill-down* the contents of cell B3 were then copied into the cells B4 to B15.

Notice, however, that in Fig. 8 the active cell B6 contains the number 30 and the formula bar indicates that this is obtained from the formula '$E$3+$E$4*A6'.

	A	B	C	D	E	F
1	t	v				
2	(s)	(m/s)				
3	0	=$E$3+$E$4*A3		u =	0	m/s
4	=A3+$E$5	=$E$3+$E$4*A4		a =	10	m/s/s
5	=A4+$E$5	=$E$3+$E$4*A5		time interval=	1	s
6	=A5+$E$5	=$E$3+$E$4*A6				
7	=A6+$E$5	=$E$3+$E$4*A7				
8	=A7+$E$5	=$E$3+$E$4*A8				
9	=A8+$E$5	=$E$3+$E$4*A9				
10	=A9+$E$5	=$E$3+$E$4*A10				
11	=A10+$E$5	=$E$3+$E$4*A11				
12	=A11+$E$5	=$E$3+$E$4*A12				
13	=A12+$E$5	=$E$3+$E$4*A13				
14	=A13+$E$5	=$E$3+$E$4*A14				
15	=A14+$E$5	=$E$3+$E$4*A15				

Figure 9

Now if we look at the formulae which appear in the cells as a result of this *filling-down* (see Fig. 9), we see that cell references which contain $ signs (e.g. **$E$5** and **$E$4**) do not change when copied from one cell to another. These are *absolute* references, which refer to particular cells. However, cell references which do not contain $ signs (e.g. **A3**) do change when copied. These are *relative* references which refer to the relative positions of cells. So, as a result of copying the formula '=$E$3+$E$4*A3' in cell B3 into the column of cells from B4 to B15 by *filling-down*, the first cell reference ($E$3) in the formula copied into each cell does not change, since it refers *absolutely* to the contents (i.e. the magnitude of the initial velocity u m/s) of the cell in column E, row 3. Similarly, '**$E$4**' is an *absolute reference* (the magnitude of the acceleration a m/s/s). However, the last cell reference in the copied formula is relative (it refers to the contents of the cell immediately to the left of the cell into which the formula is entered) so this changes as we move down column A (e.g. it is A3 in cell B3 but A6 in cell B6). This is, of course, what we want since the reference is to changing time t s.

(For further explanation of *relative* and *absolute* referencing see Chapter 2, Section 2.3).

The notion of absolute reference may cause unnecessary complications for a number of pupils. Conveniently, some spreadsheets allow us to dispense with this by *naming* cells. For example, a revised version of the spreadsheet above (i.e. Fig. 8 and Fig. 9) is shown in Fig. 10. Column A has been *named* **t**. Cells E3, E4, E5 and E6 have been named **u, a, time_interval** and **initial_time** respectively. Then the three formulae '=initial_time', '=A3+time_interval' and '=u+a*t' have been entered in cells A3, A4 and B3 respectively. The fill-down facility has then been used to copy formulae into other cells. The resulting spreadsheet would produce the same numerical results as Fig. 8 but the process of *naming* cells may be more intuitive to some pupils and may have more to offer in terms of learning algebra, particularly in the development of the concepts of variables and constants.

	A	B	C	D	E	F
1	t	v				
2	(s)	(m/s)				
3	=initial_time	=u+a*t		u =	0	m/s
4	=A3+time_interval	=u+a*t		a =	10	m/s/s
5	=A4+time_interval	=u+a*t		time interval=	1	s
6	=A5+time_interval	=u+a*t		initial time=	0	s
7	=A6+time_interval	=u+a*t				
8	=A7+time_interval	=u+a*t				
9	=A8+time_interval	=u+a*t				
10	=A9+time_interval	=u+a*t				
11	=A10+time_interval	=u+a*t				
12	=A11+time_interval	=u+a*t				
13	=A12+time_interval	=u+a*t				
14	=A13+time_interval	=u+a*t				
15	=A14+time_interval	=u+a*t				

Figure 10

No matter which cell reference style is used, pupils would be able to change the constants u and a and to ask questions such as "What would happen if the stone was falling on the moon?", since it is a simple matter to change the entries in cells E3 and E4 and to observe the effects in other cells. Used in this way the spreadsheet provides a good modelling tool.

The facilities already discussed might now be used to produce more ambitious spreadsheets especially if they were enhanced by the introduction of other operators (e.g. exponentiation '^' and percentage '%'), Scientific/Mathematical Functions (e.g. SIN(*number*), LOG(*number, base*)), Statistical Functions (e.g. MEDIAN(*number1, number2*....)) and Matrix Functions (e.g. TRANSPOSE(*array*)). These, together with graphics facilities, are but a few of the many riches provided by spreadsheets. They alone should more than satisfy the needs of most mathematics classrooms.

CHAPTER 2

Spreadsheets in Mathematics Teaching

2.1 Information Technology and Mathematics

The role of Information Technology in the mathematics curriculum has been extensively reviewed in the highly recommended *Computers in the Mathematics Curriculum* edited by WJA Mann and David Tall (1992), a report published by the Mathematical Association based on the work of a subcommittee of the Teaching Committee chaired by John Higgo. It is therefore inappropriate to repeat the process here. Some personal comments in addition may still have some value, however.

Information Technology (IT) has been around for over a decade now and a large number of mathematics teachers across the country have built up considerable expertise in some aspects of its use; not least because historically mathematics departments have supplied the majority of teachers of IT. However, there are still many other perfectly competent teachers who for one reason or another have never had occasion to use IT with their classes. Busy timetables leaving little time to learn new skills, busy IT departments with little time to help, inconvenient access to too few computers in some distant room, busy computer room timetables, the lack of departmental computers either in teaching rooms or to take home; these are all circumstances which work against the use of IT by a teacher unfamiliar with it. The authors themselves have to admit that they all too rarely use computer software with their mathematics classes, largely because of the inconvenience of having to take a class out of their normal room and walk them up to a rather distant computer lab, just for a demonstration that may only be worth five minutes of lesson time. Until many more mathematics teaching rooms are equipped with a computer and a display that all can easily see, this situation is unlikely to change.

In spite of these difficulties, IT has a great deal to contribute to the teaching of mathematics, for several reasons. Firstly, a large part of the mathematics we teach, particularly at school, consists of applying algorithms to numbers. Some examples are the solution of simultaneous equations, quadratics, solution of triangles, matrix inversion. As this is exactly what computer programs are designed to do, it seems likely that they might have something to contribute to the teaching of these processes. Using computer software that performs these same processes can de-mystify them in pupils' minds, and separate the technical difficulty of applying them accurately from the business of using them to tackle real problems. It can also enable a pupil to try out a much larger number of examples than would be possible by manual methods, and thus perhaps investigate more general properties of the method. For example, one would not normally set more than one or two problems on the effect of a zero determinant in a transformation matrix, and might only plot one graph as illustration, whereas the example spreadsheet presented later in this book (Chapter 3 page 40) would make it possible for half a dozen examples, all with graphs, to be tried out in the space of a few minutes.

Similarly, the reason for the sign of '$b^2 - 4ac$' being so important to the solution of quadratic equations is much more obvious if a range of examples with accompanying graphs can be investigated, as another of the example spreadsheets allows (see Fig. 1 and also Chapter 3 page 45 for details).

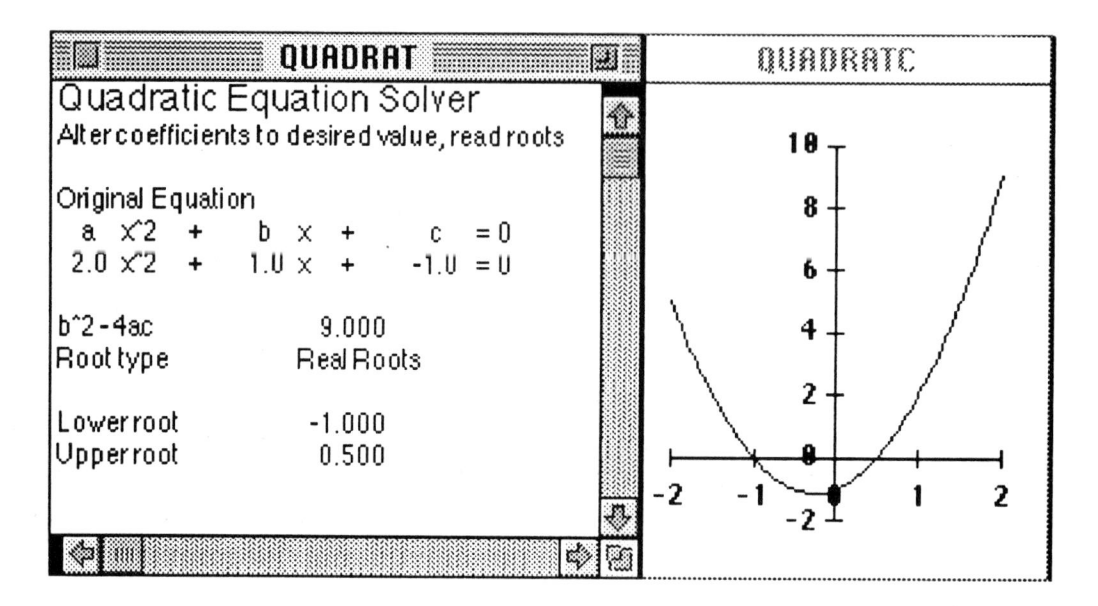

Figure 1

Of course, these points can be made on the blackboard, but with fewer and less accurate sketches. Also, in this situation, the pupil often has to take the teacher's word on trust, whereas a computer may be seen as a more impartial and personal tutor. For this reason pupils may well feel happier about accepting the truth of phenomena which they have observed for themselves on a computer screen, than about accepting statements made by a teacher in a classroom. To take an example from A level, how does one show the divergence of the Binomial expansion of $(1 + x)^n$ for $|x| > 1$ other than by using a computer to evaluate the series, as one of the example spreadsheets does? Further, a computer can not only demonstrate the divergence, but also the more subtle effect of the slowing rate of convergence as x approaches 1, thus motivating the need not just for a convergent series expansion, but an efficient one. Another topic which seems impossible to demonstrate effectively at school level without the use of a computer is the Central Limit Theorem of sampling theory in statistics; only a computer can quickly generate the masses of data needed to be convincing.

One of the important uses of the computer's calculating power in the above examples is to produce a graphical description of the mathematical phenomena being demonstrated. A graph can be far more effective than words, numerical examples or algebraic manipulations in putting across a concept. For example, the pupil who understands the concept of simultaneous solution of equations in terms of the crossing points of graphs is likely to be better equipped to apply the idea to a problem than one who only knows the algebraic procedure. Yet many pupils are so hung up on the technical difficulty of actually drawing graphs that the insight they can give is closed to them. The computer provides a way round this problem.

Of course, it is not being suggested that pupils no longer need to learn any techniques that can also be performed by computer software. At the moment it is essential that they should still do so, if only because current examination syllabuses demand them. In fact the reasons for teaching the techniques are similar to those justifying the continued teaching of arithmetic in primary schools: they are still sometimes needed when a calculator or computer isn't available, they develop general mathematical awareness, and so on. However, we shouldn't forget that the arrival of calculators dictated changes of emphasis in what we teach (largely for the better, we would suggest). Now we have statistical calculators, programmable calculators, graphic calculators and, of course, computers. It isn't going to be long before pupils have calculators that can perform algebraic manipulations, rather than purely numerical ones; such software has existed on computers for some while, and already at least one hand held machine produced by Hewlett Packard has such software as an option. The availability of such machines is increasingly causing the examination boards difficulty in setting appropriate yet fair papers. Undoubtedly this will lead to further rethinking the A-level mathematics syllabuses. (This whole area is the subject of another subcommittee of the MA's Teaching Committee.) More important than matters of syllabuses, regulations and assessment procedures, though, are the tremendous opportunities which such tools open up to deepen the understanding of the real underlying mathematics that we give our pupils. It is to be hoped that future developments of the National Curriculum and examination syllabuses will encourage teachers to take advantage of them.

For all its potential power, it is essential that computer software is properly used; it is not just a matter of sitting pupils in front of computers and leaving them to get on with it. Effective worksheets are needed to take them through the examples that will lead them to the concept the teacher wishes to impart. Often group discussion around a single computer operated by the teacher can be just as effective; the computer then becomes a 'smart glass blackboard' and we are back to an updated version of the familiar 'chalk and talk'! – not that there is anything wrong with that. Certainly some of our most productive lessons have been spent tapping functions into a graph plotting program and discussing the results with the class; often we all learn something new!

2.2 Spreadsheets and Mathematics

The many varieties of computer software relevant to mathematics teaching are reviewed in detail in the Mathematical Association's recent report (Mann and Tall, 1992). Briefly, in the early days of text-only output and crude versions of BASIC the concentration was on dedicated programs to perform numerical manipulations. There is still a place for these, as will be discussed later, but several other types of software are now available. Most have the property of generality; they are able to tackle a range of mathematical tasks rather than a single specific one. Some examples are graph plotters, databases, packages for statistical analysis, modelling and symbolic manipulation (algebra) and, of course, spreadsheets.

The main purpose of spreadsheets is to perform numerical calculations in such a way that the set of steps needed to carry out the calculation is easy to set up, modify, use with different numbers and save for future use. This description deliberately avoids computing terms, but in fact a spreadsheet is an easy way to program a computer to perform arithmetic. The main strengths of a spreadsheet from the point of view of a pupil learning mathematics (or a teacher!) are:

- The computer programming skills needed to set up simple calculations are reduced to a minimum.
- Putting numbers into the sheet ('Input') is done by 'point and press' methods, rather than by separate commands.
- Displaying the numerical results ('Output') is automatic; the results just appear on the screen.
- Formatting the results (neat layout, number of decimal places, text annotation, printed copy) is very easy.
- It is a simple matter to repeat a set of operations (though programming languages are still needed if the number of repetitions is large).
- Graphical display of results is easily added.

Spreadsheets are well suited to any area of mathematics where a fairly complicated procedure needs to be carried out, or where a simple procedure needs to be applied to a large set of numbers, or where a procedure needs to be repeated several times, or where a high degree of accuracy is required, or where an accurately drawn graph aids understanding. They are also very good for finding solutions by 'trial and improvement' methods; the 'goal seeking' feature of some software even allowing this process to be automated. Dedicated programs in a language such as BASIC, Pascal or Logo can also meet these needs, of course, but spreadsheets often simplify the setting up of the program, so allowing the pupil to take a more active part in this stage of the problem solving process. A spreadsheet may also speed up the process of altering input data and displaying the effect on the result of the process. The relative merits of spreadsheets and programming languages will be discussed in more detail later.

Below is a list of some mathematical topics that naturally make one or more of the demands listed on the previous page (an asterisk * indicates a topic covered in this book).

- **Numbers:**

    Decimal expansions of fractions *; Expansions in other bases *; Highest Common Factor *; Prime factors *.

- **Sequences:**

    Triangle numbers; AP's and GP's including graphs; and first and higher differences *; Fibonacci numbers *; Pascal's Triangle numbers *; Power series such as Binomial *, e^x *, sin *, cos *; Divergent series *.

- **Algorithms:**

    Two linear simultaneous equations in two unknowns *; Quadratic formula *; Sine and Cosine formulae.

- **Graphing:**

    Function plotter * (though a dedicated program is usually better).

- **Matrices:**

    Graphing effect of 2×2 transformation matrices *; Determinant manipulations; Solution of 3×3 matrix equations (graph of intersecting planes) *; 4×4 and higher matrix equations; Eigenvectors and eigenvalues.

- **Calculus:**

    Numerical differentiation and demonstration of limit of gradient of chord; Numerical integration by upper and lower step functions; Mid-ordinate rule; Trapezium rule; Simpson's rule *; Differential equations: Euler's method *, Modified Euler method *, Runge-Kutta.

- **Iterative methods:**

    $x=f(x)$ *; Interval Halving *; Secant; False Position *; Newton-Raphson *; Bifurcation of unstable iterative processes; Jacobi method for sets of linear equations *.

- **Data handling and Statistics:**

    Calculating mean, s.d., variance and correlation coefficient from tabulated frequency distribution *; Medians and percentiles *; Frequency distributions and histograms *; Linear regression analysis; Simulating random variables: coins *, dice *, playing cards, Binomial *, Normal *, Poisson, exponential, geometric (though programming languages are necessary for large samples); Contingency tables and Chi-squared calculations.

- **Simulation or Modelling:**

    Population growth *; Predator-prey models*; Queuing; Electrical circuits *, Chaos.

**The Index of Mathematics Topics at the back of the book
indicates where treatment of these topics is to be found.**

2.3 Fundamental Spreadsheet Concepts and Terminology

This section sets out the features which are common to most spreadsheet programs. The examples, where they are specific, refer to Microsoft's spreadsheet *Excel*, as this is probably the most widely used and powerful package available at the moment. For the most part the concepts are relevant to any other spreadsheet. Most of the basic concepts are introduced in the worksheets on sequences in Chapter 4, and it is recommended that anyone unfamiliar with spreadsheets should try working through them, on a computer, as soon as possible. Alternatively, complete beginners could refer to the elementary introduction to spreadsheets in Chapter 1 before proceeding further.

Formulae

A formula may use the contents of another cell by putting a REFERENCE to that cell in the formula in place of a number; typically a reference will denote a cell by its row and column number (or letter: typical *Excel* references are A10, Z5 or R10C1, R5C26). Some functions may need to refer to a RANGE of cells; a very useful one is SUM() which adds up rows or columns. A typical range reference might be A1:A10; other functions which might use ranges are MAX(), AVERAGE(), STDEVP(), to quote *Excel* examples. Usually it is not necessary to type these references into a formula explicitly; it is enough to select the cell being referred to with a mouse or keyboard operated cursor, the required reference being put into the formula automatically.

Most formulae are designed to produce a single number result, which is normally displayed on screen instead of the formula itself. Similarly, when a cell containing a formula is referred to in a formula elsewhere on the sheet, it is the numerical result of the formula which is passed on to the next formula (to full internal accuracy, whatever format has been chosen for display). Formulae which produce more than a single number result may or may not be available, depending on the particular spreadsheet's sophistication; *Excel* does allow ARRAY formulae, which are used primarily for matrix manipulation.

The normal structure for a spreadsheet is that the results of the sheet depend on a few 'input' values entered into cells normally at the top left of the sheet (e.g. the coefficients of a quadratic equation); cells further down or across the sheet use formulae to compute results from these values (e.g. the roots of the quadratic).

Automatic Recalculation

A very attractive feature of spreadsheets is AUTOMATIC RECALCULATION; if an input value is altered all formulae that depend on it are re-calculated and the revised results displayed immediately. Since an input value may be altered merely by selecting that cell (with mouse or keyboard cursor) and typing the new value in (probably followed by the 'Enter' or 'Return' key), results for a whole range of input values may be quickly obtained. This encourages an exploratory approach and 'trial and improvement' methods. However, cells may be so easily altered that it is possible to erase a vital formula and replace it with a number by mistake, ruining the desired structure of the sheet. For this reason it may be possible to PROTECT certain cells against accidental alteration (this has been done on many of the example *Excel* sheets). When the values in the sheet are recalculated because of changed input values, the result obtained may depend on the order in which cells are calculated, though usually the standard order of top left to bottom right suits the layout of the calculation.

Circular referencing

CIRCULAR REFERENCES occur where the result of a formula is fed back into that formula (directly or via other formulae) and can be more problematic, but this sort of iterative process is more usually carried out on a spreadsheet by laying out the stages of the iteration down a column (see Chapter 5).

Copying and pasting

The repetition of formulae down a column is a vital feature of many spreadsheets. It is the standard method of performing an iteration; an even simpler example is the generation of a sequence where each term is defined in terms of the one before by the same rule, such as adding a constant (AP), or multiplying by a constant (GP), or adding the previous two terms together (Fibonacci) (see Chapter 3 pages 38-39 and Chapter 4 Worksheet H). It is rarely necessary to laboriously type essentially the same formula all the way down the column of cells which is to contain the sequence. Instead, the desired formula is typed into the first cell where it is used, then COPIED from that cell and PASTED into all the others (this 'Copy/Paste' terminology has become almost universal in modern computer software; it is equally applicable to word processors and databases, and is quickly understood by pupils using spreadsheets for the first time, even if they haven't met it before). Formulae may normally be pasted into a complete range of cells (e.g. down a column) in a single operation, so creating a sequence is very quick. *Excel* has the special **Fill Down** command to copy down a column (and **Fill Right** to copy across columns) which was described in Chapter 1 (page 6).

Relative and absolute referencing

Referencing was briefly mentioned in Chapter 1 but it is so important that a fuller discussion is included here. When formulae are pasted from one cell to another like this, references to other cells are normally copied in a RELATIVE fashion, so that the new formula refers to cells in the same relative position to the new cell (as the cells referred to in the original formula were in relation to the original cell). For example, if cell B2 contains the formula =A2–A1 then when copied into B3 the formula will become =A3–A2, or into C3 will become =B3–B2. This illustrates how a set of first, second, and higher differences of a sequence may easily be built up, as in the example worksheets on sequences (see Chapter 3 page 38 and Chapter 4 Worksheet H) Interestingly, most uses of repeated formulae in practice seem to need relative references, so this is the DEFAULT.

However, it is sometimes necessary for a particular reference in a formula to refer to the same cell on the sheet wherever it has been copied to; an example would be a geometric progression where the common ratio between successive terms (a constant) was given by an input cell at the top of the sheet. In this case an ABSOLUTE reference to the cell containing the common ratio is needed, and this must be specified at some stage in the process of setting up the original formula or when copying the formula from one cell to another. In *Excel* a dollar sign denotes an absolute reference, so if a geometric progression were being built up (or rather down!) in column A, with the common ratio stored in B1, the formula in cell A2 would be written =A1*$B$1, and when copied from A2 and pasted into A3 would become =A2*$B$1. The $B$1 ensures that both the B and the 1 are unchanged during the move. Similarly if the formula were being copied from A2 to Z300 the formula become =Z299*$B$1.

The features described above form the core of most work with spreadsheets, and should be available in any software describing itself as such.

2.4 More Advanced Spreadsheet Features

Functions

One feature which distinguishes more advanced spreadsheets from the simpler ones is the range of STANDARD FUNCTIONS available. All the standard mathematical functions acting on single numbers should be present, including square root, log and ln, e^x, absolute value, integer part, remainder on integer division (normally called MOD), sin, cos, tan and their inverses (beware: these often accept arguments only in radians), and also the constant π. STATISTICAL FUNCTIONS should also be available, including sum, count, min, max, mean, standard deviation, which act on values stored in a range of cells.

More advanced functions which may not be present in all software include MATRIX MANIPULATION; *Excel* can multiply, invert, transpose and find the determinant of appropriate matrices, up to reasonably large orders. TEXT (STRING) FUNCTIONS may include most of such functions familiar to any programmer: to chop characters from the left, right or middle of a text string, to convert text to a number and vice versa. *Excel* includes quite powerful text functions to remove spaces, convert between upper and lower case, search for a sub-string and replace it with another string, etc.; these have been found to be very useful for converting names from a school list into a form acceptable to Examination Boards. Functions may be present to do arithmetic with calendar DATES; these can turn the chore of calculating a form's average age and each pupil's age in years and months on a given date into a simple exercise. LOOKUP FUNCTIONS can pull the relevant value out of a table; for example a table of tax rates for different income bands, or a table giving the class to which a given value belongs for making a frequency distribution.

Graphs and charts
GRAPHS are a very useful way of enhancing insight into almost any aspect of mathematics, and modern spreadsheets make it quite easy to produce them (though they may be called 'charts'). Typically, the data to be graphed is first calculated in one or more columns of the spreadsheet, then a new 'chart' sheet is opened, acting on this data. A range of graph types should be available, including pie, bar, line and scatter graphs. Be warned that the range of graph types available may reflect the needs of the businessman for whom spreadsheets were largely developed, rather than the mathematician. *Excel* uses the terms 'category' and 'value' to describe the x and y axes respectively, and imposes some unwelcome restrictions on how they may be scaled. As the software stands there is no provision to draw histograms (but see Chapter 3 page 58). On the positive side, however, scaling is usually automatic, and graphs are instantly re-drawn when the numbers on the attached spreadsheet are altered. Fig. 2 shows a chart created for a mathematical purpose (see Chapter 3 page 40).

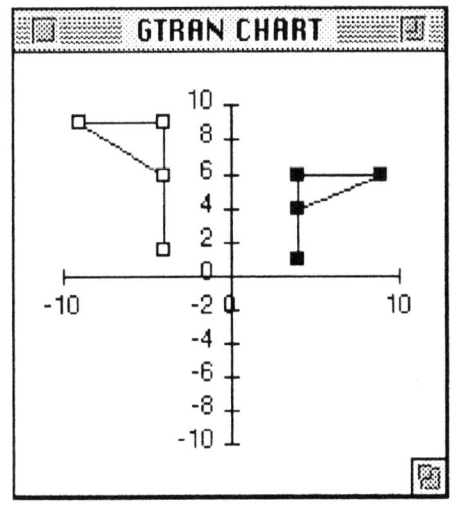

Figure 2: A chart for studying geometric transformations using matrices

Conditional tests

The CONDITIONAL FUNCTION IF() delivers either one result or an alternative result depending on the outcome of a test applied to values on the sheet. For example, the formula

=IF(b^2<4*a*c,"Complex roots","Real roots")

would print an appropriate message for a quadratic equation having real or complex roots. (Note that in *Excel* it is possible to give cells names – as was mentioned in Chapter 1 page 9. For example, the names a, b, c could refer to cells B1, B2, B3.) Such a conditional test as shown above could be used to avoid attempting to evaluate complex roots altogether, or could initiate separate evaluation of the real part and the magnitude of the imaginary part and printing an 'i' in the result – even *Excel* cannot do complex arithmetic! (see Chapter 3 page 45). A range of LOGICAL OPERATORS such as AND(), OR(), NOT() are available with many spreadsheets to widen the range of tests that can be carried out. However, such conditional functions are not nearly as powerful as conditional statements in a conventional programming language such as BASIC, Pascal or Logo which can influence which parts of a program are obeyed, and completely alter the sequence of commands carried out. A spreadsheet will always be completely evaluated in a sequence which the software decides for itself. It is usually not possible to carry out a procedure 'UNTIL' a set condition arises, and this imposes restrictions on what can be achieved. As a consequence, there are many problems which are more appropriately approached via a conventional programming language.

Macros

Many of the in-built restrictions of a spreadsheet may be overcome if it can be customised by means of its own programming language. This will probably be called a MACRO LANGUAGE; its original purpose was to automate often repeated sets of operations or 'macros'. The language built into *Excel*, however, is a full programming language in its own right with strong similarities to BASIC. It can be used to implement complex procedures such as finding the eigenvalues of a matrix, or to add new functions to the standard range available. Several of the example spreadsheets in this book use a FUNCTION MACRO. This allows the mathematical function on which a sheet acts to be easily redefined without altering the whole sheet, as in Simpson's Rule or iteration of the form x=f(x) (see Chapter 3 pages 47-51).

2.5 Availability of Spreadsheets

Spreadsheets are regarded as fundamental software applications, and so a large number of them are available for the commonly used computer systems. Of these, the most widely used in the business world are the so-called 'PC compatibles', meaning machines which are compatible at the software level with IBM PC's or PS/2's. These will almost invariably be running the MS/DOS operating system (or something compatible with it), and many MS/DOS compatible spreadsheets exist. Some major ones are Ashton Tate's *Lotus 1-2-3*, Computer Associates' *Supercalc* and Borland's *Quattro*. A more recent development has been the Windows operating system (strictly, Windows is only a 'front end' or 'user interface' to the underlying MS/DOS), which imposes a uniform and very friendly working environment across the complete range of software which may be run on the computer. The major Windows spreadsheet is Microsoft's *Excel*, though Microsoft's rivals are also bringing out Windows versions. It is part of the software library supplied by Research Machines with their network systems, and so should be available on any RM network. Microsoft *Works* is a fairly cheap compilation of a word processor, database and spreadsheet which are all reasonably capable and fairly compatible with the more powerful individual applications such as *Word* and *Excel*; it may be good value for someone who is setting up from scratch.

Windows was largely inspired by the operating system of Apple's Macintosh computers, and there are often Macintosh versions of the major Windows software applications (or vice versa; several major applications such as *Excel* or Aldus *Pagemaker* actually originated on the Macintosh). Be warned, however, that although they may look the same on the screens of their respective computers, the underlying software for PC's and Macintoshes is completely different, so if you wish to use both machines you will need to buy both versions. A more recent development is for Macintoshes to be able to read PC discs, and there is good compatibility between the Macintosh and PC versions of *Excel* at the file level, so that a sheet created on one machine can be transferred to the other without completely recreating it. There are also other spreadsheets available for the Macintosh, such as *Wingz*.

The other major educational machine, the Acorn Archimedes, is not widely used in the business world, and although it can emulate a PC (at great cost in speed) it is in no sense a PC compatible. Even in PC emulation mode, trying to run Windows probably reduces performance to an unacceptable level, though the Archimedes' own operating system is quite similar to the way Windows works. This incompatibility with the business world means that the major software suppliers have not written versions of their products for the Archimedes, and are unlikely to do so. Nevertheless, quite powerful spreadsheets such as *Logistix* and *Pipedream* are available, and the recent arrival *Eureka!* from Longman Logotron is the equal of *Excel* in many of its features.

At a lower level, it is possible to write spreadsheet software in BBC BASIC (at considerable cost in speed and flexibility). Some examples are the MA's *Algebraic Calculator*, *Spread* from the SMMIP pack and *Quickcalc* from Beebugsoft. Even these very basic programs can be quite capable of doing useful work with sequences, though their graphing capabilities are very crude. More recent is *Grasshopper* from Newman College; this is aimed mainly at the primary level, and has featured in several articles and booklets on spreadsheet use.

2.6 Spreadsheets versus Programming Languages and Other Software

It is possible to create spreadsheets to solve many mathematical problems which in the past would have been seen as the province of a conventional programming language such as BASIC, Pascal or Logo. In fact, once one starts using a powerful spreadsheet like *Excel* at the level of macro programming, there is little difference between the two approaches. At the introductory level, however, there are significant differences which make the spreadsheet approach more attractive than a program.

An obvious mode of use of software in the mathematics classroom is for pupils to load ready made spreadsheets or programs into their computer and run them. Most programs which require a set of values to be input request them in sequence and only produce output once they have all been entered. If it is desired to alter just one of them (the best approach for a methodical investigation) usually the whole sequence has to be gone through again, or a command key or menu choice has to be made to choose the value to be altered. In contrast, a spreadsheet can load with valid example values in place, and altering them merely requires clicking on the value with a mouse and typing the new one in, the display updating instantly.

Another point is that the method of calculating the result is explicitly laid out on screen (though some parts of the sheet may be scrolled out of view). Thus a pupil need not view the program as a mysterious black box out of which the answer pops; a simple method is seen to be simple. Simplicity is improved by the way the underlying software automatically takes care of inputting values and outputting results; most programs have to work very hard to achieve such friendly input and output procedures, and so appear far more complex than their actual mathematical content would appear to warrant.

The same simplicity applies to creating graphical displays; the underlying software takes care of scaling axes and matching the size of a graph to the available area on screen which take up so much of essentially simple graphical programs (Simplicity of graphical output is also one of the main virtues of graphic calculators).

Because the number of commands needed to set up a usable and attractive mathematical calculation is less than in BASIC, Pascal or Logo it becomes feasible, and worthwhile, to let pupils set up their own calculations. For example, a spreadsheet generation of a Fibonacci sequence is easy:

> Click on A1, type 1
> Click on A2, type 1
> Click on A3, type =A1+A2   [alternatively, 'A1' & 'A2' can be entered by clicking on those cells]
> Choose **Edit Copy**
> Highlight from A4 to A20
> Choose **Edit Paste**

This is likely to mean much more to pupils than a sequence produced by a program of which they may not even have seen the listing. Even so, it is not essential that pupils always construct their own sheets. In mathematics lessons a teacher's primary interest will be in teaching mathematical skills, not spreadsheet techniques, by whatever means are most effective. If facility with IT improves along the way, however, then that is a desirable by-product.

Another area where spreadsheets have an edge over conventional programming languages is in data storage. A couple of able sixth formers, who were unfortunately unaware of what spreadsheets could do, were recently witnessed writing their own BASIC program to input a set of data on pebble dimensions. Once it was running successfully they had to laboriously enter each data item into the program, without making an error (providing error correction was too complex for their programming abilities), before the required results were produced (numerically, as the graphics were again taxing them). Once the program finished, the data was lost, as they didn't know enough BASIC to save it as a data file for later use (and did not know how to use READ and DATA). In contrast, a spreadsheet solution performed the required analysis in a single cell copied down a column, and as the data formed part of the sheet it was automatically saved and reloaded with it.

The same considerations would apply to many other examples of data analysis. Incidentally, if the level of analysis required did prove beyond the capabilities of the spreadsheet, it could still be used to store the data. Most spreadsheet programs allow sheets to be saved in a simple 'text only' or ASCII format, the files so created then being readable by a program written in a conventional language. Such methods can be used to transfer data between *Excel* and *Quest/Oriel* (the popular database from The Advisory Unit, Hertford), for example.

Quite soon, of course, one does run into limitations of spreadsheets. One key problem area has already been mentioned: a spreadsheet is not easily capable of modifying the commands it obeys depending on the values it finds on the sheet (though the value produced in a given cell can be made to depend on circumstances in this way). As such 'conditional execution' is vital to the operation of most advanced software, be it mathematical or otherwise, this would appear to be a severe limitation. It has not been found to be too restricting in the range of example sheets set up to accompany this booklet, however. This is largely because they rely on either a single (though possibly quite complex) calculation that is the same whatever the values input, or on a set of calculations repeated many times. The repetition that in a programming language would normally be carried out by a FOR/NEXT loop structure, on a spreadsheet is simply implemented by copying the relevant calculations down a column of the sheet (as in the Fibonacci example above).

Problems do arise, however, when a repetition within a repetition would be needed (a 'nested loop' structure), or when a repetition needs to take place until a given condition is achieved, after which further calculation is needed (a REPEAT/UNTIL structure). The calculation of a list of primes in a programming language would usually use nested loops, and is difficult to set up on a spreadsheet, though the prime factorisation Example Sheet later in this book shows that it is sometimes possible to find a way round the problem (see Chapter 3 page 36).

As already mentioned, such problems can be circumvented by making use of a 'macro language'. One use is to input the definition of a function on which a standard procedure such as Simpson's rule or $x=f(x)$ iteration is to work, without altering large sections of the spreadsheet (see Chapter 3 pages 47-51). A similar effect can be achieved in BASIC with a user defined function, possibly input using EVAL. Once one has to write a complex procedure in a macro language, the advantages of a spreadsheet over a conventional language are less clear cut. Although the spreadsheet still offers easy input and output and possibly quite powerful built in functions, the conventional language is probably more concise and flexible, and is likely to offer much greater speed. Speed is important in statistical simulations where large samples may be required, and also in numerical analysis where a large number of iterations may be needed to achieve convergence, or a small step size used in a numerical integration or differential equation solution. Another difficulty for graphical work is that the communication between the spreadsheet and the graph only takes place once the sheet has been completely recalculated. This means that space has to be set aside on the sheet for every single point that is to be plotted; for a function whose graph is a complex curve this can be a large number, leading to a large sheet. Further, there is no chance for the graph to be built up in visible steps; this would be valuable, for instance, in statistical simulations where a sampling distribution is built up over time.

Finally, there are alternatives to both spreadsheets and programming languages; other software exists with uses in particular areas of mathematics. Function plotters such as *Omnigraph* or David Tall's *Supergraph* can do a far better job than a spreadsheet in their own domain (others are *Mouseplotter* and that included in the MEI set of programs). *Numerator* provides an approach to spreadsheet type methods which is possibly more visually attractive than a spreadsheet, though is limited as to the complexity of problem it can cope with. A range of packages exist for statistical analysis that automate the computation of sample statistics and analytical procedures which a statistician might want to use, but which are not all simply implemented in a spreadsheet; examples are *Statworks* and *Models'n'Data* for the Macintosh, and *Minitab* for PC compatibles and Macintosh. Even when using a programming language one should be aware that subroutine libraries exist that may do the desired job with greater efficiency, accuracy and reliability than the amateur is likely to be able to achieve for himself; a major example is the NAG library available on most university mainframes.

Spreadsheets, other mathematical software and programming languages like BASIC, Pascal or Logo all have their place in the toolbox of the mathematician. Some problems can be tackled equally well by any of these, other problems can benefit from the simplicity of the spreadsheet approach, while some problems need the power of a programming language or the particular focus of an off the shelf package. Mathematicians, be they teachers, pupils, or employed by other institutions need to be aware of the strengths and weaknesses of each, so that they may use them appropriately.

A very real problem is that the average classroom teacher has very little time to invest in learning to use all (or even any!) of these types of software, and is therefore wise to concentrate on one or two whose applicability is wide and which quickly repay the effort of learning. Spreadsheets fall into this category.

2.7 Adapting Mathematics for Spreadsheets

In using a spreadsheet to solve a mathematical problem, some common threads soon emerge.

First, the values which need to be input before a problem can be solved must be determined. This is natural to anyone used to writing programs, and should also be so to the analytical mind of the mathematician! It is helpful if these values are grouped together and usually they are best assigned to cells at the top left of the sheet. They should be clearly labelled by placing text in adjacent cells. If preparing a complex sheet for pupils to load ready made, it is sensible to leave these as the only unprotected cells, so that vital formulae are not accidentally overwritten.

Second, the sequence of operations leading to the result needs to be considered. If this is a single set of calculations, such as the quadratic formula, or the solution of a triangle, then no difficulty arises, though it is desirable to consider whether the layout should correspond to what the pupil might be expected to produce in an exercise book, and what in-between stages of calculation should be shown. If the process involves repetition then it needs to be structured in such a way that formulae can be copied down a column using relative references to previous cells. This means, for example, that it is more natural to set up a sequence using a definition of u_n in terms of u_{n-1} than in terms of n. Where a definition in terms of n is needed, as in a sequence of powers such as n^2, an 'n' can be made available by laying out the set of natural numbers in a column parallel to the one containing the sequence. Similarly, the distinction between absolute and relative references is vital; in the definition of a geometric sequence using $u_n = r \times u_{n-1}$ the reference to r is absolute, as it refers to the same cell throughout the sheet, whereas the reference to u_{n-1} is relative (see Chapter 4 Worksheet H). Pupils usually find the idea of relative references fairly intuitive; it is the need to make some references absolute that can be less obvious at first.

If a process involves repetition until a desired level of accuracy is achieved, as in iteration, it is not worth trying to detect this within the sheet (and it is difficult to do so in any case). It is usually sufficient to copy the iteration formulae as far down a column as seems adequate; if the process runs on to an even higher accuracy this doesn't matter, and if more steps are needed further copies of the formula can easily be made. Similarly, it is usually not easy to allow for eventualities such as, say, a zero determinant in the solution of a set of simultaneous equations. Nor is it necessary. The spreadsheet should automatically display a warning message in any cells in which it is unable to perform a calculation (and in subsequent cells that depend on it). It does not 'crash the program' in the way that a similar fault in a program would; once feasible input values are restored the sheet recalculates and performs perfectly once more. In some spreadsheets, *Excel* included, it is possible to detect such errors (using IF error ...) and so print out one's own choice of message, or cause the spreadsheet to take some appropriate action.

Data to be graphed should be laid out so as to occupy adjacent cells of a single row or column. It is feasible for a graph to overlay several different series of values on the same axes; these will generally be from different columns – for example the first, second and higher differences on the Sequences Example sheet. Some of the Example sheets build up values to be plotted in 'workspace' areas which a pupil does not need to see; they are therefore placed in a part of the sheet which is scrolled out of view. For scatter graphs in particular, it is easiest if the co-ordinates to be plotted occupy adjacent columns (or rows) with the x (or 'category') value given first.

For statistical work on tables of data it is natural to want to repeat the same analyses on samples of varying size, normally corresponding to different numbers of rows in the table. Since row sums and further calculations will probably appear at the bottom of the table this appears to create a difficulty. However, spreadsheets normally allow extra blank rows (or columns) to be inserted into a sheet even after it has been set up with formulae. It is usually best to insert new rows somewhere in the middle of the data table, as the references in SUM(), MAX(), AVERAGE(), and similar functions will then be automatically expanded to allow for them. Of course, it may not be appropriate to insert data in the middle; at the end may be the only place that it should go. A dummy end row may overcome this difficulty, but care is needed when using functions such as SUM() or STDEVP() which count the number of cells. Once a blank row has been inserted it is a simple matter to type data into the new cells and copy any formulae used in the row from the row above. The only difficulty occurs in formulae which refer across rows; for example, the formula =A5–A4 would become =A7–A4 on inserting two new rows between rows 4 and 5, not =A7–A6 as would presumably be required. Providing one is on the look-out for this it is easily corrected by copying from unaffected rows.

Other special techniques such as look-up functions, indexing into a table, and macros are noted as they arise in the examples.

2.8 Spreadsheet Reference Material

Sources of ideas for using spreadsheets in the mathematics classroom are slowly beginning to appear, though the authors are not aware of much aimed at the later stages of the curriculum. This lack of emphasis is exemplified in the interesting UNESCO book *The influence of computers and informatics on mathematics and its teaching* edited by Cornu and Ralston (1992) which in 123 pages of text only devotes $^1/_{10}$ page to spreadsheets! Below are listed some books and articles with helpful ideas for using spreadsheets in mathematics teaching.

- Many good ideas are to be found within the pages of *Exploring Mathematics with Spreadsheets* by Lulu Healy and Rosamund Sutherland.
- The NCET has published a booklet *Thinking About Spreadsheets* which discusses different modes of spreadsheet use and identifies general areas of applicability; it also reviews available software, complete with addresses of suppliers.
- Another good booklet is *Simply Spreadsheets* by Roger Keeling and Senga Whiteman which is full of practical spreadsheet projects, mostly applicable up to around Key Stage 3 and possible with relatively simple software such as Grasshopper.
- Articles in the MA's journal *Mathematics in School* occur from time to time, and one issue (Vol 22 No 5, Nov 1993) is devoted to the use of computers in mathematics teaching. Richard Bridges (Vol 20 No 5, Nov 1991) published an article along the lines of some of the material in this book. Alan Pritchard (Vol 21 No 5, Nov 1992) described a Key Stage 2 activity about choosing quantities of various confectionery bars to cost exactly £2.00. Mike Hammond (Vol 22 No 1, Jan 1993) described the use of spreadsheets for Data Handling.
- The ATM publication *MicroMath* often contains spreadsheet articles.
- Dave Miller's books of photocopiable worksheet masters *MicroMathematics* contain some material on spreadsheets, using *Grasshopper*.
- Czes Kosniowski's book *Fun Mathematics on your Microcomputer* contains many short BASIC programs and ideas that would adapt readily to spreadsheets.
- Thelma Aspin has compiled for the Hertfordshire Mathematics Centre a booklet with 18 activities (each set out as one or two photocopiable pages) which should be particularly suitable for 11-16 year olds.
- The Centre for Statistical Education at Sheffield has produced a 28 page booklet giving ideas for using spreadsheets for data handling (and a video is available).
- A different sort of book altogether is the *Handbook of Mathematical Functions* by Abramowitz and Stegun. Although more of a 'laptop' or 'luggable' then a 'notebook' it has good sections on numerical integration, the simulation of random variables and accurate series approximations to useful functions such as the Normal probability integral, as well as extensive tables of functions.

References

Abramowitz M and Stegun I A (1965). *Handbook of Mathematical Functions*, Dover.

Aspin T (1990). *Spreadsheets in the Mathematics Classroom*, Hertfordshire Mathematics Centre.

Bridges R (1991). Graphical Spreadsheets, *Mathematics in School* Vol 20 No 5 pp 2-5.

Cornu B and Ralston A (1992). *The influence of computers and informatics on mathematics and its teaching*, Science and technology education 44, UNESCO.

Centre for Statistical Education (1992). *Using Databases and Spreadsheets in Teaching Data Handling (Mathematics 11-16)*, Centre for Statistical Education, Sheffield University, S3 7RH.

Hammond M (1992). Handling Data with Spreadsheets and Databases, *Mathematics in School* Volume 22 No 1 pp 2-5.

Healy L and Sutherland R (1991). *Exploring Mathematics with Spreadsheets*, Blackwell.

Keeling R and Whiteman S (1990). *Simply Spreadsheets*, KW Publications, 42 Compton Drive, Streetly, Sutton Coldfield, West Midlands, B74 2DB.

Kosniowski C (1983). *Fun Mathematics on your Microcomputer*, CUP.

Mann W J A and Tall D eds. (1992). *Computers in the Mathematics Curriculum*, Mathematical Association, 259 London Road, Leicester, LE2 3BE.

Miller D (1990). *Micromathematics, Levels 5&6 and Levels 7&8*, Causeway Press Ltd.

NCET (1990). *Thinking About Spreadsheets*, NCET, Sir William Lyons Road, University of Warwick Science Park, Coventry, CV4 7EZ.

Pritchard A (1992). Modelling with a Spreadsheet at Key Stage Two, *Mathematics in School* Vol 21 No 5 pages 34-35.

Rothery A. (1990). *Modelling with a Spreadsheet,* Chartwell-Bratt.

Addresses for journals

Mathematics in School:
Longman, 6th Floor, Westgate House, Harlow, Essex CM20 1NE.
All other M.A. publications:
The Mathematical Association, 259 London Road, Leicester, LE2 3BE. Tel. 0533 703877.
MicroMaths:
The Association of Teachers of Mathematics, 7 Shaftesbury Street, Derby DE23 8YB.

Spreadsheet software highlighted in this book is available as follows:

Excel (RM Nimbus, PC compatibles, Apple Macintosh):
Available directly from Microsoft, though it is more sensible to go through a dealer or educational authority to obtain Microsoft's substantial educational discount. Note that *Excel* is part of Research Machines' Nimbus network bundle.

Grasshopper (RM Nimbus, BBC):
Newman College, Genners Lane, Bartley Green, Birmingham, B32 3NT

Eureka! (Acorn Archimedes):
Longman Logotron, 124 Cambridge Science Park, Milton Road, Cambridge, CB4 4ZS.

CHAPTER 3

Example Spreadsheets

This chapter describes spreadsheets which have been designed for and used in secondary school mathematics classes. They are available on disc – details are to be found in the Foreword.

The main purpose in developing the spreadsheets is to show teachers with limited knowledge of spreadsheets what can be done. It is not intended that the suggestions be used with classes 'off the shelf' but rather that the teacher try them out and adapt them as seems most appropriate. There are several possible modes of use with pupils. The teacher could operate a single computer in front of the class, loading in a ready made sheet and manipulating it to demonstrate whatever point is desired. The bolder and more experienced teacher could construct the sheet on screen in front of the pupils, possibly according to their suggestions. Both of these modes allow relatively quick progress through a planned set of demonstrations. If it is desired to put more emphasis on the pupils discovering things for themselves the class would need to be split up into groups working around a number of computers and would also need worksheets for guidance. They could load in ready made spreadsheets, or construct their own; in some cases it is the investigation that a sheet makes possible that is of value, rather than how it works, whereas in other cases it is the construction process itself that is most mathematically worthwhile.

The motivation for the individual examples is various: some were stimulated by the deficiencies of teaching a particular topic by 'chalk and talk' methods, others originated in the need to solve a particular problem, yet others were a challenge to produce the same result more simply than could be achieved using a program, while others just seemed like a nice idea. A wide range of spreadsheet techniques is used, deliberately, as the examples are meant to be informative and a stimulus to further work, as well as useful teaching tools in themselves.

The commentary assumes that *Excel* (version 2 or later) is being used to implement the sheet. It should be easy to adapt most of the ideas to other spreadsheets. Most examples require a combination of 'worksheets' and 'chart' sheets; it is usually best to give these nearly identical names, but to make sure the chart sheet has a name later in alphabetical order than the corresponding worksheet. Then the 'workspace' can be saved, also with the same name, creating an XLW file (XLS files are *Excel* spreadsheets, XLC files are *Excel* charts). Then when a pupil later opens the XLW file it automatically opens the correct combination of sheets and charts with the windows correctly sized. (N.B. *Excel* 4 uses 'workbooks', which are compatible with 'workspaces' but are set up slightly differently.)

Occasionally an XLM macro file is used, FNMACRO in particular being used by several of the workspaces to enable different function definitions to be used with the same sheet. Most of the sheets should be 'protected' so that only a few specific cells can be altered, to avoid pupils needlessly getting into a mess by erasing or corrupting vital formulae. Similarly, most of the sheets can have gridlines and row/column headings turned off.

3.1 Domestic Arithmetic

Domestic Arithmetic – Car Mileage

The workspace MILEAGE lists a set of mileometer readings and amounts of fuel bought, and calculates performance in miles per litre. Moving averages over the last three and the last five fillings are also calculated, and the three performance measures plotted on the same graph (Fig. 1). The calculations are very simple, and could easily be set up by pupils using a worksheet. The sheet is a good illustration of the usefulness of moving averages for ironing out randomly fluctuating data. A similar sheet could be constructed for a class's own version of the Retail Price Index, or the annual index of inflation, and could be made to exhibit the effect on the index of price jumps moving in or out of the twelve month averaging period.

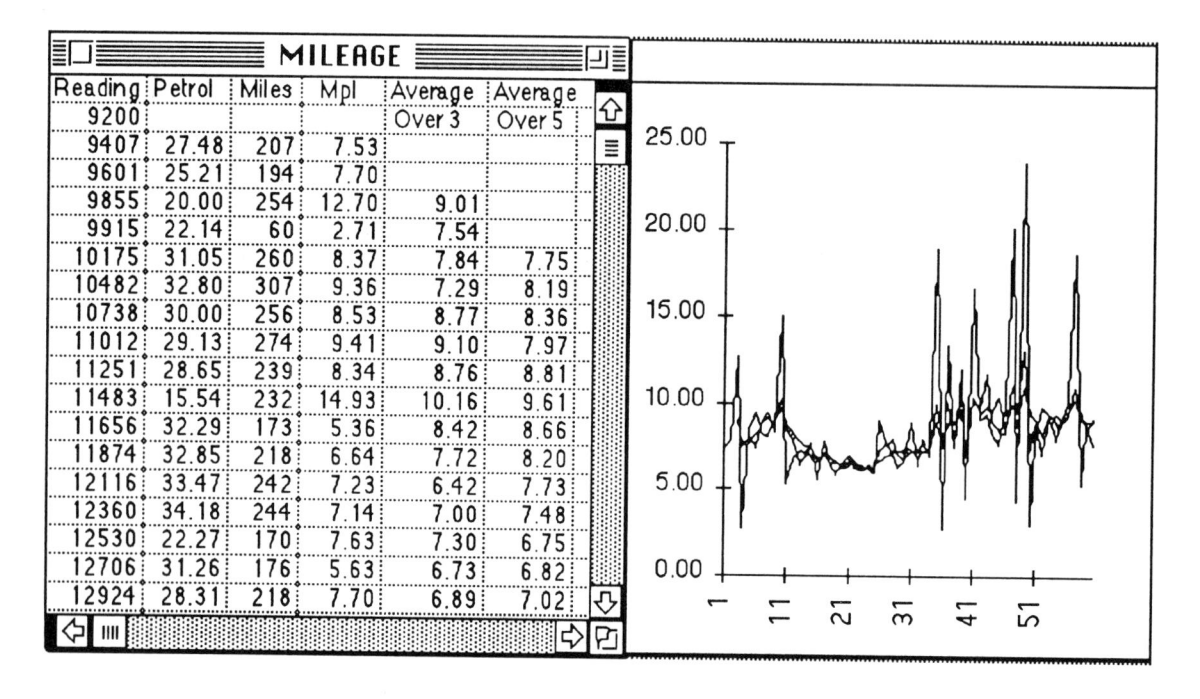

Reading	Petrol	Miles	Mpl	Average Over 3	Average Over 5
9200					
9407	27.48	207	7.53		
9601	25.21	194	7.70		
9855	20.00	254	12.70	9.01	
9915	22.14	60	2.71	7.54	
10175	31.05	260	8.37	7.84	7.75
10482	32.80	307	9.36	7.29	8.19
10738	30.00	256	8.53	8.77	8.36
11012	29.13	274	9.41	9.10	7.97
11251	28.65	239	8.34	8.76	8.81
11483	15.54	232	14.93	10.16	9.61
11656	32.29	173	5.36	8.42	8.66
11874	32.85	218	6.64	7.72	8.20
12116	33.47	242	7.23	6.42	7.73
12360	34.18	244	7.14	7.00	7.48
12530	22.27	170	7.63	7.30	6.75
12706	31.26	176	5.63	6.73	6.82
12924	28.31	218	7.70	6.89	7.02

Figure 1: Car mileage workspace screen display

Domestic Arithmetic – Annual Percentage Rate (APR)

This is an ideal topic for a spreadsheet, as the calculations are simple, but repetitive and tedious. The sheet APR lays out the accumulation of interest over a twelve month period, given an initial amount and a monthly interest rate, and works out the APR from the final amount (Fig. 2). This would be easily set up by pupils using a worksheet, and they could be expected to produce the correct percentage formulae for themselves. It should be instructive to see how an apparently small monthly rate translates into a swingeing APR!

		APR		
Monthly interest rate %:	3.00	Month number	Amount	Interest
Initial Amount	1000.00	0	1000.00	
		1	1000.00	30.00
		2	1030.00	30.90
		3	1060.90	31.83
		4	1092.73	32.78
		5	1125.51	33.77
		6	1159.27	34.78
		7	1194.05	35.82
		8	1229.87	36.90
		9	1266.77	38.00
		10	1304.77	39.14
		11	1343.92	40.32
		12	1384.23	41.53
		Final Amount	1425.76	
		Total Interest		425.76
		Initial Amount		1000.00
		Annual Percentage Rate		42.58

Figure 2: Annual Percentage Rate (APR) calculation

Domestic Arithmetic – Mortgage

The sheet MORTGAGE is an extension of the APR sheet where a constant repayment is made each month; the idea is to find the correct repayment to exactly pay off the debt over the 25 year term. To solve this problem analytically needs a clear head and knowledge of GP methods, but pupils should have no problem finding the answer by trial and improvement. Again, the sheet is simple enough to be set up by pupils themselves. As the sheet is long, extending over 12 × 25 months, it is useful to split its window into two 'panes', one being scrolled to the top of the sheet and the other to the bottom (Fig. 3). Also, the month and year numbers should not be entered manually; they may be calculated from row numbers, then using integer division and remainders (this tricky aspect could be omitted altogether). There is some scope for plotting graphs of the debt against time.

\=\= MORTGAGE \=\=					
PAYING OFF A MORTGAGE					
Amount Borrowed		30000.00			
Interest Rate (% per year)		15.00			
Monthly Payment		384.25			
Year No.	Month	Amount	Interest	Payment	Capital Paid
0	0	30000.00			
	1	30000.00	375.00	384.25	9.25
	2	29990.75	374.88	384.25	9.37
	3	29981.38	374.77	384.25	9.48
	4	29971.90	374.65	384.25	9.60
	5	29962.30	374.53	384.25	9.72
	6	29952.58	374.41	384.25	9.84
	9	1487.62	18.60	384.25	365.65
	10	1121.97	14.02	384.25	370.23
	11	751.74	9.40	384.25	374.85
25	12	376.89	4.71	384.25	379.54
Amount left to pay		-2.65			
Totals Paid			85272.35	115275.00	30002.65

Figure 3: Mortgage repayment spreadsheet

Domestic Arithmetic – Compound Interest

If pupils are prepared to derive a formula for the amount after compound interest they could set up a sheet such as COMPOUND (Fig. 4). An additional feature of the sheet as set up is that it calculates the effect of compounding the interest several times a year. Many savings institutions do this; also, there is an obvious tie-up with APR.

Interest Rate per Annum	10
Initial Amount	100
Period (Years)	1
No. of Times Compounded per Year	2
Rate per Compounding Period	5
No. of Compounding Periods	2
Final Amount	110.25

Figure 4: Compound interest calculation

Possibly more interestingly, the effect of compounding more and more often can be investigated; this doesn't lead to larger and larger amounts of money, as pupils often expect, but to a finite limiting amount. If the interest rate is 100% (!) and the initial amount 1, the amount after one year approaches e (Fig. 5).

Interest Rate per Annum	100
Initial Amount	1
Period (Years)	1
No. of Times Compounded per Year	365
Rate per Compounding Period	0.273973
No. of Compounding Periods	365
Final Amount	2.714567

Interest Rate per Annum	100
Initial Amount	1
Period (Years)	1
No. of Times Compounded per Year	100000
Rate per Compounding Period	0.001
No. of Compounding Periods	100000
Final Amount	2.718268

Figure 5: Compound interest calculations, showing the approach to e

3.2 Properties of Numbers

Properties of Numbers − Decimal Expansions

This was inspired by reading about 'REPPAT', a BBC BASIC program published by Keele University Mathematical Publications. The sheet DECIMAL shows the decimal expansion of a given rational to about 50 places (more is possible); numerator and denominator can be altered. A line graph shows the digit value of each place in the expansion; even quite long recurring patterns show up clearly (Fig. 6).

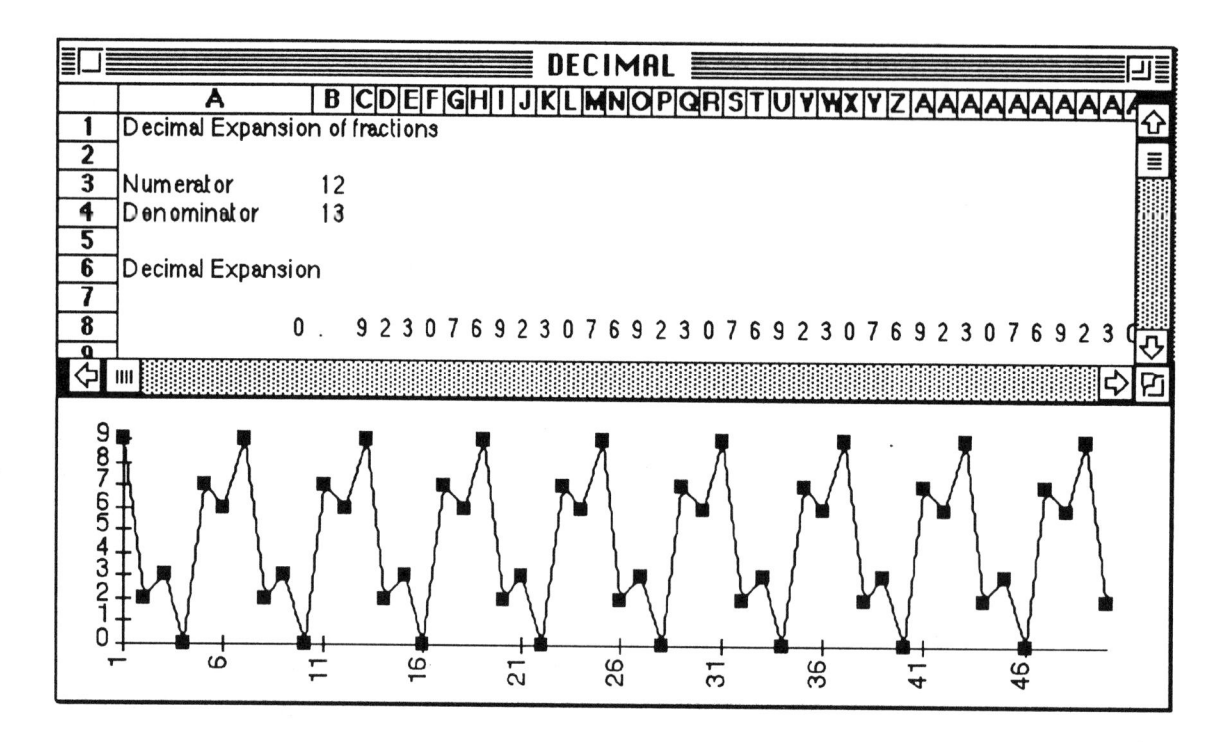

Figure 6: Decimal expansion workspace showing 12/13

The sheets work by performing an integer division of a remainder by the denominator of the fraction to produce the next digit of the expansion, and multiplying the remainder after the division by 10 (or other base value) to produce the remainder for the next step. This gives a pair of formulae that can be copied along a row indefinitely.

Assuming the denominator is held in cell B4, the remainders in row 7 and the digits in row 8, the formulae are:

>   New remainder   =(D7−D8*$B$4)*10   (in cell E7)
>   New digit   =INT(E7/$B$4)   (in cell E8)

and similarly in columns F, G, etc.

A second sheet, FRACTION, does the same for other bases less than 10. As an example, the expansion of 1/10 in base 2 shows clearly why most BASICs go wrong when asked to do: FOR x = 0 TO 1000 STEP 0.1: PRINT x: NEXT
because 0.1 recurs in binary arithmetic which the computer uses, but will be truncated to a number differing slightly from 0.1 (Fig. 7).

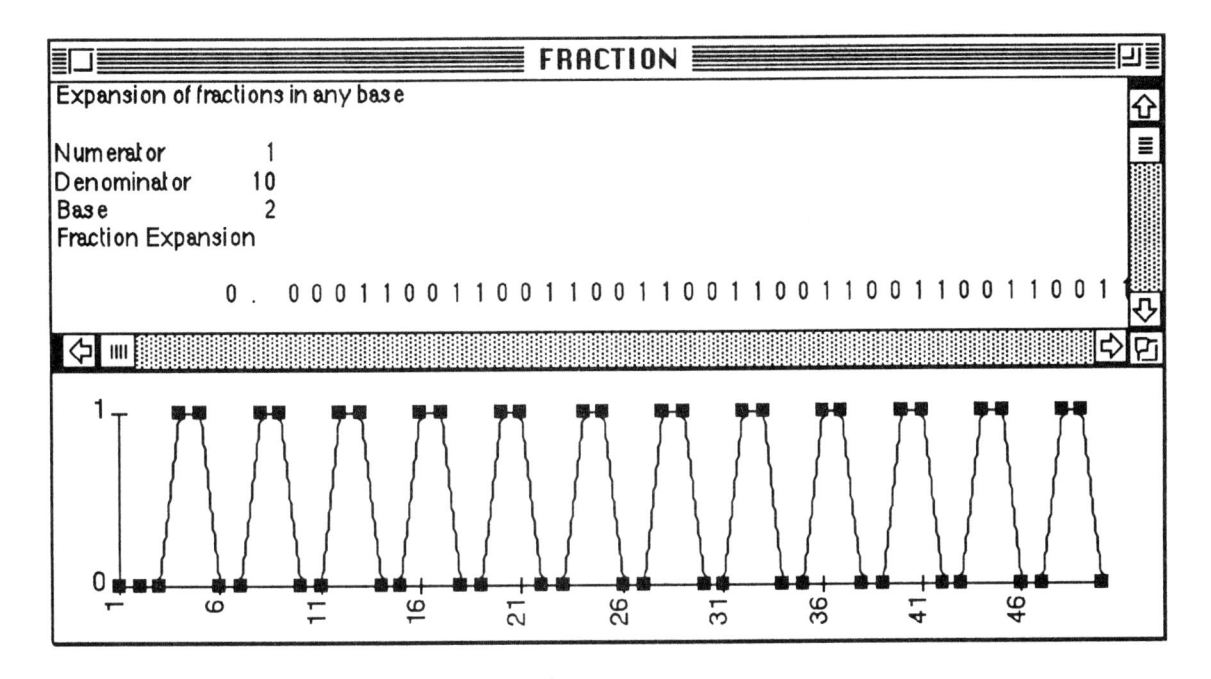

Figure 7: Recurring expansion of 1/10 in base 2

The patterns produced are a good topic for investigation (Fig. 8 shows another chart, for 1/7 base 3). This ties in with work on prime factors and also on the working of the long division algorithm. Worksheet J in Chapter 4 (page 89) is a possible approach, though its usefulness would very much depend on what the teacher was trying to achieve.

This is an informative example of how computers can be made to do arithmetic to arbitrary precision, rather than the limited number of significant figures used by most programming languages. The method is perhaps a little too tricky to be worth pupils setting up for themselves; in this case it is the end result that is the main point of interest.

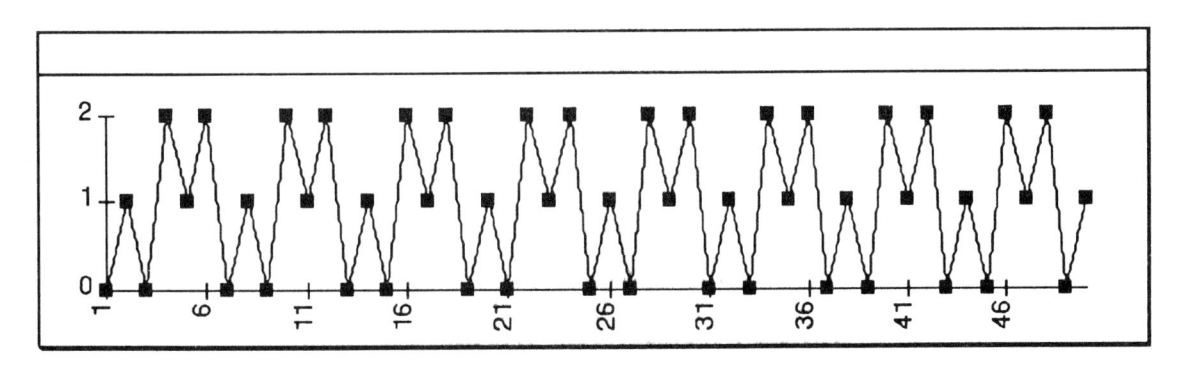

Figure 8: Recurring expansion of 1/7 in base 3

Properties of Numbers – Prime Factors

This staple example of IT performing a tedious but essentially simple arithmetic task is possibly more easily done using a programming language, but the sheet PRIME shows a spreadsheet can do it too (Fig. 9). A reference list of primes is entered into the sheet by hand, and column C is assigned to an index number which gradually works down this list as divisibility by each prime is tested. This uses the INDEX() function to refer to the array of prime numbers (by the name 'primes' rather than the reference D3:D26, achieved by using **Formula Define Name**); this function is only likely to be available in relatively sophisticated spreadsheet software. Divisibility is tested by an IF() function using MOD(); if the remainder is zero the relevant prime is copied out of the reference list into the prime factors column. If the number is not divisible by the prime being tested, the index number is increased. The following cell contents are copied down the three columns used:

=IF(MOD(A3,INDEX(primes,C3))=0,A3/B3,A3)   (divides number in column A if necessary)
=IF(MOD(A3,INDEX(primes,C3))=0,INDEX(primes,C3),"")   (checks divisibility in column B)
=IF(MOD(A3,INDEX(primes,C3))=0,C3,C3+1)   (increases index as required in column C)

This is a slightly tricky procedure that might not be worthwhile for pupils to attempt to reproduce themselves.

The example on disc contains =2^3*3^2*11*13 in cell A3, showing that it is possible to put formulae into input cells as well as numbers. It is useful in this case, as a large number with desired prime factors can be worked out as a product of smaller ones.

	A	B	C	D
1	Number to be	Prime factors	Number of prime	List of primes
2	factored	found	being tested	
3	10296	2	1	2
4	5148	2	1	3
5	2574	2	1	5
6	1287		1	7
7	1287	3	2	11
8	429	3	2	13
9	143		2	17
10	143		3	19
11	143		4	23
12	143	11	5	29
13	13		5	31
14	13	13	6	37
15	1		6	41

Figure 9: Prime factor spreadsheet

Properties of Numbers – Highest Common Factor by Euclid's Algorithm

This is very easily implemented by the sheet HCF, and pupils could do it for themselves (Fig. 10). If the two initial numbers are entered into cells A3 and B3 the pair of formulae:
=MIN(A3,B3)   and   =MAX(A3,B3) – MIN(A3,B3)
copied from A4 and B4 down columns A and B produce the HCF eventually in column B; the LCM is then the product of the original numbers divided by the HCF. This sheet also splits the window into panes, as the algorithm can take many steps. This sheet might profitably be used alongside the prime factors sheet.

	A	B	C	D
1	Finding Highest Common Factor (HCF) by Euclid's Algorithm			
2	First Number	Second Number		
3	17640	9000		17640
4	9000	8640		18375
5	8640	360		441000
6	360	8280		19173.913
7	360	7920		20045.4545
8	360	7560		21000
9	360	7200		22050
10	360	6840		23210.5263
11	360	6480		24500
12	360	6120		25941.1765
13	360	5760		27562.5
14	360	5400		29400
15	360	5040		31500
16	360	4680		33923.0769
17	360	4320		36750
31	0	360		441000
32	0	360		441000
33		HCF		LCM
34				

Figure 10: Euclid's Algorithm for Highest Common Factor

3.3 Sequences and Number Patterns

Sequences and Number Patterns – Differences

The workspace SEQUENCE consists of a sheet containing a sequence and its first, second and third differences; the natural numbers are in the first column for use when the sequence is defined in terms of n, as for the sequence of fourth powers shown (Fig. 11). The linked graph sheets show line graphs of the sequence and its differences on linear, log-linear and log-log scales, two of which fit beside the spreadsheet itself at any given time.

The spreadsheet is shown finished merely to demonstrate what can be achieved; pupils should certainly construct this for themselves. Worksheets H and I in Chapter 4 (pages 83-88) have been used successfully with classes (who had not used *Excel* before), though other approaches are possible. These worksheets would be quite a good starting point for a teacher unfamiliar with spreadsheets to get used to some of their features.

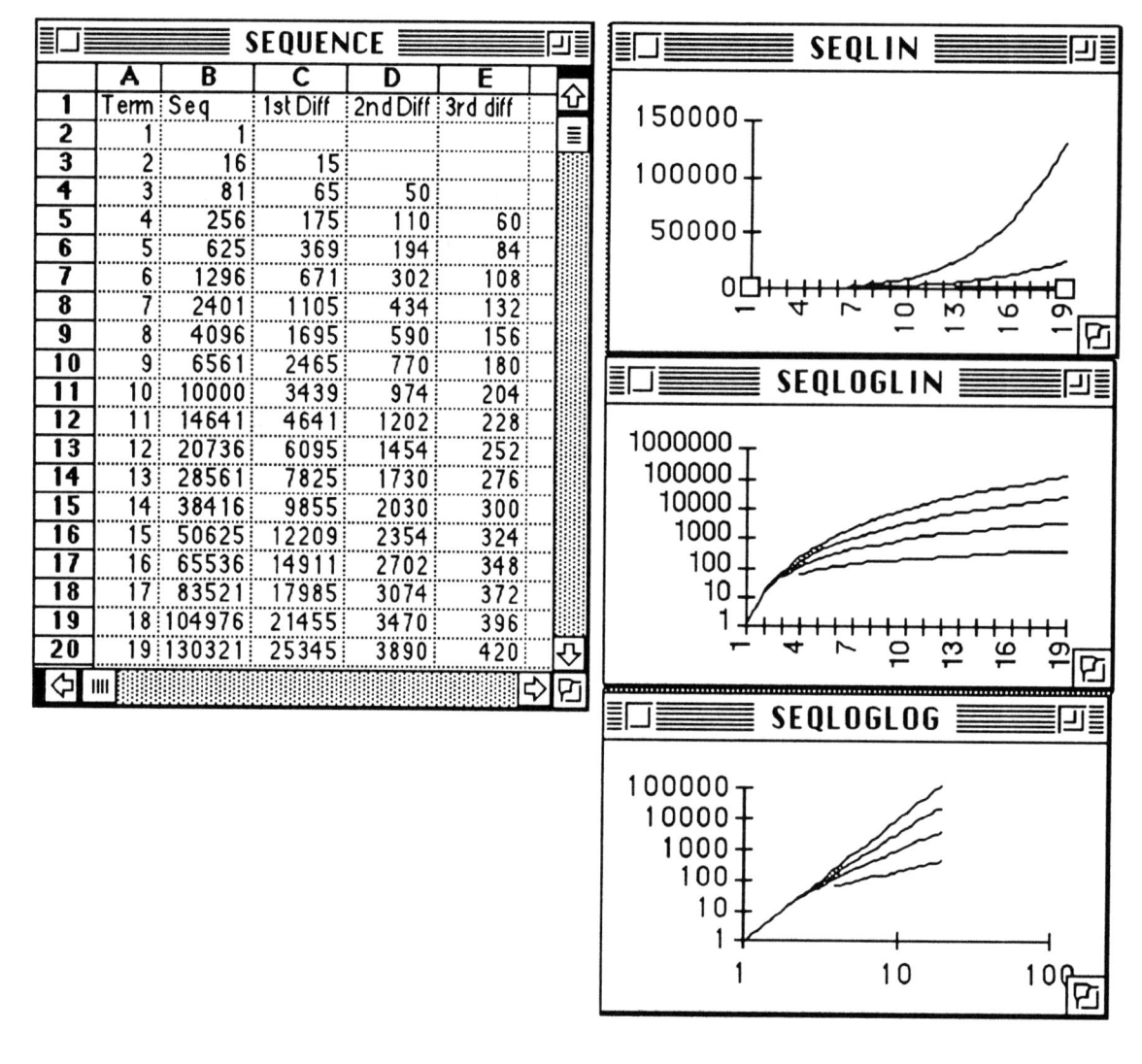

	A	B	C	D	E
1	Term	Seq	1st Diff	2nd Diff	3rd diff
2	1	1			
3	2	16	15		
4	3	81	65	50	
5	4	256	175	110	60
6	5	625	369	194	84
7	6	1296	671	302	108
8	7	2401	1105	434	132
9	8	4096	1695	590	156
10	9	6561	2465	770	180
11	10	10000	3439	974	204
12	11	14641	4641	1202	228
13	12	20736	6095	1454	252
14	13	28561	7825	1730	276
15	14	38416	9855	2030	300
16	15	50625	12209	2354	324
17	16	65536	14911	2702	348
18	17	83521	17985	3074	372
19	18	104976	21455	3470	396
20	19	130321	25345	3890	420

Figure 11: Sequence workspace showing spreadsheet with fourth powers and their differences and Linear, log-linear and log-log charts

Sequences and Number Patterns – Fibonnacci and other patterns

The workspace SEQUENCE discussed in the previous section has considerable potential. Simple modification of the formulae in the sequence column (modify formula in top cell, then copy down column) allows triangle numbers, squares, cubes, Fibonacci, APs and GPs to be investigated. This is implemented as FIBSEQ with an embedded chart (Fig. 12).

It is striking that the software allows conventionally difficult ideas like log axes to be used in a simple way, and hence much lower down the school than would normally be the case. This is a very good thing; the whole point of such axes is to simplify the picture conveyed by a graph, not complicate it, and they are widely used in practice for this reason. A simple classification of sequences into linear (AP), log-linear (GP) and log-log (powers) can be easily achieved, along with other important observations such as the differencing of a power sequence leading to a sequence of degree one less, while the difference of a geometric sequence is a geometric sequence with the same common ratio (same gradient on log-linear axes). The Fibonacci sequence is clearly 'almost geometric'; if the ratio of successive terms is subtracted from the 'best estimate' of the Golden Ratio (the bottom ratio in the column, used as an absolute reference) and the results plotted on log-linear axes, the convergence to the Golden Ratio clearly is geometric as well (Fig. 12).

Pascal's triangle and similar 'two dimensional' patterns can be readily created. For Pascal's Triangle, 1's should be entered into the left hand column and 0's into the rest of the top row, and every other cell should contain the formula adding the cell above and above left (a single formula can be Copied/Pasted into a highlighted rectangle to achieve this). See Worksheet D, Chapter 4 page 67.

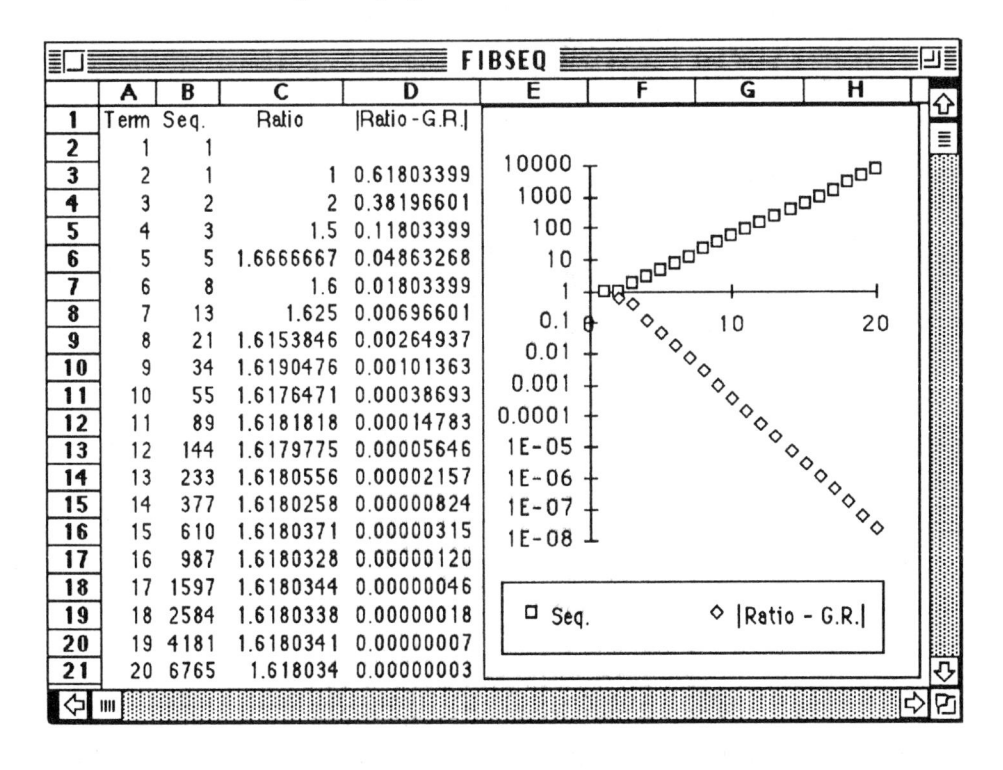

	A	B	C	D
1	Term	Seq.	Ratio	|Ratio - G.R.|
2	1	1		
3	2	1	1	0.61803399
4	3	2	2	0.38196601
5	4	3	1.5	0.11803399
6	5	5	1.6666667	0.04863268
7	6	8	1.6	0.01803399
8	7	13	1.625	0.00696601
9	8	21	1.6153846	0.00264937
10	9	34	1.6190476	0.00101363
11	10	55	1.6176471	0.00038693
12	11	89	1.6181818	0.00014783
13	12	144	1.6179775	0.00005646
14	13	233	1.6180556	0.00002157
15	14	377	1.6180258	0.00000824
16	15	610	1.6180371	0.00000315
17	16	987	1.6180328	0.00000120
18	17	1597	1.6180344	0.00000046
19	18	2584	1.6180338	0.00000018
20	19	4181	1.6180341	0.00000007
21	20	6765	1.618034	0.00000003

Figure 12: The convergence to the Golden Ratio in a Fibonacci sequence

3.4 Geometrical Transformations and Matrices

The workspace GTRAN consists of a sheet showing a 2×2 transformation matrix multiplying a 2×4 matrix representing a quadrilateral and producing a 2×4 matrix representing its image under the transformation. A linked graph displays the original shape and its image (Fig. 13). All matrix elements may be modified, varying either the transformation or the shape it acts on; the graph changes to reflect each alteration.

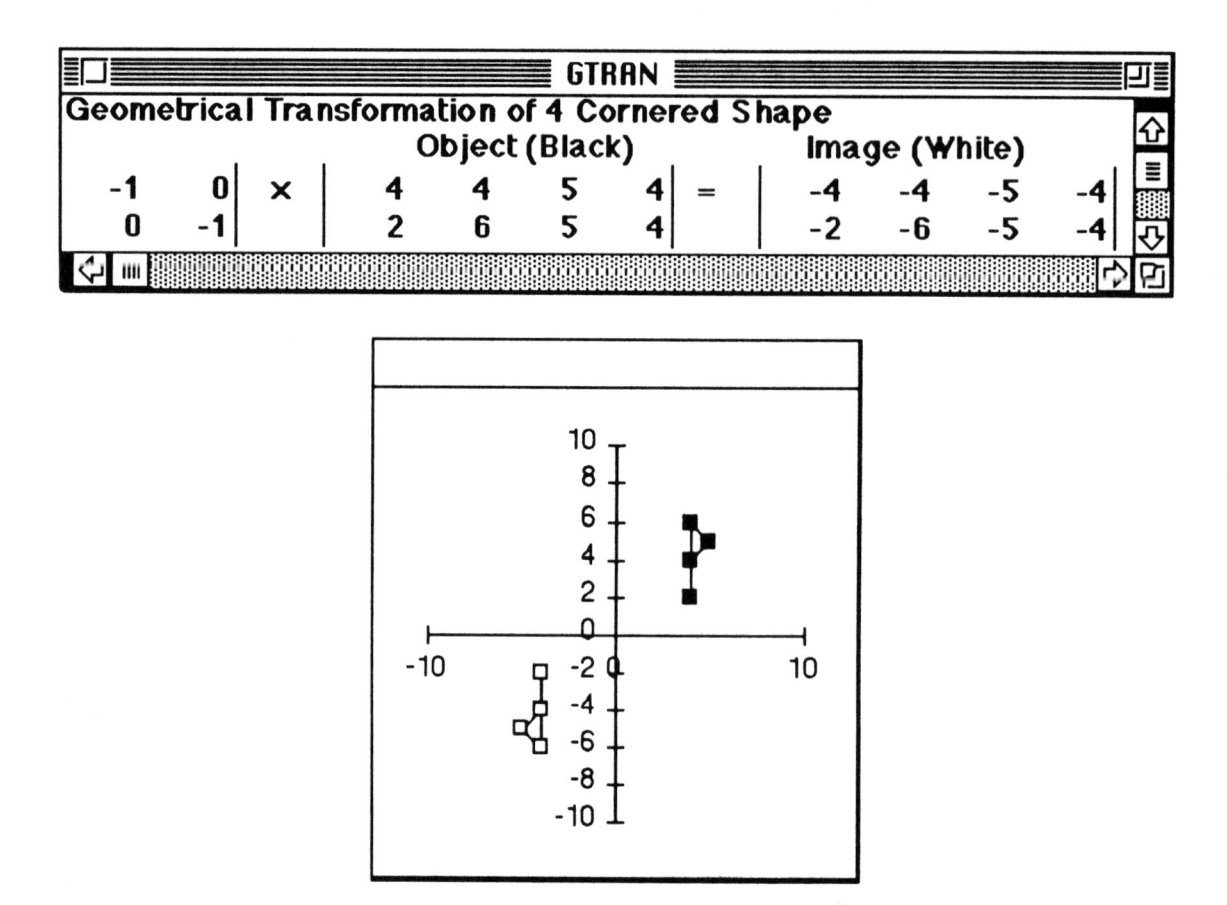

```
================================ GTRAN ================================
Geometrical Transformation of 4 Cornered Shape
                Object (Black)              Image (White)
    -1   0   ×    4   4   5   4    =    -4   -4   -5   -4
     0  -1        2   6   5   4         -2   -6   -5   -4
```

Figure 13: Geometrical transformation workspace

The sheet uses array functions to do the matrix manipulation which may not be available in all spreadsheet software, though, if not, the necessary arithmetic would not be too difficult to enter manually. Once the transformation and object matrices have been laid out (in ranges A3:B4 and C3:F4) the cells to contain the image are highlighted and the formula =MMULT(A3:B4,C3:F4) is typed in. This is terminated with CTRL/SHIFT/Enter rather than just Enter to indicate that it's an array formula, and braces { } are put round it to show this on screen. The highlighting ensures that it is entered into all cells of the image matrix. The graph is effectively a joined up scatter graph, which is the only way of making *Excel* plot points from co-ordinates. The object matrix is highlighted and **Edit Copy** selected, then the chart is activated and **Edit Paste Special** used, then **Values in Rows**, then

Categories in First Row chosen. The same is then done for the image. This rather complex procedure for scatter graphs is one of *Excel*'s defects from the mathematician's point of view.

Worksheets M and N in Chapter 4 (pages 93-98) give one way of using this sheet to investigate properties of geometrical transformations and of 2×2 matrices in general. The worksheets also show how formulae can be put into the input cells of the transformation matrix that compute the correct elements for a rotation through an arbitrary angle, though *Excel*'s use of radians in its trigonometric functions is a slight inconvenience.

3.5 Solution of Equations

Solution of Equations – Two linear simultaneous equations

The workspace SIMEQ shows two equations whose numerical coefficients may be altered, and the actual solution using the inverse of a 2×2 matrix. A linked graph shows the two straight lines and their crossing point, coinciding with the solution obtained algebraically (Fig. 14).

The only input cells are the coefficients of the two equations. These are copied down into a 2×2 matrix whose inverse is computed using the MINVERSE() array function. The inverse is then multiplied by the right hand side vector using MMULT() to produce the solution vector. The lines on the chart are plotted from a pair of end points worked out for $x = -10$ and $+10$, using **Paste Special** into a joined up scatter graph as for geometrical transformations. Though possible, it would probably not be profitable for pupils to set this up for themselves.

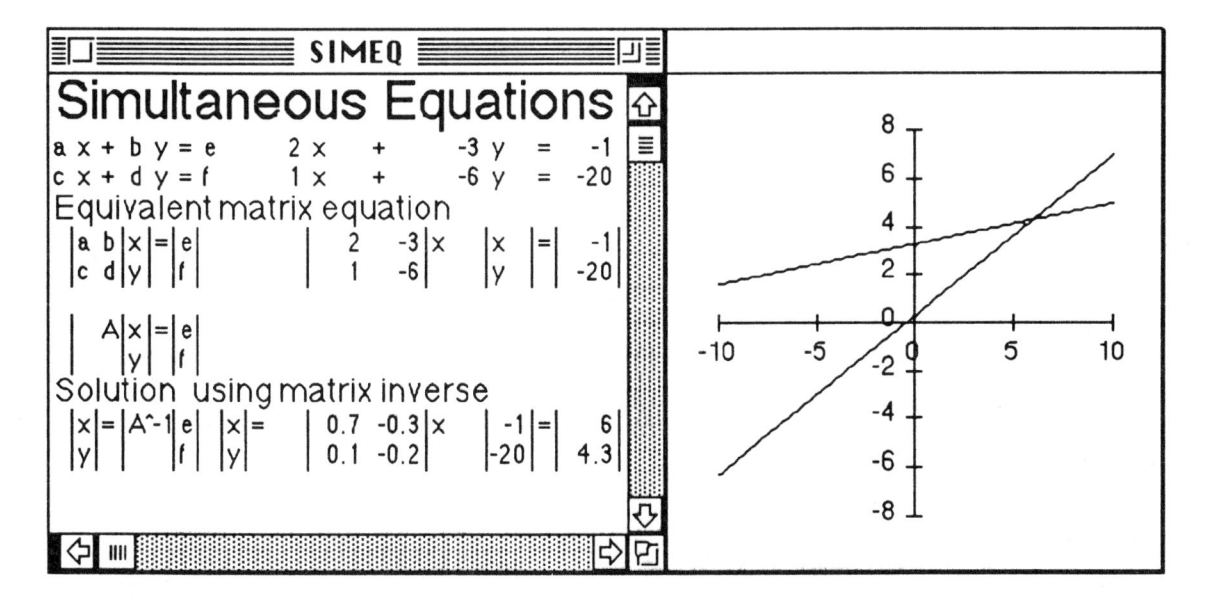

Figure 14: Workspace for solution of two linear simultaneous equations

Solution of Equations – Three linear simultaneous equations

The workspace SIMEQ3D is an attempt to show the solution of three linear simultaneous equations in three unknowns graphically as the intersection of three planes, as well as the algebraic solution using a 3×3 matrix. A linked graph displays a simulated three dimensional view of the three planes and their lines of intersection. The direction of view may be altered to 'walk round' the planes and see more clearly cases such as two parallel planes, or planes intersecting in three parallel lines (Fig. 15).

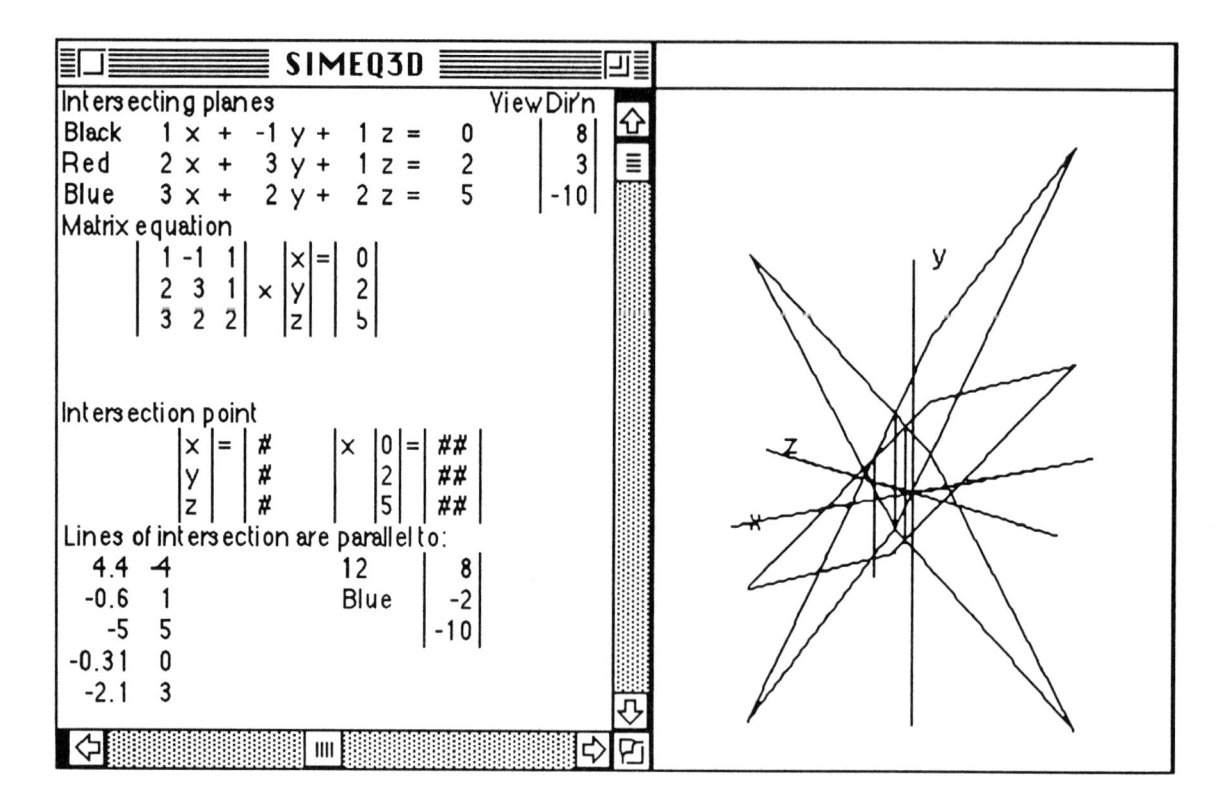

Figure 15: Workspace for solution of three linear simultaneous equations

On screen, and in Fig. 15, # and ## appear where columns are too narrow to display the numbers. Widening the relevant columns will eliminate this (as shown in Fig. 16), but at the expense of reducing the number of columns which will fit in. Note that the use of colour makes the screen diagram more intelligible than Fig. 15 would suggest.

The matrix algebra is essentially the same as for SIMEQ, but the simulation of the 3D view is more tricky. The components of the view direction vector (v_x, v_y, v_z) are used to compute θ, its angle above the x/z plane and ϕ, its angle of rotation about the y axis from the x/y plane (alternatively θ and ϕ could be entered directly):

$$\theta = \tan^{-1}(v_y/(v_x^2 + v_z^2)^{1/2}), \quad \phi = \tan^{-1}(v_z/v_x)$$

These are then used to compute two unit vectors in the directions to be used for screen x and y co-ordinates:

$$x_s = (\sin\phi, 0, -\cos\phi), \quad y_s = (-\sin\theta\cos\phi, \cos\theta, -\sin\theta\sin\phi).$$

Conversion from (x, y, z) co-ordinates to screen (x_s, y_s) co-ordinates is achieved by multiplying the 2×3 matrix formed by the x_s and y_s vectors by the 3×n matrix formed by the set of points it is desired to transform. If these are appropriately placed on the sheet the array function MMULT() can be used. Four points are computed for each plane, having x and z co-ordinates of +5 and –5, and transformed into screen co-ordinates. Similarly, the two points where the lines of intersection of each pair of planes have a z co-ordinate of +5 or –5 are computed and transformed. A set of points representing the ends of the x, y and z axes is transformed also. The sets of screen x and y co-ordinates are then copied into a joined up scatter diagram using **Paste Special** as before. Finally, vectors parallel to each line of intersection are computed and displayed; this helps in choosing good view directions and clarifies situations of parallel intersection. Needless to say, this is a sheet to load and use ready made!

The final 3D view is not particularly easy to interpret, and probably something better could be organised using a programming language. However, this is a fairly advanced topic, so the sheet would probably only be used by quite able A level pupils. It would be appropriate for investigating the relationship between the plane equations needed to give intersection in three parallel lines, or in a single line, or parallel planes.

```
                           SIMEQ3D
       K    L  M N    O    P Q R S T    U       V   W
 1  Intersecting planes                       View Dir'n
 2  Black    1 x +   -1 y +   1 z =     0          8
 3  Red      2 x +    3 y +   1 z =     2          3
 4  Blue     3 x +    2 y +   2 z =     5        -10
 5  Matrix equation
 6           1 -1  1        |x|=| 0
 7           2  3  1  ×     |y|  | 2
 8           3  2  2        |z|  | 5
 9
10
11  Intersection point
12          |x|=| -5E+15       |0|=| 1.4E+16
13          |y|   1.2E+15   ×  |2|   -3.6E+15
14          |z|    6E+15       |5|   -1.8E+16
15  Lines of intersection are parallel to:
16    4.4  -4              12           8
17   -0.6   1              Blue        -2
18     -5   5                          -10
19  -0.31   0
20   -2.1   3
```

Figure 16: Spreadsheet for SIMEQ3D expanded to reveal numbers

Solution of Equations – Skew Lines

The workspace 3DLINES uses a similar 3D view to project two lines whose equations are given in the vector form **r** = **a** + **b**t (Fig. 17). The view direction and transformation to screen co-ordinates work exactly as before. The portions of the lines chosen for plotting are the 5 units of length nearest to the origin; the two end points required are:
a + [(5/|**b**|) –(**a.b**/**b.b**)]**b** and **a** + [–(5/|**b**|) –(**a.b**/**b.b**)]**b**.
Intersection is checked by solving the x and y equations simultaneously for the parameters t and s and then checking if the z equation is consistent with these values also.

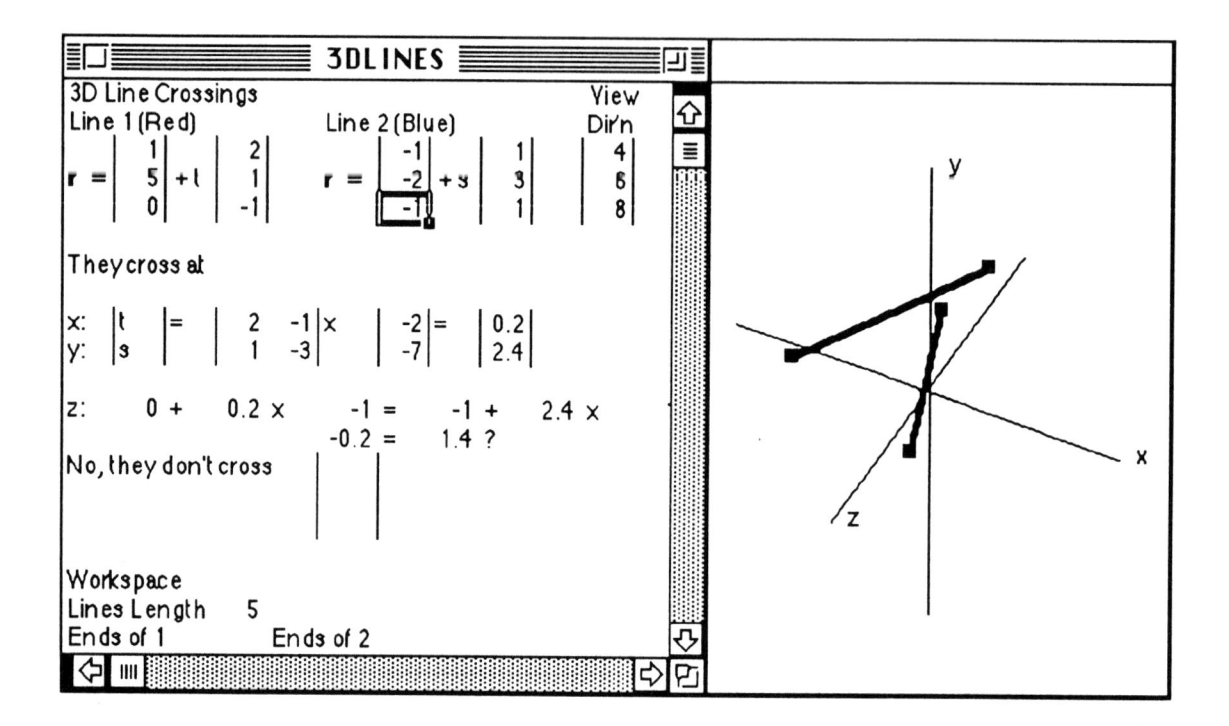

Figure 17: Skew lines in three dimensions

Solution of Equations – Quadratic Equations

The workspace QUADRAT solves quadratic equations using the standard formula, and plots a graph of the quadratic so that the graphical interpretation of distinct, equal and imaginary roots can clearly be seen (Fig. 18).

The quadratic formula is straightforwardly implemented. The discriminant $b^2 - 4ac$ is checked using an IF() function which prints a message about imaginary roots if it is negative. The only tricky feature is to find the correct plotting range for the quadratic. If r is defined as $|b^2 - 4ac|^{1/2}/|a|$ then a suitable range over which to plot the values is from $-b/(2a) - r$ to $-b/(2a) + r$. This range is divided into 100 steps and the appropriate x and f(x) values laid out down two adjacent columns. These are then copied into a joined up scatter diagram using **Paste Special** as previously.

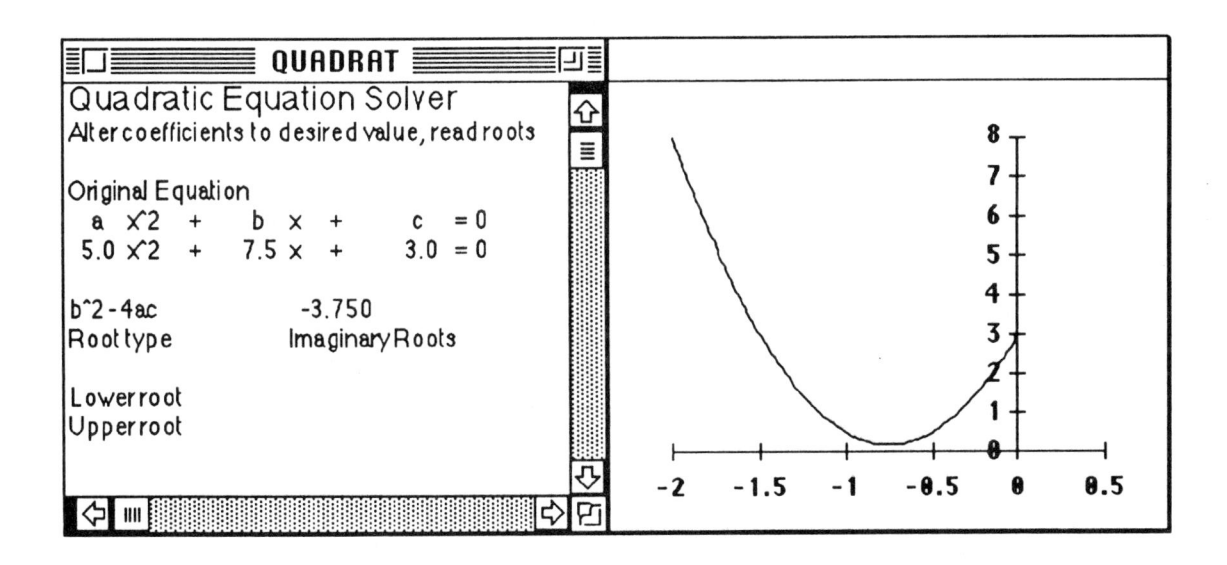

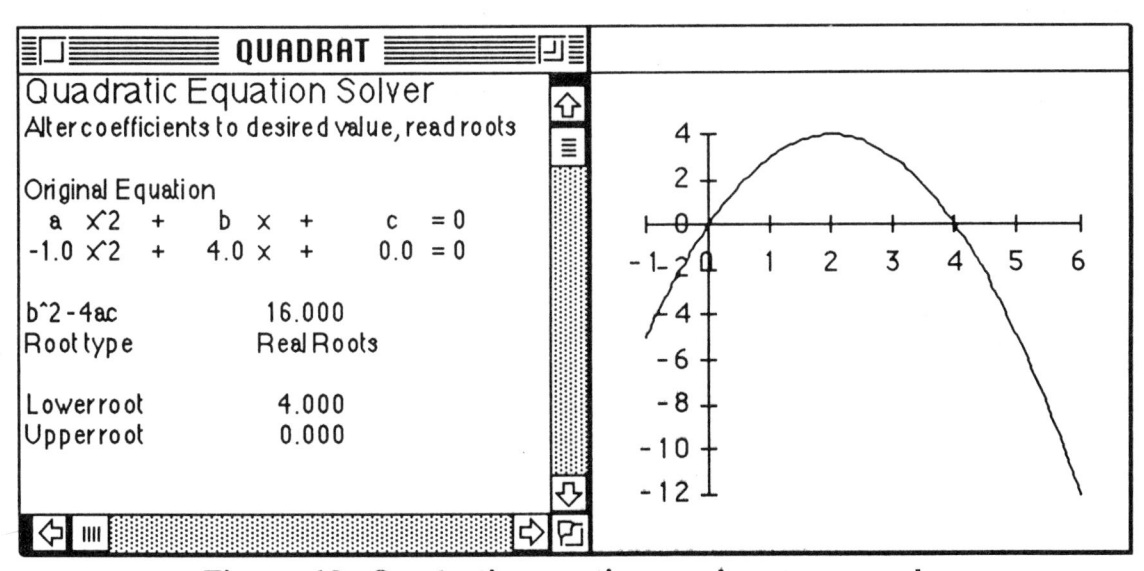

Figure 18: Quadratic equation workspace examples

3.6 Function Plotting

Straight Line Function Plotting

The workspace STRTLINE allows y=mx+c equations to be investigated, the graph giving an instant response to alteration of the coefficients. Once one of the cells containing a coefficient is highlighted a whole series of values can be run through very quickly by typing: value, Enter, value, Enter, etc. Gradients much greater than 10 appear to cause errors in the plotting of the line, so be prepared for these. The sheet computes y values for x = +10 and –10 and pastes the co-ordinates into a joined up scatter diagram using **Paste Special**.

General Function Plotter

The workspace FNPLOT allows more general functions to be plotted. The function definition is entered into the FNMACRO window in normal 'computer language', such as =COS(2*PI()*x/360) (to illustrate how the radian problem is handled). The range of x values for plotting is entered into the FNPLOT window, and the graph plotted (the y axis is scaled automatically by *Excel*). This is a very 'cheap and cheerful' function plotter; the self-scaling means that any function such as 1/x or tan x is scaled into invisibility (though an axis may be rescaled by selecting it and choosing **Format Scale**). Dedicated plotters such as SPA's *Omnigraph* or David Tall's *Supergraph* are far better!

The 'macro sheet' FNMACRO.XLM is just about the minimum possible macro. A full listing is:

B2	f	The name by which the function is called.
B3	=ARGUMENT("x",1)	Defines the function's single argument, a number.
B4	=RESULT(1)	Defines the function's result to be a number.
B5	=x^3–3*x	The function definition, alterable by the user.
B6	=RETURN(B5)	Returns the value in stated macro cell to the calling sheet.

The syntax, though a little cumbersome, makes sense. To create this macro **File New Macro Sheet** is chosen and the cells entered as above. In order to use it the name of the function needs to be made known to other sheets. This is done by clicking on cell A1 and selecting **Formula Define Name** and clicking on 'Function' in the Macro section of the dialogue box obtained. This adds the new function FNMACRO.XLM!f to the list of functions available from the **Formula** menu **Paste Function** option; it will be available whenever sheet FNMACRO is open. Several functions can be defined on the same macro sheet in a similar way.

The function is used by the normal worksheet FNPLOT which computes a set of x values spanning the input range, and the corresponding f(x) values in an adjacent column whose cells contain formulae such as =FNMACRO.XLM!f(A10) (entered simply by selecting **Formula Paste Function**). These co-ordinates are then copied into a joined up scatter graph using **Paste Special** as previously.

3.7 Numerical Methods

These were the original *raison d'être* of computers for mathematicians, but syllabuses still seem to concentrate on the exceptional analytically soluble problems at the expense of these powerful general methods. Modern A level syllabuses such as the MEI's modular scheme are beginning to look this way, however, and it seems that the need for simple teaching implementations of such methods will be increasingly in demand. They are particularly appropriate for spreadsheets.

Numerical Methods – Numerical Integration by Simpson's Rule

The workspace SIMPSON allows a general function defined on the same sheet (FNMACRO as described on page 46) to be integrated. The spreadsheet allows choice of range and number of double-strips, then shows the table of x values, function evaluations and multiplying factors going into the formula (Fig. 19). Exact results up to cubics are easily shown. There is no graph, as the approximating parabolas would be too close to the curve to show. There is a built in limit of 10 double strips as the sheet stands (easily increased by copying formulae further down the sheet); the sheet checks if this has been exceeded and displays a warning message if so.

The layout of the sheet is self evident, but a hidden complication is the method of allowing for a choice of number of double strips, which utilises IF() functions. This is rather cumbersome and devious as implemented, and not worth going into here. Pupils would be quite capable of setting up a sheet to use a specified number of double strips, however.

	A	B	C	D	E
1	Numerical Integration: Simpson's Rule				
2					
3	Ensure correct function defined in cell A5 of FNMCRO sheet				
4					
5	Lower limit	0			
6	Upper limit	2			
7	No. of double-strips	3			
8	Strip width	0.333333333			
9	Sum of f(x) terms	-14.3703704			
10	Approx integral	-1.59670782			
11					
12		x values	f(x) values	Mult'n factor/contribution	
13	1	0	0	1	0
14	2	0.333333333	-1.32099	4	-5.283951
15	3	0.666666667	-2.46914	2	-4.938272
16	4	1	-3	4	-12
17	5	1.333333333	-2.17284	2	-4.345679
18	6	1.666666667	1.049383	4	4.1975309
19	7	2	8	1	8
20	8				

	A	B
2		f
3		=ARGUMENT("x",1)
4		=RESULT(1)
5	Function Definition f(x)	=x^4-4*x
6		=RETURN(B5)

Figure 19: Simpson's rule workspace to integrate $f(x) = x^4 - 4x$

Numerical Methods – Interval Halving

The workspace INTHALVE uses the sheet FNMACRO to define the function to which this *Interval Halving* method of finding roots is applied. Upper and lower estimates for the root are entered, for which f(x) should be of opposite sign. The sheet then calculates about 20 steps of the method (Fig. 20).

The only technical point of the sheet is the use of IF functions to detect the pair of f(x) values that are of equal sign (by taking their product). If the lower, upper and mid x values are in cells A6, C6, E6 respectively, and their corresponding f(x) values in B6, D6 and F6, then the requisite formulae to calculate the appropriate new lower and upper x values are:

In A7   =IF(B6*F6>0, E6, A6)
In C7   =IF(D6*F6>0, E6, C6)

Pupils could in principle do this for themselves. The more rapidly convergent method of *False Position* is described in detail in Chapter 5 (pages 121-123).

	A	B	C	D	E	F
1			Method of Interval halving			
2	Initial x values, giving f(x) of opposite signs					
3	x1	1	f(x1)	-2		
4	x2	2.5	f(x2)	8.125		
5	Lower x	f(x)	Upper x	f(x)	Middle x	f(x)
6	1	-2	2.5	8.125	1.75	0.109375
7	1	-2	1.75	0.109375	1.375	-1.52539
8	1.375	-1.52539	1.75	0.109375	1.5625	-0.8728
9	1.5625	-0.8728	1.75	0.109375	1.65625	-0.42538
10	1.65625	-0.42538	1.75	0.109375	1.703125	-0.16923
11	1.703125	-0.16923	1.75	0.109375	1.726563	-0.03277
12	1.726563	-0.03277	1.75	0.109375	1.738281	0.037585
13	1.726563	-0.03277	1.738281	0.037585	1.732422	0.002227
14	1.726563	-0.03277	1.732422	0.002227	1.729492	-0.01532
28	1.732051	-9E-07	1.732051	1.24E-06	1.732051	1.71E-07
29						
30	Approximate Root:		1.732051			
31	f(x) at root:		1.71E-07			

Figure 20: Interval halving workspace to solve $x^3 - 3x = 0$

Numerical Methods – Newton-Raphson method

The workspace NEWTRAPH uses both f and a further function df/dx defined on sheet FNMACRO; clearly this must correspond to the definition given to f! The improvement of the *Newton-Raphson* method over *Interval Halving* should be obvious (Fig. 21).

This sheet has no technical difficulties of implementation given that FNMACRO exists already, and could easily be done by pupils themselves.

```
                    NEWTRAPH
              Newton-Raphson Method
Estimate of root
        x                  f(x)              f'(x)
        2                   2                  9
   1.777777778         0.285322359        6.481481481
   1.733756614         0.010249962        6.017735987
   1.732053322         1.5085E-05         6.000026128
   1.732050808         3.28448E-11        6
   1.732050808         8.88178E-16        6
   1.732050808        -8.88178E-16        6
   1.732050808         8.88178E-16        6
   1.732050808        -8.88178E-16        6
   1.732050808         8.88178E-16        6

              Approximate Root:        1.732050808
              f(x) at root:            8.88178E-16
```

	A	B
2		f
3		=ARGUMENT("X",1)
4		=RESULT(1)
5	Function Definition f(x)	=x^3-3*x
6		=RETURN(B5)
7		df/dx
8		=ARGUMENT("X",1)
9		=RESULT(1)
10	Function Derivative df dx	=3*x^2-3
11		=RETURN(B10)
12		

Figure 21: Newton-Raphson workspace to solve $x^3 - 3x = 0$

Numerical Methods – Iteration x=f(x)

The workspace ITERATE uses FNMACRO again. The sheet shows the iteration proceeding and a linked graph displays the curves y=x and y=f(x), hopefully crossing, and the iterates spiralling in (even more hopefully) to the crossing point (Fig. 22). There is some potential here to show bifurcation series developing as the constant a is increased from 1 to 4 in f(x) = ax(1–x), though programs written in BASIC are probably better.

The 'cobweb plot' co-ordinates are calculated in pairs; typically the cells B4:C5 contain:

=C3   =FNMACRO.XLM!f(B4)
=C4   =B5

An alternating pair of rows like this is easily copied down a column: highlight the block of cells to be copied, **Edit Copy**, then highlight the rest of the pair of columns and **Edit Paste**. The pasted formulae alternate correctly, just like the copied originals. A separate workspace area of the sheet calculates x,f(x) values at regular intervals so that the cobweb can be superimposed on a plot of the function. The graph is slightly tricky to create, but the method itself could be very easily set up by pupils.

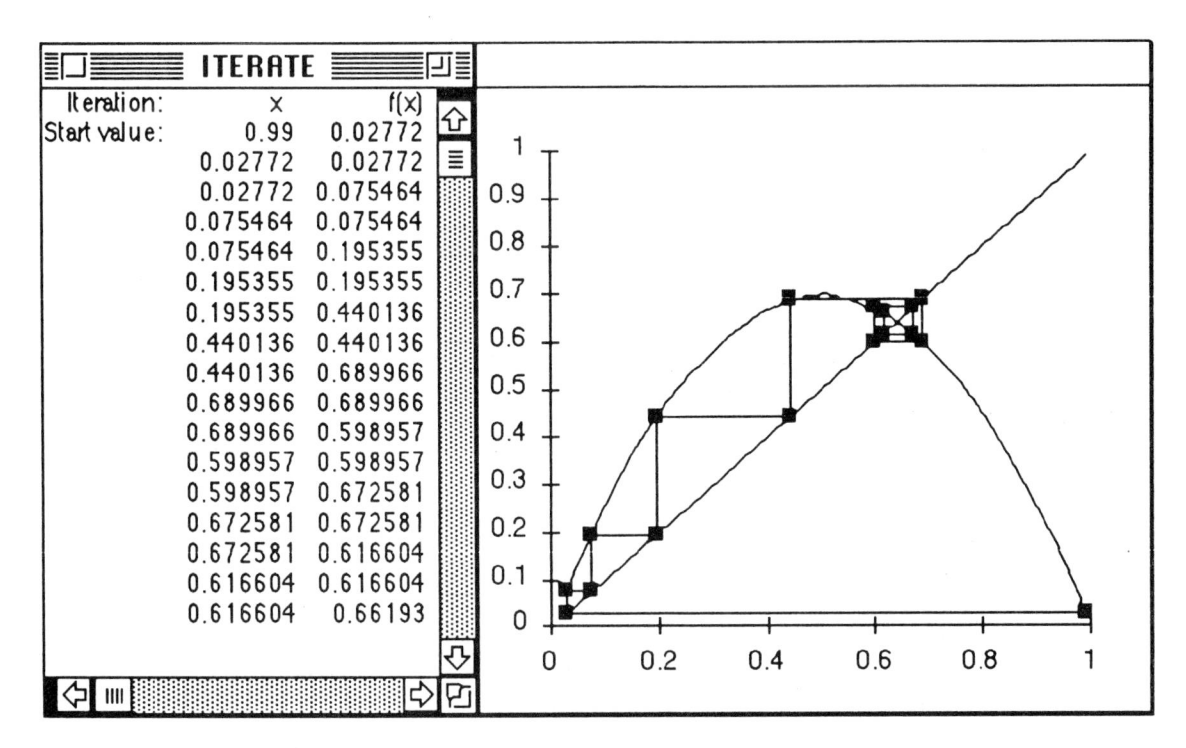

Iteration:	x	f(x)
Start value:	0.99	0.02772
	0.02772	0.02772
	0.02772	0.075464
	0.075464	0.075464
	0.075464	0.195355
	0.195355	0.195355
	0.195355	0.440136
	0.440136	0.440136
	0.440136	0.689966
	0.689966	0.689966
	0.689966	0.598957
	0.598957	0.598957
	0.598957	0.672581
	0.672581	0.672581
	0.672581	0.616604
	0.616604	0.616604
	0.616604	0.66193

FNMACRO.XLM

	A	B
2		f
3		=ARGUMENT("x",1)
4		=RESULT(1)
5	Function Definition f(x)	=2.8*x*(1-x)
6		=RETURN(B5)

Figure 22: Iteration workspace for $x_{n+1} = 2.8x_n(1 - x_n)$

3.8 Series Expansions and Limits

Series Expansions and Limits – Binomial Series

The workspace BINOMIAL calculates the coefficients, terms and partial sums of the Binomial expansion of $(a + b)^n$, and a linked graph shows the terms. The sheet can be used to demonstrate convergence if $|b/a|<1$ but divergence if $|b/a|>1$, even if a+b is the same (to calculate $2^{1/2}$ for example) (Fig. 23).

Implementation of the sheet is straightforward; a key computing technique is to calculate each term from the one before it rather than to use factorial formulae. This avoids problems that would arise when the size of the factorials would overflow the computer's arithmetic, even though the final term is small. Assuming that a, b, n are in A4, B4, C4 and that columns A, B, C, D contain the Term number r, the Binomial coefficient nCr, the r'th term of the series expansion, and the corresponding partial sum, then the formulae to be entered into row 11 and copied into subsequent rows are:

=A10+1	in cell A11
=B10*($C$4 – A11 + 1)/A11	in cell B11
=B11*$B$4/$A$4	in cell C11
=D10 + C11	in cell D11

There are other, possibly more economical, ways of doing this.

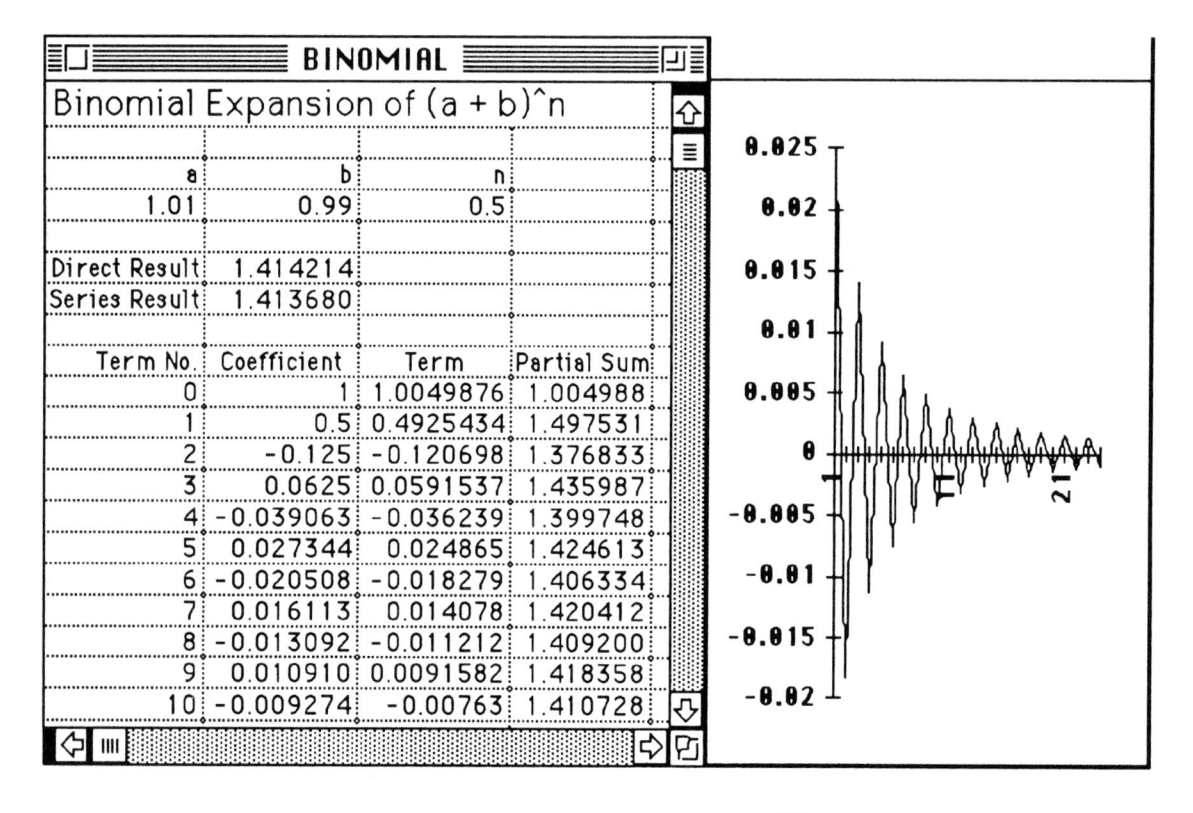

Figure 23: Binomial expansion of $(1.01 + 0.99)^{1/2}$ and graph of Term

Series Expansions and Limits – Exponential Limit and Series

The workspaces E and EX illustrate how spreadsheets can be used to show e as the limit of $(1 + 1/n)^n$ and e^x as the limit of $(1 + x/n)^n$ as n tends to infinity. They also demonstrate that the power series for e^x does work! Pupils should be able to set these up for themselves. Certain inaccuracies of computer arithmetic manifest themselves, and make an appropriate topic for discussion (Figs. 24-25).

ELIMIT

	A	B
1	Limit of $(1+1/n)^n$ as	
2	n increases to infinity	
3	n	$(1+1/n)^n$
4	1	2
5	10	2.59374246
6	100	2.704813829
7	1000	2.716923932
8	10000	2.718145927
9	100000	2.718268237
10	1000000	2.718280469
11	10000000	2.718281694
12	100000000	2.718281798
13	1000000000	2.718282052
14	10000000000	2.718282053
15	1E+11	2.718282053
16		
17	Computer's e	2.718281828
18		

ESERIES

	A	B	C
1	Series for e		
2			
3	Term No	Term	Partial Sum
4	0	1	1
5	1	1	2
6	2	0.5	2.5
7	3	0.166667	2.666666667
8	4	0.041667	2.708333333
9	5	0.008333	2.716666667
10	6	0.001389	2.718055556
11	7	0.000198	2.718253968
12	8	2.48E-05	2.718278770
13	9	2.76E-06	2.718281526
14	10	2.76E-07	2.718281801
15	11	2.51E-08	2.718281826
16			
17		Computer's e	2.718281828
18			

Figure 24: The constant e as a limit and as the sum of a power series

EXLIMIT

	A	B
1	Limit of $(1+x/n)^n$ as	
2	n increases to infinity	
3	x=	3
4		
5	n	$(1+x/n)^n$
6	1	4.00000000
7	10	13.78584918
8	100	19.21863198
9	1000	19.99553462
10	10000	20.07650227
11	100000	20.08463311
12	1000000	20.08544654
13	10000000	20.08552788
14	100000000	20.08553610
15	1000000000	20.08553736
16	10000000000	20.08554190
17	1E+11	20.08554191
18		
19	Computer's e^x	20.08553692
20		

EXSERIES

	A	B	C
1	Series for e^x		
2			
3	x=	3	
4			
5	Term No	Term	Partial Sum
6	0	1	1
7	1	3	4
8	2	4.5	8.5
9	3	4.5	13
10	4	3.375	16.375
11	5	2.025	18.4
12	6	1.0125	19.4125
13	7	0.433928571	19.84642857
14	8	0.162723214	20.00915179
15	9	0.054241071	20.06339286
16	10	0.016272321	20.07966518
17	11	0.004437906	20.08410308
18			
19	Computer's e^x		20.08553692
20			

Figure 25: Limit and power series for e^x

Series Expansions and Limits – Power Series for Sin and Cos

The workspace SINCOS demonstrates these two power series; again, pupils should be capable of setting them up for themselves. The alternate zero terms in the series were deliberately included; thus alternate rows contain different formulae, but these are easily copied and pasted in pairs as noted under x=f(x) iteration (page 51). Again, possible inaccuracies in evaluating the series would make a worthy topic for discussion (Fig. 26).

SINSERIES

	A	B	C
1	Series for sin(x) x =		3
2			
3	Term No.	Term	Partial Sum
4	0	0	0
5	1	3	3
6	2	0	3
7	3	-4.5	-1.5
8	4	0	-1.5
9	5	2.025	0.525
10	6	0	0.525
11	7	-0.433928571	0.091071429
12	8	0	0.091071429
13	9	0.054241071	0.1453125
14	10	0	0.1453125
15	11	-0.004437906	0.140874594
16			
17		Computer's sin(x)	0.141120008
18			
19			

COSSERIES

	A	B	C
1	Series for cos(x) x =		1
2			
3	Term No.	Term	Partial Sum
4	0	1	1
5	1	0	1
6	2	-0.5	0.5
7	3	0	0.5
8	4	0.041666667	0.541666667
9	5	0	0.541666667
10	6	-0.001388889	0.540277778
11	7	0	0.540277778
12	8	2.48016E-05	0.540302579
13	9	0	0.540302579
14	10	-2.75573E-07	0.540302304
15	11	0	0.540302304
16			
17	Computer's cos(x)		0.540302306
18			
19			

Figure 26: Power series for sine and cosine

3.9 Data handling and Statistics

Data handling and Statistics – Mean and Variance

The built-in functions AVERAGE() and STDEVP() will produce the mean and (population) standard deviation for a column of figures; it is important to use STDEVP() if the divisor n is wanted in the calculation of variance (s.d. = $\sqrt{\text{variance}}$), as the function STDEV() uses divisor n–1 to give an unbiased sample estimate of variance. Mean and variance of frequency distributions are not built in functions, however, so the workspace FRQTABLE shows how the necessary working can be built up. It assumes that the distribution has been grouped into classes and that the frequency for each class appears in the table alongside the lower class boundary; the necessary class mid-values x, fx and fx^2 are then easily laid out (Fig. 27). A similar sheet could easily be constructed for covariance and correlation between a set of pairs of values. Pupils should be able to construct these for themselves, working from an appropriate worksheet (e.g. Worksheet P, Chapter 4 pages 100-102).

Lower Boundary	Frequency	x (mid class)	fx	fx^2
9.5	6	10.5	63	661.5
11.5	5	12.5	62.5	781.25
13.5	5	14.5	72.5	1051.25
15.5	3	16.5	49.5	816.75
17.5	3	18.5	55.5	1026.75
19.5	9	20.5	184.5	3782.25
21.5	3	22.5	67.5	1518.75
23.5	7	24.5	171.5	4201.75
25.5	4	26.5	106	2809
27.5	5	28.5	142.5	4061.25
29.5	0			
Sums	50		975	20710.5
Mean		19.5		
Variance		33.96		
Std.Deviation		5.827521		

Figure 27: Spreadsheet for frequency table calculations

Data handling and Statistics – Cumulative Frequency Polygon & Percentiles

The workspace CUMFREQ shows how a cumulative frequency polygon can be constructed for a grouped frequency distribution laid out as discussed on page 55; the repetition of the column of lower class boundaries is purely to create two adjacent columns of x and y values for pasting into a scatter diagram (with **Paste Special,** as usual). The workspace also loads in the macro sheet PERCENT which calculates percentiles from a grouped frequency table of the above form by linear interpolation (Fig. 28) (see related Worksheet P, Chapter 4 pages 100-102).

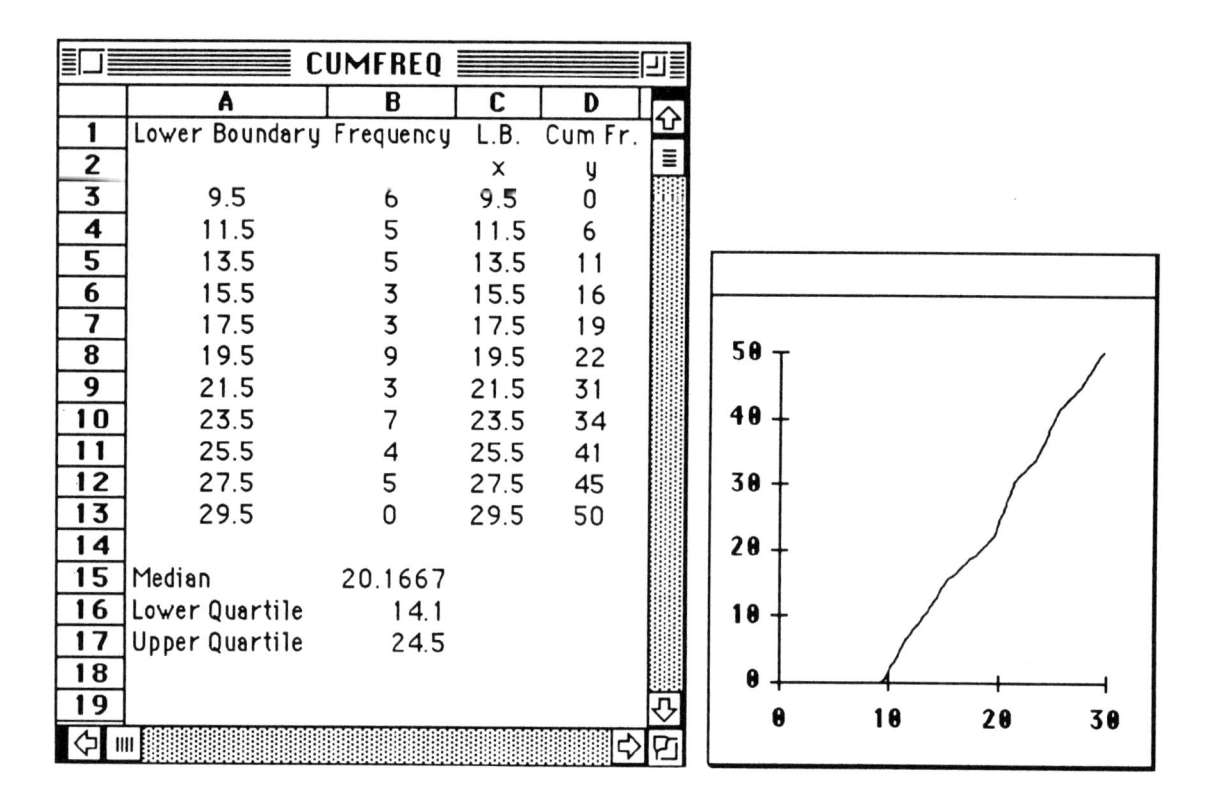

	A	B	C	D
1	Lower Boundary	Frequency	L.B.	Cum Fr.
2			x	y
3	9.5	6	9.5	0
4	11.5	5	11.5	6
5	13.5	5	13.5	11
6	15.5	3	15.5	16
7	17.5	3	17.5	19
8	19.5	9	19.5	22
9	21.5	3	21.5	31
10	23.5	7	23.5	34
11	25.5	4	25.5	41
12	27.5	5	27.5	45
13	29.5	0	29.5	50
14				
15	Median	20.1667		
16	Lower Quartile	14.1		
17	Upper Quartile	24.5		

Figure 28: Cumulative frequency polygon workspace

Data handling and Statistics – Counting Frequencies and Histograms

If it is desired to group raw data into a frequency distribution a problem arises: *Excel* is not able to do this as it stands (at least, in the earlier versions 2 and 3 that many users will have). Two relatively complex macro sheets have therefore been produced to go some way to filling in the gap. *Excel 4* does include some macros to perform similar tasks.

The purpose of COUNTER is to count frequencies of occurrence of different values in a column of data on a standard *Excel* worksheet. It is used as follows:
    Create or open a sheet containing the data to be counted (e.g. REACTION on disc).
    Open the sheet COUNTER.XLM. Highlight the data to be counted (*only* the data!).
    Choose **Macro Run** and click on COUNTER.XLM!countf to select it, and click **OK**.
The default is to produce both a pie chart and a table of frequencies; either can be de-selected by clicking on the appropriate 'check-boxes' that appear in the dialogue box shortly before the macro finishes.

COUNTER is primarily designed to count qualitative or non-numerical data; it will not work well on a continuous distribution of numbers (use instead GROUPFRQ described on the next page), or if a large number of different values is present. It operates fairly slowly if a large number of data (in the hundreds, say) are being counted (Fig. 29).

	REACTION				
	A	B	C	D	E
1	Name	Sex	Time	Games	Hand
2			sec.	ability	L/R
3					
4	Brace	Boy	0.29	9	R
5	Bryce	Girl	0.25	7	R
6	Bunker	Boy	0.23	7	L
7	Campbell	Boy	0.27	7	R
8	Carter	Boy	0.33	6	R
9	Hamadi	Girl	0.32	9	R
10	Hart	Boy	0.33	7	R
11	Ingle	Girl	0.29	8	R
12	Junior	Girl	0.29	3	R
13	Kodaki	Girl	0.31	3	L
14	Layton	Girl	0.33	7	R
15	McKay	Girl	0.30	5	R
16	Mistry	Boy	0.27	5	R
17	Preston	Girl	0.28	9	R
18	South	Boy	0.26	7	L
19	Teak	Boy	0.26	6	R
20	Tower	Girl	0.32	6	R
21	Twinning	Boy	0.27	8	L

	Worksheet1	
	A	B
1	Category	Frequency
2	3	3
3	5	2
4	6	4
5	7	6
6	8	2
7	9	3

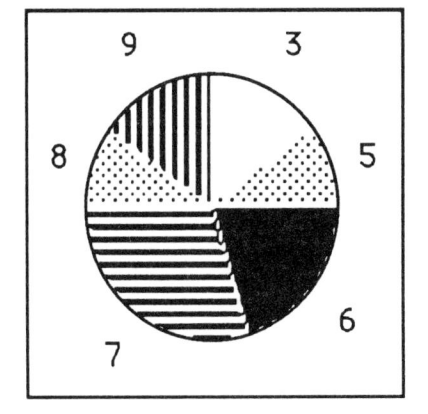

Figure 29: Counting frequencies (games ability) and drawing a pie chart

The macro sheet GROUPFRQ does a similar job for columns of numerical data which are to be grouped into classes. It is operated in a similar way, except that after highlighting the data it is activated by choosing **Macro Run** and clicking on GROUPFRQ.XLM!groupf to select it and clicking **OK**. It attempts to assign class boundaries correctly according to the scale of the data, and whether it is discrete and rounded or continuous and unrounded; if unequal class widths are required the classes can be entered manually. After counting, the options to produce a table of data and to plot a histogram are offered (Fig. 30) (see Worksheet P, Chapter 4 pages 100-102).

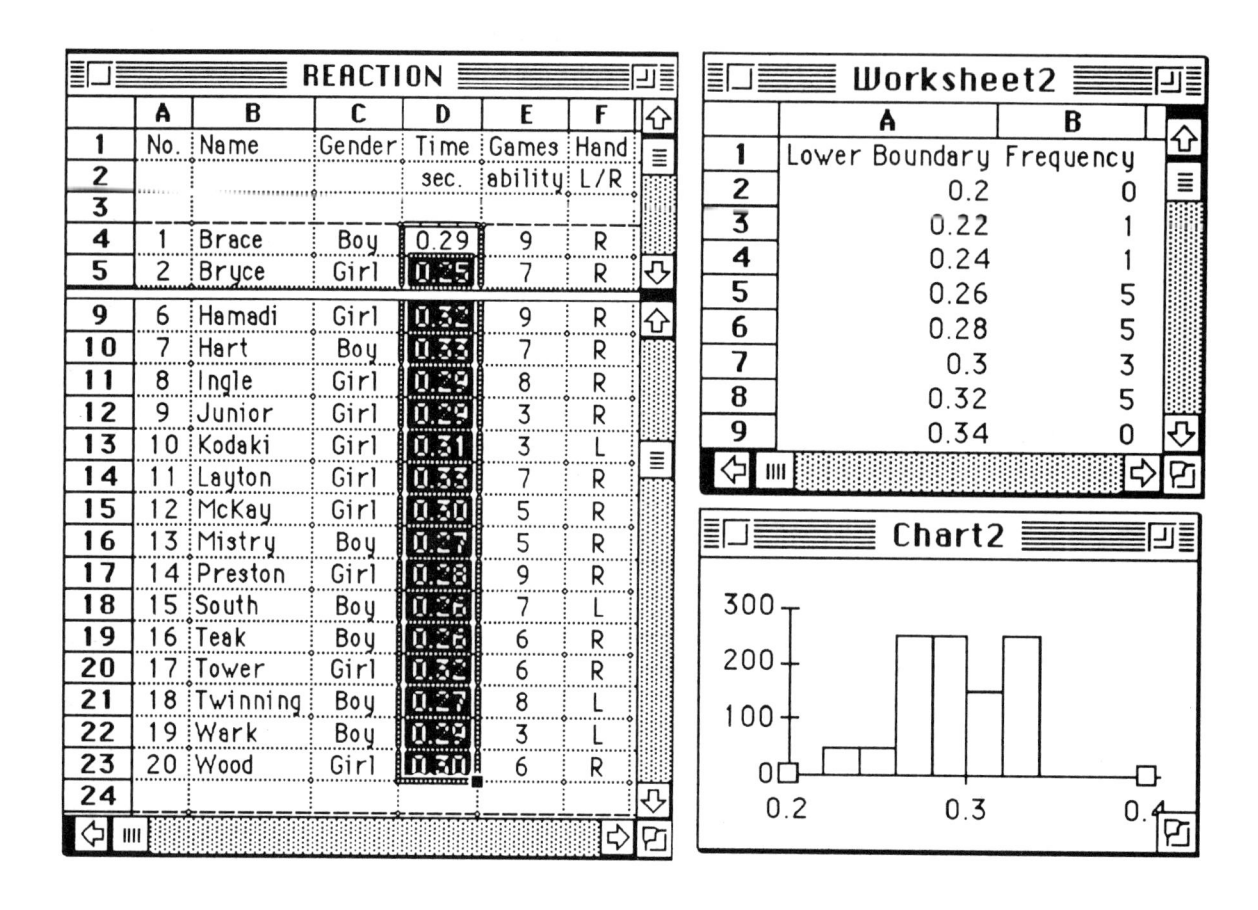

Figure 30: Counting frequencies in classes and plotting histogram

Data handling and Statistics – Random variable simulation

The workspace DIECOIN demonstrates how simple discrete random variables such as scores from coins or dice may be simulated. In COINS20 or DICE2, in order to have the spreadsheet calculate a new set of results use **Options Calculation Calc Now** or more simply just use the key combination **Command =** (for Macintosh) or **CTRL =** (for PCs)

In COINS20 it would be quite easy to increase the number of coins by inserting more rows and using **Fill Down**.

In DICE2 one changes the entry in B23 to find the frequency for any particular score from 2 to 12. This actually causes the spreadsheet to recalculate and so produces a new set of random numbers to which the analysis applies. It would be quite easy to set up further columns to calculate the frequencies for all scores, by using **Fill Right** and adjusting the IF() tests.

COINS20

	A	B
1	Coin Toss	H
2	T	0
3	T	0
4	H	1
5	H	1
6	H	1
7	H	1
8	H	1
9	T	0
16	H	1
17	H	1
18	H	1
19	T	0
20	H	1
21	T	0
22		
23	No. of Heads	11
24	No. of Tails	9
25	% Heads	55
26		

DICE2

	A	B	C	D
1	Red Die	Blue Die	Sum	COUNT
2	3	2	5	0
3	1	2	3	0
4	3	1	4	0
5	1	6	7	0
6	3	5	8	0
7	6	1	7	0
8	4	4	8	0
9	4	3	7	0
16	4	6	10	0
17	1	5	6	1
18	4	1	5	0
19	2	5	7	0
20	1	4	5	0
21	4	5	9	0
22				
23	No. of:	6	scores is	2
24				
25				
26				

Figure 31: Coin and dice experiment workspace

The workspace BINNORM uses similar techniques, in conjunction with the macro sheet STATRVS, to simulate a Binomial random variable, but this crude method is a bit slow for large n (see Fig. 32 for STATRVS). A Normal random variable is also simulated by generating it from the appropriate combined transformation of two values from the Uniform(0,1) built-in random number generator RAND().

Data handling and Statistics – Significance Testing

The workspace SIGDIFF shows how the working for a significance test can be laid out in spreadsheet form. A potential difficulty is the need for the tables of values of the integral of the N(0,1) distribution $\Phi(z)$ and its inverse. Fortunately, accurate numerical approximations to these are available (Abramovitz and Stegun, 1970) and these have been implemented as macro functions on the sheet STATRVS. Again, *Excel 4* comes with some ready-made macros to perform certain statistical tests, including quite complex ones such as ANOVA.

SIGDIFF

	A	B
1	Significance of difference of xbar from mu	
2		
3	Ho Population mean mu	5
4	Known population S.D. sigma	0.1
5	Size (% level) of test	5
6		
7	Sample size n	90
8	Sample mean xbar	5.02
9		
10	Standard Error of xbar (=sigma/root n)	0.01054093
11	Equivalent N(0,1) deviate for xbar (=(xbar-mu)/SE)	1.8973666
12		
13	Significance level (2 sided test)	0.0577798
14	Not significant evidence to reject H0	
15	Level of matching confidence interval:	95
16	Lower confidence limit for mu	4.99933562
17	Upper confidence limit for mu	5.04066438
18		

STATRVS.XLM

	A	B
1	Binomial	
2	=ARGUMENT("n",1)	
3	=ARGUMENT("p",1)	2
4	=RESULT(1)	
5	=SET.VALUE(x,0)	0
6	=SET.VALUE(count,0)	
7	=SET.VALUE(count,count+1)	4
8	=IF(RAND()<p,1,0)	
9	=SET.VALUE(x,x+A8)	
10	=IF(count<n,GOTO(A7),GOTO(A11))	
11	=RETURN(x)	
12		

Figure 32: Spreadsheet SIGDIFF and part of macro sheet STATRVS simulating a Binomial random variable

CHAPTER 4

Example Worksheets

Introduction

This chapter contains a selection of worksheets, in a variety of styles, which have been used in secondary school and college mathematics courses. They could be used as they are or modified by the teacher for different groups of students or for different spreadsheet packages. Some of these worksheets – clearly marked DISC NEEDED – require support material on disc. This may be prepared by the teacher or, alternatively, is available for purchase – see page (vi) at the front of the book.

The worksheets are divided somewhat arbitrarily into three categories; the teacher may find material suitable for a class in any section.

4.1 Worksheets A - G Lower Secondary pages 64-82

4.2 Worksheets H - P Upper Secondary pages 83-102

4.3 Worksheets Q - U Sixth Form/College pages 103-110

Some worksheets do not require the use of a computer, some have instructions specific to *Excel*, some require software. A list summarising this information for each worksheet is provided in Table 1 on page 62.

The links between the worksheets and the relevant sections of Chapters 3 and 5 are given in Table 2 on page 63.

Table 1: Computer, spreadsheet and support material requirements for Worksheets

Worksheet	Computer	Excel	Software
A	no	no	no
B	yes	no	no
C	no	no	no
D	no	yes	no
E	yes	yes	no
F1	no	no	no
F2	no	no	no
F3	optional	no	optional
G1	yes	yes	yes
G2	yes	yes	yes
G3	yes	no	yes
G4	yes	no	yes
G5	yes	yes	yes
G6	yes	yes	yes
H1	yes	yes	no
H2	yes	no	no
H3	yes	no	no
H4	yes	yes	no
H5	yes	yes	no
I1	yes	yes	no
I2	yes	yes	no
I3	yes	yes	no
I4	yes	yes	no
J	yes	no	yes
K	yes	no	no
L	yes	no	no
M	yes	yes	yes
N	yes	yes	yes
O	yes	yes	optional
P1	yes	yes	yes
P2	yes	yes	yes
P3	yes	yes	yes
P4	yes	yes	yes
P5	yes	yes	yes
Q	yes	yes	no
R	yes	no	no
S	yes	no	no
T	yes	yes	no
U	yes	no	no

Table 2: Worksheet titles and references to relevant pages of Chapters 3 and 5

Page	Worksheet	Title/Topic	Page references to Chapter 3 (unless otherwise stated)
64	A	Number Patterns	38
65	B	Number Patterns	38
66	C	Number Patterns	38
67	D	Pascal's Triangle	39
68	E	Pascal's Triangle	39
69	F	Processing Data	55
74	G	Processing Data	55
83	H	Sequences	38
86	I	Further Sequences	39
89	J	Decimal Expansions	34
91	K	Mystic Square	
92	L	Magic Square	
93	M	Matrices & Geometrical Transformations	40
97	N	Matrices and Simultaneous Equations	41
99	O	Data Analysis	55
100	P	Further Data Analysis	56-58
103	Q	Miscellaneous Problems	40, 51, 55, Chapter 5: 124
104	R	Miscellaneous Problems	38, 59
105	S	Optimisation Problems	Chapter 5: 127
107	T	Excel Charts	38-39; Chapter 2: 19
110	U	Further Excel Charts	38-39, Chapter 2: 19

WORKSHEET A – Number Patterns: (not using a computer)

The table below is a printout of the formulae on a computer spreadsheet. Some of the formulae are partly hidden, for example the formula in cell A11 should read "= 1 + A10".

	A	B	C	D	E	F	G
1	1	=2*A1-1	1			1	
2	=1+A1	=2*A2-1	=C1+B2			1	=F2/F1
3	=1+A2	=2*A3-1	=C2+B3			=F1+F2	=F3/F2
4	=1+A3	=2*A4-1	=C3+B4			=F2+F3	=F4/F3
5	=1+A4	=2*A5-1	=C4+B5			=F3+F4	=F5/F4
6	=1+A5	=2*A6-1	=C5+B6			=F4+F5	=F6/F5
7	=1+A6	=2*A7-1	=C6+B7			=F5+F6	=F7/F6
8	=1+A7	=2*A8-1	=C7+B8			=F6+F7	=F8/F7
9	=1+A8	=2*A9-1	=C8+B9			=F7+F8	=F9/F8
10	=1+A9	=2*A10-1	=C9+B10			=F8+F9	=F10/F9
11	=1+A10	=2*A11-1	=C10+B11			=F9+F10	=F11/F10
12							

1. Look at the pattern followed by the formulae shown and try to work out what the formulae in cells A12, B12, C12, F12 & G12 would be if we *filled down* to row 12.
2. When the computer calculates according to these formulae, the values it shows in Row 2 are: 2, 3, 4 ... 1, 1. You are now invited to be the computer and fill in all the values in columns A, B, C, F and G on the blank worksheet, down to row 11. (You will need a calculator for column G).
3. See if you can continue the patterns down to rows 12 and 13.
4. Can you give names to the sequences in columns A, B, C and F?
5. Try to predict what numbers would be in row 100 if we filled all the way down. (Column F is too difficult).

	A	B	C	D	E	F	G
1							
2							
3							
4							
5							
6							
7							
8							
9							
10							
11							
12							
13							
14							
15							

WORKSHEET B – Number Patterns (using a computer)

Test your answers to question 5 of Worksheet A by actually setting up this spreadsheet, as follows:

1. You should have a blank spreadsheet open on the computer in front of you. (If not, and you need help, ask your teacher).

2. Type the 1's and formulae into cells A1, B1, C1, A2, B2, C2.

3. Click on cell A2.

4. Hold down the shift key, move down to cell C100, and click. (This "selects" a block of cells from A2 down to C100).

5. Copy the formulae down (*Excel* commands: **Edit Fill Down**)

6. Use a similar method for columns F and G.

WORKSHEET C – Number Patterns

The formulae for another spreadsheet are shown below.

	A	B	C	D	E	F	G	H	I	J	K	L
1	1											=SUM(A1:K1)
2	1	=B1+A2	=C1+B1	=D1+C1	=E1+D1	=F1+E1	=G1+F1	=H1+G1	=I1+H1	=J1+I1	=K1+J1	=SUM(A2:K2)
3	1	=B2+A3	=C2+B2	=D2+C2	=E2+D2	=F2+E2	=G2+F2	=H2+G2	=I2+H2	=J2+I2	=K2+J2	=SUM(A3:K3)
4	1	=B3+A4	=C3+B3	=D3+C3	=E3+D3	=F3+E3	=G3+F3	=H3+G3	=I3+H3	=J3+I3	=K3+J3	=SUM(A4:K4)
5	1	=B4+A5	=C4+B4	=D4+C4	=E4+D4	=F4+E4	=G4+F4	=H4+G4	=I4+H4	=J4+I4	=K4+J4	=SUM(A5:K5)
6	1	=B5+A6	=C5+B5	=D5+C5	=E5+D5	=F5+E5	=G5+F5	=H5+G5	=I5+H5	=J5+I5	=K5+J5	=SUM(A6:K6)
7	1	=B6+A7	=C6+B6	=D6+C6	=E6+D6	=F6+E6	=G6+F6	=H6+G6	=I6+H6	=J6+I6	=K6+J6	=SUM(A7:K7)
8	1	=B7+A8	=C7+B7	=D7+C7	=E7+D7	=F7+E7	=G7+F7	=H7+G7	=I7+H7	=J7+I7	=K7+J7	=SUM(A8:K8)
9	1	=B8+A9	=C8+B8	=D8+C8	=E8+D8	=F8+E8	=G8+F8	=H8+G8	=I8+H8	=J8+I8	=K8+J8	=SUM(A9:K9)
10	1	=B9+A10	=C9+B9	=D9+C9	=E9+D9	=F9+E9	=G9+F9	=H9+G9	=I9+H9	=J9+I9	=K9+J9	=SUM(A10:K10)
11	1	=B10+A11	=C10+B10	=D10+C10	=E10+D10	=F10+E10	=G10+F10	=H10+G10	=I10+H10	=J10+I10	=K10+J10	=SUM(A11:K11)
12												

1. You be the computer and fill in the values on the blank sheet below. When you have finished, compare with a neighbour and discuss some of the patterns you see.
2. What is the sequence of numbers in column C called?

3. Comment on any patterns you notice.

4. What number would go into (i) cell C12? (ii) cell L12?

Now ask your teacher if you can try to produce this spreadsheet for yourself on a computer. You will find instructions for doing this on Worksheet D.

WORKSHEET D – **Number Patterns** (Pascal's triangle on a computer)

1. ***To get started:***
   You should have a blank spreadsheet open on the computer in front of you. (Ask the teacher for help if necessary.)

1.1 Keeping the mouse button depressed, drag the pointer across the column headings so as to blacken from A to R.

1.2 Click on **Format**, keeping the button pressed. A pull-down menu will appear in a window. Move down to select **Column Width**, release the mouse button and type 3 and click **OK**.

2. Click with the mouse on cell A1 to highlight that cell. Type the number 1 and then click in the tick box.

3. Now place the cursor on cell A1. Depress the mouse button and, holding it down, drag all the way down to cell A10 and then let go.
   The first (A) column should now be black, down to cell A10.

4. Click on **Edit** keeping the button pressed.
   A pull-down menu will appear in a window.
   Still keeping the button pressed, move the arrow down until **Fill Down** is highlighted, and let go.
   You have used the Edit menu to fill down the contents of cell A1 to cell A10.

5. To put a formula rather than a number or word into a cell, you simply type = followed by the formula. Try this by clicking on cell B2 and typing =A1+B1.
   N.B. After typing in a formula, always "click on the tick" before doing anything else.

6. Now fill the formula down to B10 in the same way as you did in steps 2 to 3.
   Can you explain what happens and why?
   What formula is now in B10? *Consider and discuss carefully what has happened here. It is a very important feature of how spreadsheets work.*
   *It is called **relative replication**. It is the way Excel always replicates unless you tell it otherwise. (To help understand this, you might try repeating steps 5 and 6 in column C. What do you get if you add pairs of numbers from Column C?)*

7. Now highlight (blacken) all the way from B3 to R10 and use **Edit Fill Right**.
   And there it is: Pascal's Triangle.

8. To get totals in column S, move to cell S1 and type in the formula =SUM(A1:R1).
   Then **Fill Down** from S1 to S10 in the usual way.
   Note: When entering a formula, you can enter a cell reference number simply by clicking on that cell, or to enter a range of cell numbers drag across the group of cells (from top left cell to bottom right cell will do).

WORKSHEET E – Number Patterns (Extension)

1. Look at the numbers in Column C from the spreadsheet used with Worksheet D. What are these numbers and why?
   What is the next number in this column, that is in cell C11?
   Fill down the formulae from C10 to C11 to check whether you were right.

2. Explain how the numbers in column D are related to those in column C. These are called **pyramid numbers**. Can you explain why?
   In cell C12, type in a formula to add up all the numbers in column C from C1 to C10. You could either type = and then click on each cell in turn, or use the formula =SUM(C1:C10)

3. **Fill Down** from D10 to D11. What do you notice?

4. Can you predict what you get when the formula in C12 is filled right?
   Perhaps you should fill row 11 right first.

5. What other patterns do you see in Pascal's Triangle, either when drawn this way or as drawn in your book?

6. What pattern do the totals of the numbers in the first few rows give?

   Now find another way of getting the same numbers in column T as in column S, without referring to any of the entries in columns A to S. Start with 1 in cell T1...

68

WORKSHEET F – Statistics: Reaction Time Database

Processing Tabulated Data and Drawing Conclusions

Last term twenty Y9 pupils measured their reaction times using the computer program *Times* (from the package Teaching Maths with a Micro 3 produced by the Shell Centre for Mathematics Education, Nottingham University). They entered their results (actually the median of 100 times each) and other personal statistics into a computer database. The data in the form of a printout of an *Excel* spreadsheet are given in Table 1 below.

	A	B	C	D	E	F	G	H	I	J	K	L	M	N
1	No.	Name		Year	Set	Age		Time	Spread	Gender	Games	Hand	Height	Mass
2						year	mon	s	s	m/f	ability	L/R	m	kg
3														
4	1	Bryce	Liz	Y9	2	13	8	0.25	0.060	f	7	R	1.63	50.4
5	2	Preston	An	Y9	2	14	5	0.28	0.085	f	9	R	1.70	69.9
6	3	Ingle	Lo	Y9	2	14	1	0.29	0.030	f	8	R	1.55	44.5
7	4	Junior	Na	Y9	2	14	6	0.29	0.070	f	3	R	1.63	49.0
8	5	McKay	Jea	Y9	2	13	7	0.30	0.050	f	5	R	1.60	48.6
9	6	Wood	He	Y9	2	14	4	0.30	0.030	f	6	R	1.70	54.0
10	7	Kodaki	Ni	Y9	2	14	4	0.31	0.065	f	3	L	1.52	40.9
11	8	Hamadi	Ro	Y9	2	14	1	0.32	0.070	f	9	R	1.70	54.0
12	9	Tower	Ta	Y9	2	14	2	0.32	0.120	f	6	R	1.63	38.1
13	10	Layton	Ro	Y9	2	14	5	0.33	0.070	f	7	R	1.60	50.8
14	11	Bunker	Ma	Y9	2	13	5	0.23	0.060	m	7	R	1.50	34.5
15	12	South	Lu	Y9	2	14	3	0.26	0.060	m	7	L	1.68	53.6
16	13	Teak	Pe	Y9	2	14	9	0.26	0.060	m	6	R	1.55	40.9
17	14	Campbell	Ed	Y9	2	14	2	0.27	0.050	m	7	R	1.60	44.5
18	15	Mistry	Ra	Y9	2	14	1	0.27	0.040	m	5	R	1.57	43.1
19	16	Twinning	Mi	Y9	2	13	10	0.27	0.050	m	8	L	1.55	43.1
20	17	Brace	An	Y9	2	13	10	0.29	0.080	m	9	R	1.73	74.5
21	18	Wark	Jo	Y9	2	14	4	0.29	0.060	m	3	L	1.57	43.6
22	19	Carter	He	Y9	2	13	7	0.33	0.060	m	6	R	1.50	41.3
23	20	Hart	Ad	Y9	2	14	5	0.33	0.060	m	7	R	1.60	42.7

Table 1

THREE EXERCISES F1, F2, F3 WHICH USE THESE DATA
ARE FOUND ON THE FOLLOWING SHEETS.

Exercise F1

Use Table 1 to answer the following questions:

1. Who has the quickest reactions (shortest time)?

2. Who has the slowest reactions?

3. What is the **range** of reaction times? (Subtract your answers above).

4. Who had the most consistent reactions (smallest spread)?

5. Who had the better reactions - the males or the females? Why do you say so?

You will have noticed that the rows of the spreadsheet have been sorted by gender and then by time, in ascending order. This makes it very easy to answer questions such as:

6. What was the **median** (i.e. middle) time for (a) the males and (b) the females?

7. What was the **mode** of the male's times, i.e. the time that came up most often? And for the females?

8. Draw separate frequency tables and frequency diagrams for the male's and females' reaction times.

9. Find the **range** of (a) the males' times (b) the females' times.

10. Copy and complete this two-way table ('Carroll diagram'):

	Males	Females
Times under 0.28 s		1
Times of at least 0.28 s		

    Would this be a fair way to answer question 5?

11. Find the **mean** reaction time   (i) for males   (ii) for females   (iii) for all 20 pupils. Comment.

12. Find the **mean** reaction time of the left-handers. Comment.

13. Notice that the lightest person has the quickest reactions. Is this a trend? Find some way of checking for **correlation** between mass and time, e.g. a scatter diagram or a two-way table.

Exercise F2

In Table 2 on the next page the same spreadsheet has been sorted by rows, in ascending order of reaction times (column H).

1. What is the median of all the times?

2. Copy and fill in the numbers in following two-way tables:

   (a)

	Males	Females
Time ≤ median		
Times > median		

   (b)

	Left-handed	Right-handed
Time ≤ median		
Times > median		

   (c)

	Age under 14	Age over 14
Time ≤ median		
Times > median		

   Compare the proportions of fast times and slow times in the two columns of each table. Do your results suggest any possible trends (correlations)?

3. From your results in question 2, suggest approximate probabilities (on a scale from 0 to 1) for each of the following events:

   (a) the next person I meet from the list in column B is a female.

   (b) the next person I meet from the list in column B is left-handed.

   (c) the next person I meet from the list in column B is right-handed.

   (d) the next person I meet from the list in column B has a reaction time less than the median.

   (e) the next person I meet from the list in column B was over 14 years old when the spreadsheet was set up.

   (f) the next person I meet from the list in column B is a left-handed person with a reaction time less than the median.

   (g) the next female I meet from the list in column B has a reaction time less than the median.

	A	B	C	D	E	F	G	H	I	J	K	L	M	N
1	No.	Name		Year	Set	Age		Time	Spread	Gender	Games	Hand	Height	Mass
2						year	mon	s	s	m/f	ability	L/R	m	kg
3														
4	1	Bunker	Ma	Y9	2	13	5	0.23	0.060	m	7	R	1.50	34.5
5	2	Bryce	Liz	Y9	2	13	8	0.25	0.060	f	7	R	1.63	50.4
6	3	South	Luk	Y9	2	14	3	0.26	0.060	m	7	L	1.68	53.6
7	4	Teak	Pe	Y9	2	14	9	0.26	0.060	m	6	R	1.55	40.9
8	5	Campbell	Edv	Y9	2	14	2	0.27	0.050	m	7	R	1.60	44.5
9	6	Mistry	Ral	Y9	2	14	1	0.27	0.040	m	5	R	1.57	43.1
10	7	Twinning	Mic	Y9	2	13	10	0.27	0.050	m	8	L	1.55	43.1
11	8	Preston	Ann	Y9	2	14	5	0.28	0.085	f	9	R	1.70	69.9
12	9	Brace	Ann	Y9	2	13	10	0.29	0.080	m	9	R	1.73	74.5
13	10	Wark	Joh	Y9	2	14	4	0.29	0.060	m	3	L	1.57	43.6
14	11	Ingle	Lou	Y9	2	14	1	0.29	0.030	f	8	R	1.55	44.5
15	12	Junior	Na	Y9	2	14	6	0.29	0.070	f	3	R	1.63	49.0
16	13	McKay	Jea	Y9	2	13	7	0.30	0.050	f	5	R	1.60	48.6
17	14	Wood	Hel	Y9	2	14	4	0.30	0.030	f	6	R	1.70	54.0
18	15	Kodaki	Nir	Y9	2	14	4	0.31	0.065	f	3	l	1.52	40.9
19	16	Hamadi	Ro	Y9	2	14	1	0.32	0.070	f	9	R	1.70	54.0
20	17	Tower	Tar	Y9	2	14	2	0.32	0.120	f	6	R	1.63	38.1
21	18	Carter	He	Y9	2	13	7	0.33	0.060	m	6	R	1.50	41.3
22	19	Hart	Ada	Y9	2	14	5	0.33	0.060	m	7	R	1.60	42.7
23	20	Layton	Ro	Y9	2	14	5	0.33	0.070	f	7	R	1.60	50.8

Table 2

Exercise F3   [DISC OPTIONAL]

Table 3 below is another copy of Table 2, with only the following changes:
  (i)   The formulae entered in column A are shown instead of the cell values.
  (ii) Column H has been widened.
  (iii) Rows 1 and 2 have been copied and pasted in rows 25 and 26.
  (iv) Cell A23 has been given the name n.
  (v)   Formulae have been typed into H29 to H36 to show how to calculate the reaction time statistics typed in cells B29 to B36.

1. Work out the sample size, range, median and mean of the times in column H and check that these are the same as given by the formulae, using a computer if available.
2. Now, suppose we want, instead, to find the sample size, range, median and mean of the heights in column M. If we were to copy the formulae in cells H29:H36 and paste them into cells M29:M36 (so that all H's in the formulae change to M's), would the formulae still work? Which ones would and which ones would not, and why?

	A	B	C	D	E	F	G	H	I	J	K	L	M	N
1	No.	Name		Year	Set	Age		Time		Spread	Gender	Games	Hand	Height	Mass
2						year	mon	s		s	m/f	ability	L/R	m	kg
3															
4	1	Bunker	M	Y9	2	13	5	0.23	0.06	m	7	R	1.5	34.5
5	=1+A4	Bryce	Li	Y9	2	13	8	0.25	0.06	f	7	R	1.63	50.4
6	=1+A5	South	Lu	Y9	2	14	3	0.26	0.06	m	7	L	1.68	53.6
7	=1+A6	Teak	P	Y9	2	14	9	0.26	0.06	m	6	R	1.55	40.9
8	=1+A7	Campbell	Ed	Y9	2	14	2	0.27	0.05	m	7	R	1.6	44.5
9	=1+A8	Mistry	R	Y9	2	14	1	0.27	0.04	m	5	R	1.57	43.1
10	=1+A9	Twinning	Mic	Y9	2	13	10	0.27	0.05	m	8	L	1.55	43.1
11	=1+A10	Preston	A	Y9	2	14	5	0.28	0.085	f	9	R	1.7	69.9
12	=1+A11	Brace	A	Y9	2	13	10	0.29	0.08	m	9	R	1.73	74.5
13	=1+A12	Ingle	L	Y9	2	14	1	0.29	0.03	f	8	R	1.55	44.5
14	=1+A13	Junior	N	Y9	2	14	6	0.29	0.07	f	3	R	1.63	49
15	=1+A14	Wark	J	Y9	2	14	4	0.29	0.06	m	3	L	1.57	43.6
16	=1+A15	McKay	Je	Y9	2	13	7	0.3	0.05	f	5	R	1.6	48.6
17	=1+A16	Wood	H	Y9	2	14	4	0.3	0.03	f	6	R	1.7	54
18	=1+A17	Kodaki	N	Y9	2	14	4	0.31	0.065	f	3	L	1.52	40.9
19	=1+A18	Hamadi	R	Y9	2	14	1	0.32	0.07	f	9	R	1.7	54
20	=1+A19	Tower	T	Y9	2	14	2	0.32	0.12	f	6	R	1.63	38.1
21	=1+A20	Carter	H	Y9	2	13	7	0.33	0.06	m	6	R	1.5	41.3
22	=1+A21	Hart	A	Y9	2	14	5	0.33	0.06	m	7	R	1.6	42.7
23	=1+A22	Layton	R	Y9	2	14	5	0.33	0.07	f	7	R	1.6	50.8
24														
25	No.	Name		Year	Set	Age		Time		Spread	Gender	Games	Hand	Height	Mass
26						year	mon	s		s	m/f	ability	L/R	m	kg
27														
28														
29		Count, n						=n						
30		Smallest						=H4						
31		Biggest						=H23						
32		Range						=H31-H30						
33		Median						=(H13+H14)/2						
34		Total						=SUM(H4:H23)						
35		Mean						=H34/n						
36		Mean						=AVERAGE(H4:H23)						

Table 3

WORKSHEET G [DISC NEEDED]

STATISTICS: REACTION TIME DATABASE FURTHER ANALYSIS

Uses the files REACT20.and REACT79.

Exercise G1
(Using the file REACT20)

Your screen should show a spreadsheet called REACT20, as given in Table 3 for Exercise F3. If not, ask your teacher.

In this Exercise, answers to the questions in italics should be written in your book.

1. **Checking cell contents**
   Use the mouse to press the pointer on the arrow pointing downwards at the bottom right hand corner of the screen to step through the rows and see what the entries are in cells H29:H36. Click on each of the cells H29 to H36 in turn and watch the formula shown at the top of the screen change.
   Are these the correct formulae as shown in Table 3?
   Now look at the values in these cells.
   Are these what you expected from your calculations in Exercise F3?

2. **Column Width**
   In the course of this work you may need to widen or narrow down some of the columns. There are two ways to do this described below. Try them on column C.

2.1 Move the pointer to the dividing line between C and D (in the heading at the top) and drag this to the right to widen column C. You should now be able to see the full first name of each person.

2.2 Alternatively, select (i.e. 'black') column C by clicking on the heading C. Then press the pointer on the **Format** menu, drag down to **Column Width** and release. Enter a number such as 5 and the **OK**.

   Note: From now on we shall give instructions like this in shortened form:

   Format Column Width 5 OK.

   [You could try 2.1 or 2.2 on rows as well as columns.]

3. **Copying, pasting and replicating**
   Select cells H29:H36. (You do this by first clicking on the top cell, H29, and, keeping the mouse depressed, dragging down to the bottom and releasing.) Except for starting cell, which will be outlined in black, this block of cells should now be all black.

   3.1 Now copy the contents of these cells: **Edit Copy**. (Note how the computer shows that you have made a copy - in memory- of this block.)

   3.2 Select cells M29:M36 and paste into this area: **Edit Paste**.

   3.3 If you now click on each of these cells in turn, you will see that you have replicated the formulae in column H into column M just as described in Exercise F3 No 2.
   Do the values in column M confirm your answers to Exercise F3?
   What is the mean height of the pupils?

   3.4 Get the computer to put the means of the numbers in columns F and G into cells F36 and G36. (You could, for example, simply copy and paste the formula from H36.)

4. **Using a formula**
   Explain why the numbers in F36 and G36 do not give the correct average age (on the day the figures were entered last term) of these third-formers in years and months.
   What do we need to do to ages in years and months to convert them to ages in months?
   What was Mark Bunker's age in months?
   Make this into a formula using the symbols F4 and G4.

   4.1 Use the arrows at the bottom of the screen to move to cell O4.
   Enter your formula (for Mark's age in months) into cell O4. (Always "click on tick" after entering a formula.)
   Does your formula work? (Did you remember the = sign?)

   4.2 Type the appropriate heading (Age/months) into cells O1 and O2. Copy and paste this into cells O25 and O26. You may now wish to narrow down column O.

   4.3 Now replicate your formula from O4 all the way down to O23. A quick way of doing this is to select (i.e. "black) O4:O23 with the mouse as described in 3 above and then:
   Edit Fill Down.
   Check that this gives the right values.

   4.4 Now put the average of O4:O23 into cell O36. *How does it compare with F36, G36?*

5. **Scatter diagrams:**
   You could investigate the correlation between height and mass by drawing and analysing a scatter diagram. However, since different versions of *Excel* work in different ways you would need to consult your teacher first. When you have mastered the techniques and you have produced your scatter diagram, try the exercises below.

5.1 *Does there appear to be any correlation between height and mass?*

5.2 Use the same method to draw some more scatter diagrams to find any correlation you suspect to be there *and state the degree of correlation in each case.*

   Here are some suggestions:
   (a) Time and spread. (Spread was actually the interquartile range of the 100 reaction times.)
   (b) Age in months and mass.
   (c) Games and time. (Games was the person's own estimate of ability at ball games on a scale from 1 (lowest) to 10. (highest).)

6. **Averages: Mean**

6.1 If all 20 people were laid end to end across the school field (or playground), how far would they reach? (Give your answer, in metres).
   You will remember that the answer is in cell M34. *Why?*
   (You will need to widen the column to read the answer.)

6.2 Now we could get the mean height of all the people in the database by dividing your answer by the number of people. This should have been done already in cell M35. *What is the formula and what is the answer?*

6.3 But we have seen that there is an easier way: Click on cell M36 and look at the formula displayed at the top under the heading.
   Is the answer the same as in M35? What is the formula this time?

6.4 Select M36:O36 and **Edit Fill Right** to put the mean mass into cell N36 and the mean age into cell O36. *Note these down.*
   Is the mean age the same as you got in 4.4?

6.5 Select F36:O36 and **Edit Fill Right**.
   (a) What is the mean spread?
   (b) What is the mean games ability?
   (c) Why does the computer appear to be unhappy in cells J36 and L36?
   (d) Why could we not find the medians by just replicating formulae in the same way?

7. **Defining Names**

   Carefully select the block of data from A4 to O23, either by dragging or as follows: Click on cell O23 and, while holding down the shift key, click on cell A4.

7.1 To find medians and for other reasons we are going to need to sort the data. For when we do sort, it is a good idea now to give this block a *name*, e.g. SortArea. Do it like this (making sure the right block remains black):
   Formula Define Name SortArea **OK**.

7.2 This lets us to get back to the sort area any time we want to. Click anywhere on the worksheets and then get back by:
   Formula Goto SortArea **OK**.

   [Instead of **OK**, at any time, you may press the Enter button.]

8. **Sorting – range and median**

   Medians can be found by sorting the data in ascending order and finding the value in the middle. What (two) numbers are in the middle of the counting column (A)? Remember them. As an example, we now find the median height of the entries. First we shall sort by height and then see which heights come in the middle.

8.1 Whatever you want to sort always needs to be selected first:
   Formula Goto SortArea **OK**

8.1.1 **Data Sort.** If the Sort box which you get is in a bad place you can move it by clicking on the lines (blue on the Nimbus) at the top and dragging with the mouse.

8.1.2 Click anywhere in Column M (height) **OK**. The result should be that you have sorted the rows in ascending order of height. The median height is now the mean of M13 and M14.

8.1.3 (a) Why?
   (b) Write down the median height and compare with the mean.
   (c) What is the mode? Type the word "mode" into cell B37 and enter its value in M37.
   (d) What is the range of heights?

8.1.4 Check that cells M32 and M33 give the range and median, respectively, of the heights. *Now explain why cells H32 and H33 no longer give the range and median of the times.*

8.2 Your aim now is to find the median, range and mode of each of columns I, K, M, N, O and record these in rows 32, 33 and 37.

8.2.1 Start by replicating the block H29:H36 across to column O, using
   Edit Fill Right.

8.2.2 Of course, next time we sort the data according to a different column, we shall have the same problem with M32 and M33 as we had with H32 and H33: they will no longer give the correct range and median. We can get round this problem by pasting values instead of formulae into these cells: Select M29:M33 and **Edit Copy** then **Edit Paste Special**, click on **Values** and **OK**.

8.2.3 Now use the same sorting procedure as in 8.2 above, for each column in turn, to complete the task set in 8.3. You will, of course, need to Paste values as in 8.3.2 each time after sorting.

8.2.4 If you would like to tidy up J29:J36 and/or L29:L36, select and use **Edit Clear**.

Exercise G2 – Using a larger data set　　　　　　　　**[DISC NEEDED]**
(Using the file REACT79)

Process the data on the larger file of 79 pupil's reaction times (called REACT79) in the same way as in Exercise G1.
Find means and medians of each column and draw some scatter diagrams.
By sorting appropriately, can you detect any differences between:

- Males and Females?
- Left- and right-handers?
- Younger and older pupils?
- Those in top Maths sets and those who are not?
  etc.

Exercise G3 – Using data collected by the class

Use data collect by the class and process it in the kinds of ways suggested in Exercises G1 and G2.

Exercise G4 – Sorting further, seeking correlations　　**[DISC NEEDED]**
(Using the file REACT79)

Following on from Exercise G2 we could look for correlations by sorting further, into males and females for examples, and then comparing half-sample statistics with those for the whole sample.

1. Select a file of data, e.g. the one used in Exercise G1 and load it onto a computer as before. Now sort the data into Males and Females.

2. Select a statistic, such as mean or median, and use the computer to work it out for the columns of interest. Compare with each other and/or the corresponding values for the whole sample.

3. Draw some scatter diagrams to compare females with males (It is possible to superimpose by pasting into an existing chart.)

4. Try this with the data divided into two in some other way, e.g. left-/right- handers.

We could, alternatively, sort further and look for correlations through two-way tables, as in Exercises F1 and F2.

Exercise G5 – Further Data Analysis [DISC NEEDED]
(Using either the file REACT20 or REACT79)

You need to have a spreadsheet open on a computer as in Exercise G1 or Exercise G2

1. Suppose we want to find all the left-handed males in Y9. You could first sort by Year and then by Hand and then by Gender. Or you could do all this in one go like this:

1.1 **Edit Goto** SortArea **OK** or select the right area by clicking/dragging.

1.2 **Data Sort**

1.3 Click anywhere in the Year column, e.g. D19. This will put $D$19 into the box for 1st key.

1.4 Click on the box for 2nd key (or press TAB) and click anywhere in the Hand column (probably Column L).

1.5 Click on the box for 3rd key (or press TAB) and click anywhere in column J (Gender).

1.6 *Is Michael Twinning the only left-handed male in Y9 on this database? How many left-handed females are there?*

1.7 If the answer is not clear, try sorting again by Year, Gender and Hand in that order instead.

2. Use the methods of question 1 to answer the questions below.

    (a) Which 14 year old females have surnames between A and H?

    (b) How many females with heights between 1.40m and 1.50m (inclusive) weigh under 45kg?

    (c) Ask a similar question, answer it and get a friend to check.

    (d) Copy and complete the following two-way tables:

Males	Reaction Time	
	Over 0.28 s	0.28 s or less
Left-handed	4	1
Right-handed	12	
Females	Reaction Time	
	Over 0.28 s	0.28 s or less
Left-handed		
Right-handed		
All	Reaction Time	
	Over 0.28 s	0.28 s or less
Left-handed		
Right-handed		

Does there seem to be any correlation between reaction time and which hand is used?

3. Use a similar method to 2(d) to check some other correlations.
   (Discuss with your teacher or a friend.)

Exercise G6 – **Alphabetical Order Sort**   [DISC NEEDED]

Computers sort names alphabetically but figures in numerical order. There ought, of course, to be no particular correlation between the position of your name in the alphabet and any of your statistics. Nevertheless, the following exercise can be quite fun.

You need to have a spreadsheet open on a computer as in Exercise G1 or Exercise G2.

1. Sort the data by surname (column B) as described in Exercise G5.

2. Now select column A and convert the formulae to values by using **Edit Copy** and **Edit Paste Special Values OK**. The figures in column A should now give the alphabetical ranking of the pupils.

3. Now look for correlations between column A and other columns, e.g. by drawing scatter diagrams.

WORKSHEET H – Sequences

H1 Arithmetic Sequences (Copy and Paste Formulae)
In arithmetic sequences each term is a constant amount more than the term before it:
$$u_n = u_{n-1} + d.$$

a: Type a 1 into cell A1.

b: Click the cursor into cell A2 and type =A1+1 (then enter); it should show 2 on screen.

c: Still with the cursor in A2, choose **Copy** from the **Edit** menu.

d: Click on A3 and drag down the column so that A3 down to, say A15 are highlighted.

e: Choose **Paste** from the **Edit** menu.
This puts the same formula that you previously copied into all the highlighted cells. You should see the arithmetic sequence 1, 2, 3, 4, 5, ... appear.

f: Click on A3 to see the formula that has been copied; you should see that it says =A2+1 (not =A1+1 as you might expect). This is because formulae are usually copied so that they act in a 'relative' fashion; i.e. the formula should really say 'cell above' +1 and so A1 is called a 'relative reference' to a cell. Click on other cells to see the formulae.

g: Click on A1 again. This is the only cell that contains a number, not a formula. Type a different number in, then press Enter. You should see the new sequence displayed right away.

h: Now try altering the step in the sequence. Into A2 type =A1+4 (or any number you wish. This will only work for the whole sequence if you now go through the **Copy** and **Paste** procedure into the rest of the A.. cells; see if you can get it to work.
Try others.

H2 Geometric Sequences (Including Absolute References)
In geometric sequences each term is a constant multiple of the one before it; $u_n = u_{n-1} \times r$.

a: Click on A1 and type in 3, click on B1 and type in 2.

b: Click in A2 and enter the formula =A1*$B$1 (i.e. using dollar signs as shown). **Copy** and **Paste** this formula into the other A... cells, and you should see the geometric sequence 3, 6, 12, 24, 48, ... appear.

c: Click in A3 and you should see the formula =A2*$B$1. The dollar signs tells the computer always to keep B1 in the formula even when it is copied; $B$1 is called an 'absolute reference' because it stays the same even when copied to a different part of the grid.

d: Try altering the number in A1 to alter the starting point of the sequence, or the number in B1 to alter the 'common ratio'.

H3 Natural Number Sequences and their Differences (Multiple Columns)

Now we'll look at sequences like 1, 4, 9, 16, ... or 1, 8, 27, where $u_n = n^2$, $u_n = n^3$ or some other power of n.

a: Set up the sequence of natural numbers 1, 2, 3, 4, ... in cells A1, A2, etc using a formula =A1+1 copied from A2 into the other A.. cells.

b: Put the formula =A1*A1 into cell B1. You can shorten your typing by doing it with the mouse: type the = then click on A1, then type the * then click on A1 again, and finally Enter.

c: Copy the formula from B1 into the rest of the B.. column; you should see the sequence of squares 1, 4, 9, 16, ... (NB relative references only used).

d: Put the formula =B2-B1 into cell C2 (using the mouse if you wish). Then copy it into the rest of the C.. column. You should see the sequence of 'first differences' 3, 5, 7, ... appear (NB all relative again).

e: Copy from C2 into D3 and the rest of the D.. column (all relative again) to get the column of second differences 2, 2, 2, ... Have a look at the formulae in the D's to make sure you understand what has happened. N.B. You'll get an error if you copy into D2, as there's nothing in C1 for it to refer to. If you make this mistake, click on D2 and choose Edit, Clear.

f: Copy into E4 and the rest of the E.. column to get the 'third differences'; starting from the squares these are all 0.

g: Save the sheet calling it SEQUENCE (if using *Excel* use the **File Save As** option).

h: Now return to B1 and alter the formula to =A1^3 (using the ^ for a power; this will give the cubes). Then copy this into the rest of the B.. column, and see what happens in the difference columns.

H4 Triangular Numbers (Printing)

These count the numbers of dots in triangles giving: 1, 3, 6, 10, ... from rule $u_n = u_{n-1} + n$.
To set this up on your SEQUENCE sheet, alter B1 to =A1, alter B2 to =B1+A2
Then **Copy** from B2 and **Paste** into the rest of the B.. column.
Make sure you notice what the difference columns look like for the triangular numbers.

Printing: first you have to make a few changes to the print options, or you'll get extremely slow and fairly poor quality results.
From the **Format** menu choose **Fonts Printer Fonts Roman 10cpi** (or whatever other font your teacher tells you).
From the **File** menu choose **Page Setup** and click in the **Print Gridlines** and **Print Row & Column Headings** boxes so that the crosses disappear (i.e. you are choosing not to print these items). Finally, choose **Print** from the **File** menu.

H5 Fibonacci Sequence (Charts)

This is the sequence 1, 1, 2, 3, 5, 8, 13, ... from the rule $u_n = u_{n-1} + u_{n-2}$ To set it up:

a: Choose **File New Worksheet**. Type 1 into A1 and A2. Type =A1+A2 into A3, then **Copy** it and **Paste** into the rest of the A.. column.

b: To look at the ratio of successive terms (which converges to the Golden Ratio 1.618....., enter the formula =A2/A1 into B2, then copy it into the rest of the B.. column.

c: To plot a graph of this ratio, drag over the cells of the B.. column so that they are highlighted in black. Then choose **File New Chart** and a graph will be drawn. It will probably appear as a bar chart, so choose **Gallery Line** and then click on the sort of line chart you want. You can print the chart if you like, but first go to **File Page Setup** and choose **Match Size to Screen**.

WORKSHEET I – Further Work with Sequences

USING GRAPHS TO RECOGNISE SEQUENCE TYPES

This section will show you how to recognise the difference between ARITHMETIC, GEOMETRIC and POWER sequences purely from their graphs.

Get into Excel and if possible re-load the SEQUENCE sheet you saved before (which should include columns for first, second and third differences). Alternatively, there may be an example sheet on your computer system which will do; ask your teacher. Or you could type it in from scratch, according to the instructions on the previous worksheet. Whichever you do, you should have a sheet which has the numbers from 1 down to about 15 in column A, the main sequence in column B, and its first, second and third differences in columns C, D, E.

11 Graphs of Arithmetic Sequences

Modify column B so that it contains an Arithmetic Sequence (using the Copy/Paste techniques you learnt on the previous sheet). Now draw a graph of it:

1) Highlight the numbers in columns B-E and **Edit Copy**
2) Choose **File New Chart**. When the new chart window appears it will probably be blank, so choose **Edit Paste** to put the number data into it.
3) You will probably get a Bar Chart, which isn't really the right type, so choose **Gallery Line**, and click on type 2. You should now get a normal straight line graph.
4) It's best to arrange the screen so you can see the graph and the sheet at the same time. To achieve this, choose **Window Arrange All**. You may find it best to click on 'Sheet 1', which you're probably not using, and **File Close** it, then **Window Arrange All** again.

Now try modifying the sequence in column B to other Arithmetic Sequences (alter the starting value, alter the common difference or step size), and see how the graph is affected – it should re-draw automatically each time you change the sequence.

I2 Graphs of Geometric Sequences

Now modify column B so that it contains a Geometric Sequence, as on the previous worksheet. You should find that cell C1 is free to hold the common ratio - remember that in the formula =B1*$C$1 the dollar signs mean an 'Absolute' reference. Look at the graph that is produced. you should find that its curved, and that there are other curved graphs in different colours corresponding to the difference columns.

Try a common ratio of 2 and a starting value of 1.
Do the graphs of the differences look similar to the graph of the main sequence?
Now look at the difference columns on the spreadsheet to see why they do.
Try other ratios and other starting values to see if they all show the same effect.

It isn't very easy to see that the shapes of the difference graphs are the same as the shape of the main sequence graph. It shows more clearly if you choose a different type of graph: click on the **Chart** window and choose **Gallery Line** and click on type 6. The display will be a bit messy, so choose **Chart Gridlines**, and click on the boxes so that only the 'Value Axis' Major Gridlines box has a cross in it.

You should now find that the graphs are parallel straight lines, the upper one being the main sequence, and the others being the differences. Look at the axis scales: the x axis (the 'Category Axis', as Excel calls it) is normally labelled, but the y axis (the 'Value Axis') is labelled 10, 100, 1000, 10000, etc., evenly spaced. A scale like this is called a LOGARITHMIC or LOG scale: a graph with a normally scaled x axis and a log scaled y axis is called a LOG-LINEAR graph. As you can see, it's very useful for geometric sequences, as it turns them into straight lines.

Try other geometric sequences: try common ratios less than one (not all the differences will be plotted because negative values can't be plotted on log scales). Another possibility is to see what an Arithmetic Sequence looks like on a log-linear scale: you can use the C1 value as the Common Difference by altering the B2 formula to =B1+$C$1 and **Copy** and **Paste** it down the column. Does an Arithmetic Sequence give a straight line?

I3 Graphs of Power Sequences

Now put the sequence of fourth powers into column B – make B1 contain the formula =A1^4, then **Copy** and **Paste** it down the column. Does this give straight lines on the log-linear graph? Use **Gallery Line** and click on type 2 to go back to a linear-linear graph – does this give straight lines?

Now change the graph type to **Gallery Scatter** and click on type 5 – and clean up the display with **Chart Gridlines Only Major Gridlines**.
This sort of graph has a log scale on both axes, so it's called a LOG-LOG graph.
Do you get straight lines now?
Are they parallel this time?
Which is the steepest, the main sequence or the differences?
What are the gradients of the straight lines for the main sequence, first difference, etc?

You can make the power you use into a variable by changing B1 to the formula =A1^$C$1 and Copy/Pasting this down the column – now, the value you type into C1 will be the power you're using.
Try power 4 again to check it works.
Try squares, cubes, higher powers.
Try power 0.5 (what does power 0.5 mean?).
Try power –1 (what does power -1 mean?).
Can you see any rule governing the power, the gradient of the main sequence graph and the gradient of its differences?

I4 Identifying Special Sequences

Now modify column B to contain the sequence of triangle numbers, using the formula $u_n = u_{n-1} + n$ as on the previous worksheet. By switching between the three graph types (linear-linear, log-linear and log-log) identify whether it is an Arithmetic, a Geometric or a Power type sequence.

Now modify column B to contain a Fibonacci sequence using the formula $u_n = u_{n-1} + u_{n-2}$ and use the three graph types to identify what sort of sequence it is.

WORKSHEET J – Decimal expansions [DISC NEEDED]

A Number Investigation: Decimal Expansion of a Fraction

This exercise uses a computer spreadsheet to let you look at how fractions such as 3/7, 5/13, 6/17 appear when written as decimals. It shows you many more decimal places than any calculator, and a graph helps you see some of the interesting patterns that are involved.

Getting Started

Load the spreadsheet program into your computer and start the DECIMAL spreadsheet running (see end of sheet for further details). The sheet is constructed for you; all you have to do is enter figures for the numerator (top) and denominator (bottom) of the fraction and observe the results. As soon as you alter the figures the spreadsheet will work out the correct decimal and the graph will display the pattern formed by the digits of the decimal.

Denominator 7

Move to the denominator (bottom) of the fraction using a mouse or keyboard cursor keys and type in the number 7. Move to the numerator and type in 1. Look at the decimal and the graph. Now try numerator 2 and look again. Then try numerators 3, 4, 5, 6. Write a brief description of the patterns that you saw, particularly what they all had in common. Check different numerators again to see if there was anything you missed last time. Try numerators 7, 8, 9. Do you discover anything new? Is it worth looking at bigger numerators?

Denominators 2 to 6

Try denominator 2 with numerators 1, 2, 3. What is different from the denominator 7 patterns? Then try denominators 3, 4, 5, 6, with various numerators. The sort of patterns you get should fall into two types: list out the set of denominators that have patterns of one type, and the set that have patterns of another type. Would you say that denominator 7 should be included in either of these sets, or should it be put in a third set?

Denominators 8 to 12

Investigate the patterns formed by the decimal expansions of fractions with these denominators. Which fall into the sets you have already formed, and do you get any new types of pattern so that you need a new set? Can you think of any rule that might be involved in deciding which set a given denominator will belong to?

Denominator 13

This one is particularly interesting, so investigate it carefully. Does it deserve a new set? You may even think that the possible numerators for fractions with denominator 13 could be divided into more than one set – if so, list the sets and say why they are different.

Bigger denominators

Now try even bigger denominators: 14, 15, 16, etc. You should be beginning to get a feel for which ones will produce the most interesting patterns, whether a new pattern type will be found or which of the previous sets the denominator can be put with. Can you give any sort of rule for which numbers produce the most interesting patterns? Can you give any rule for how long the pattern takes to repeat, and are there any denominators that break the rule? Can you predict interesting denominators to investigate, and do their patterns look as you expected?

WORKSHEET K – Mystic Square

In the centre of the spreadsheet enter the numbers 1-9 in a 3 by 3 square.
At the end of the top row enter a formula to **multiply together** the numbers in this row.
Do the same for the bottom row and for the left hand column and the right hand column.
Finally enter a formula to **add together** all these four totals.

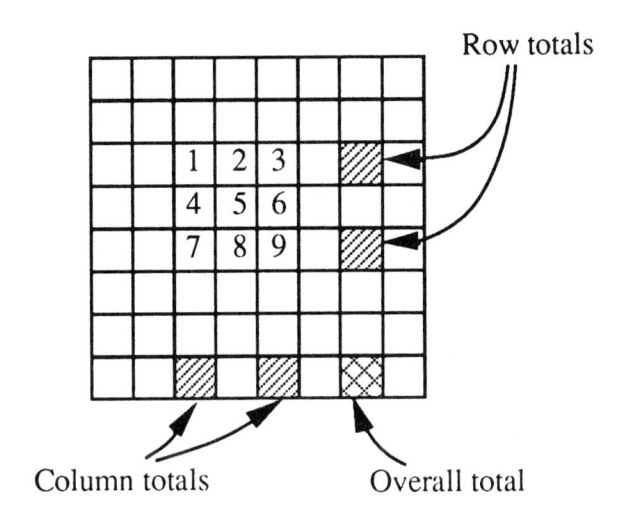

Row totals

Column totals   Overall total

Record your results in some way.

Which arrangement of the 9 numbers gives the smallest overall total?

Which arrangement of the 9 numbers gives the largest overall total?

What do you notice about your arrangements?

Try the numbers 1-16 in a 4 by 4 grid ....

WORKSHEET L – Magic Square

(a) Enter the numbers 1-9 in a three by three grid in the spreadsheet.
To the right of each row enter a formula that totals up the row:

1	2	3	xxx	Row 1 total
6	5	4	xxx	Row 2 total
7	8	9	xxx	Row 3 total

(b) Repeat for each column, placing the column totals below each column:

1	2	3
6	5	4
7	8	9
xxx	xxx	xxx
Col 1	Col 2	Col 3
total	total	total

(c) Rearrange the 9 numbers so that all the six totals are the same.

(d) Add formulas to calculate the sums of the two diagonals.

(e) Find an arrangement of the 9 numbers that makes ALL eight totals the same.

If you find this too easy try the numbers 1-16 in a four by four grid. GOOD LUCK!

WORKSHEET M – Matrices and [DISC NEEDED]
Geometrical Transformations

The purpose of this set of exercises is to allow you to investigate which 2×2 matrices correspond to which geometrical transformations by plotting their effect on screen, using the Excel spreadsheet.

Starting Up
Switch on you computer system in the normal way, logging on if you are using a networked machine. Start up Windows, then double click on the Excel icon. To load the geometrical transformation spreadsheet that has already been set up, choose **Open** from the **File** menu, click on the drive letter that your teacher tells you in the directories box, then possibly a sub-directory, and finally scroll down to GTRAN.XLW in the Files box and **Open** that. Just click **OK** on any 'Read Only' warning messages which appear. A matrix calculation and graph window should appear. Click on the up arrow at the top right of the Excel window to make sure you use the full screen.

Simple Transformations
The top window shows a 2×2 transformation matrix multiplying a 2×4 object matrix to produce a 2×4 image shape matrix. The object and its image are plotted on the graph in red and blue respectively. Initially the shape is a little 'flag' and the transformation matrix corresponds to a 180 degree rotation about the origin. To alter the transformation matrix, click on the element you want to alter, type the new number and then Enter. Alter the transformation matrix to each of the following in turn, and write down in your book what transformation it gives.

Q1.

a) $\begin{pmatrix} 1 & 0 \\ 0 & -1 \end{pmatrix}$
b) $\begin{pmatrix} -1 & 0 \\ 0 & 1 \end{pmatrix}$
c) $\begin{pmatrix} 0 & -1 \\ 1 & 0 \end{pmatrix}$
d) $\begin{pmatrix} 0 & 1 \\ -1 & 0 \end{pmatrix}$

e) $\begin{pmatrix} 1.5 & 0 \\ 0 & 1.5 \end{pmatrix}$
f) $\begin{pmatrix} -0.5 & 0 \\ 0 & -0.5 \end{pmatrix}$
g) $\begin{pmatrix} 2 & 0 \\ 0 & 1 \end{pmatrix}$
h) $\begin{pmatrix} 0.7 & 0.7 \\ -0.7 & 0.7 \end{pmatrix}$

Moving the object shape:
The object shape matrix is set up so that the base of the flag is always at the co-ordinates given by the first column, and if you alter just the first column the object 'flag' just changes position. Try typing in the following transformation, which represents a SHEAR: $\begin{pmatrix} 1 & 1 \\ 0 & 1 \end{pmatrix}$ and observe its effect as you move the flag around.

Q2.

(a) Look at the position of the image relative to the object as you vary the x co-ordinate of the base of the flag (keeping the y co-ordinate on 0). How does the relative position vary?

(b) Now vary the y co-ordinate of the base of the flag (keeping the x co-ordinate on 0). Now how does the relative position of image and object vary?

(c) Click on element 1, 2 (i.e. 1st row of 2nd column).
Which part of the flag is this? Write down the formula in this cell that makes sure the flag moves around as you alter the first column of the object matrix.
Write down also the formula in element (2, 2).

*Hint: If you accidentally type over and alter some of these formulae and destroy your flag, just **Open** the GTRAN.XLS sheet; this will restore the original formulae.*

(d) Alter the transformation matrix to: $\begin{pmatrix} 1 & -1 \\ 0 & 1 \end{pmatrix}$

Investigate and write down the way the SHEAR you get now differs from before.

(e) The transformation in (a) and (d) represent shears parallel to the x axis. Experiment until you can find two matrices that represent shears parallel to the y axis, one going each way. Write the matrices down.

Rotation Matrices

Now you will set up a matrix that will rotate through any angle about the origin.
To do this:

(a) Click in the blank cell above element (1,1) of the transformation matrix and type in an angle in degrees (45° is a good one to start with).

(b) Now click in the cell next to it on the right (i.e. above 1, 2) and enter a formula into it: type the '=' key, then click the mouse on your angle, then finish off the formula by typing *2*PI()/360
You should end up with this formula: =A2*2*PI()/360 and when you click Enter a number will appear in the cell. It is the angle measured in a different set of units called RADIANS, which computer software and advanced mathematicians often use in preference to degrees.

(c) Now click in element (1, 1) of the transformation matrix and enter a formula: type =COS(then click the mouse on your angle in radians, then finish the formula with a bracket and Enter. It should end up as: =COS(B2)
In element (1, 2) put the formula = –SIN(B2)
In element (2, 1) put the formula =SIN(B2)
n element (1, 2) put the formula =COS(B2)
Now look at your image; if you've done all this correctly it should be rotated. Check that rotations of 90 and –90 agree with your previous matrices by clicking on the angle in degrees (not the formula for radians) and altering it.

Q3.
Set the rotation angle to 120 degrees. Write down the rotation matrix you get. What is the value of cos(120°)?
Print the resulting sheet by choosing **Print** from the **File** menu. Click on the chart and print it too in the same way.

Altering the object shape
If you have some time left, try altering some of the other co-ordinates in the object shape, so you get something different from a flag. Typing numbers in will erase the formulae, but this doesn't matter. Adding extra vertices to the shape is more difficult and requires altering the matrix multiplication formula built into the sheet; don't try this at the moment.

Setting up your own matrix multiplication in Excel
Now you will find out how the matrix multiplication which does the geometrical transformation on the GTRAN sheet is actually set up. It is done using a more complicated form of formula.

First, choose **File New Worksheet** to give yourself a new blank spreadsheet to work with (in fact you can **Close** the GTRAN sheets now if you wish). Type the following matrix of numbers into the square block of four cells from A1 to B2:
$\begin{pmatrix} 2 & 1 \\ -1 & 2 \end{pmatrix}$ and into the square block from D1 to E2 type $\begin{pmatrix} 0 & 1 \\ 2 & 3 \end{pmatrix}$

For what you're going to do next you really need more columns displayed on the screen, which you can do by setting the columns to be narrower. Click the mouse on the A column heading and drag it sideways across to the H heading so that columns A to H are completely highlighted in black. then pull down the **Format Column Width** command and type width 5 into the box.

Now highlight the square block of cells from G1 to H2 by clicking and dragging with the mouse. Start entering the formula you need to multiply the two matrices like this:
=MMULT(

Now click and drag the mouse over the first matrix: A1:B2 should appear in the formula. Now type a comma.
Now click and drag the mouse over the second matrix, giving D1:E2.
Now type a closing bracket.
Finally, don't just press Enter, but hold down CTRL and SHIFT as you press Enter; this puts the 'array formula' into all four cells from G1 to H2, which is shown by { } round it.

Q4.

The correct answer to the matrix multiplication should appear; write the answer in your book and check that it is correct. In cells G4 to H5 enter an array formula to multiply the same two matrices the other way round. Write the answer down.

By altering the numbers in the original two matrices, find and write in your book the values of AB and BA where the pair of matrices A and B are:

a) $\begin{pmatrix} 1 & 2 \\ 2 & 1 \end{pmatrix}, \begin{pmatrix} 3 & -1 \\ -1 & 3 \end{pmatrix}$ b) $\begin{pmatrix} 1 & 2 \\ 3 & 4 \end{pmatrix}, \begin{pmatrix} -1 & 0 \\ 0 & 2 \end{pmatrix}$ c) $\begin{pmatrix} 1 & 2 \\ 3 & 4 \end{pmatrix}, \begin{pmatrix} 4 & -2 \\ -3 & 1 \end{pmatrix}$

For each pair, state whether or not they COMMUTE, i.e. whether AB = BA. Do also for:

d) $\begin{pmatrix} 1 & 2 \\ -2 & 1 \end{pmatrix}, \begin{pmatrix} 2 & -3 \\ 3 & 1 \end{pmatrix}$ e) $\begin{pmatrix} 1 & 2 \\ 3 & 4 \end{pmatrix}, \begin{pmatrix} 1 & 3 \\ 2 & 4 \end{pmatrix}$ f) $\begin{pmatrix} 1 & 2 \\ 2 & 4 \end{pmatrix}, \begin{pmatrix} 1 & 3 \\ -3 & -9 \end{pmatrix}$

State any conclusions you think you may be able to draw about which types of matrix commute, and test your hypotheses with matrices of your own choosing.

If the end of the lesson arrives while you're still working on this, save your spreadsheet as you'll need it for the next section.

WORKSHEET N – Matrices and Simultaneous Equations [DISC NEEDED]

A simple spreadsheet function evaluates determinants for you. Continuing with the same spreadsheet as you used for matrix multiplication, type the following formula into cell B4 (i.e. below matrix A):

=MDETERM(A1:B2)

and finish with CTRL/SHIFT/Enter. Check the answer it gives for the determinant is correct. Enter formulae into E4, J2 and J5 to work out the determinants of B, AB and BA respectively.

Q1.
For each of the pairs of matrices below (met in **Q4** of Worksheet M), use your spreadsheet to find det(A), det(B), det(AB), det(BA) and write them down in your book. State any conclusion you draw (refer back to your results for Worksheet M).

a) $\begin{pmatrix} 1 & 2 \\ 2 & 1 \end{pmatrix}, \begin{pmatrix} 3 & -1 \\ -1 & 3 \end{pmatrix}$ b) $\begin{pmatrix} 1 & 2 \\ 3 & 4 \end{pmatrix}, \begin{pmatrix} -1 & 0 \\ 0 & 2 \end{pmatrix}$ c) $\begin{pmatrix} 1 & 2 \\ 3 & 4 \end{pmatrix}, \begin{pmatrix} 4 & -2 \\ -3 & 1 \end{pmatrix}$

d) $\begin{pmatrix} 1 & 2 \\ -2 & 1 \end{pmatrix}, \begin{pmatrix} 2 & -3 \\ 3 & 1 \end{pmatrix}$ e) $\begin{pmatrix} 1 & 2 \\ 3 & 4 \end{pmatrix}, \begin{pmatrix} 1 & 3 \\ 2 & 4 \end{pmatrix}$ f) $\begin{pmatrix} 1 & 2 \\ 2 & 4 \end{pmatrix}, \begin{pmatrix} 1 & 3 \\ -3 & -9 \end{pmatrix}$

Inverses
Another function will work out the inverse of a matrix for you. We will use it to solve the following pair of simultaneous equations:

$7x + y = 8$
$2x + y = -3$

which are equivalent to the single matrix equation:

$$\begin{pmatrix} 7 & 1 \\ 2 & 1 \end{pmatrix} \begin{pmatrix} x \\ y \end{pmatrix} = \begin{pmatrix} 8 \\ -3 \end{pmatrix}$$

for which the solution is (as you should know):

$$\begin{pmatrix} x \\ y \end{pmatrix} = \left\{ \text{Inverse of } \begin{pmatrix} 7 & 1 \\ 2 & 1 \end{pmatrix} \right\} \begin{pmatrix} 8 \\ -3 \end{pmatrix}$$

and the inverse should be:

Choose **File New Worksheet** to get a new blank spreadsheet, and type the matrix $\begin{pmatrix} 7 & 1 \\ 2 & 1 \end{pmatrix}$ into cells A1 to B2.

Highlight the square block of cells from A4 to B5 and into them type the formula:
=MINVERSE(A1:B2)
and then CTRL/SHIFT/Enter. The correct inverse should appear. Now enter the column vector $\begin{pmatrix} 8 \\ -3 \end{pmatrix}$ into cells C4 and C5. Finally, highlight cells E4 to E5 and enter the correct formula to multiply the inverse matrix by the column vector to produce the two solutions to the equation. Write these solutions down and verify that they are correct.

Q2.

Use your inverse spreadsheet to solve the following pairs of equations:

a) $\quad x - 3y = 2$
$\quad\quad 2x - 5y = -3$

b) $\quad 2x + 4y = 1$
$\quad\quad x + 3y = -5$

c) $\quad 3x + 5y = 3$
$\quad\quad x + y = -7$

d) $\quad 2x - 3y = -2$
$\quad\quad -3x + 2y = 0$

and state what happens when you try these:

e) $\quad x + 3y = 2$
$\quad\quad 3x + 9y = 6$

f) $\quad 2x - 3y = 4$
$\quad\quad -4x + 6y = 2$

Do either of these last two actually have solutions?
If so, find a pair and write them down.

Q3.

Modify your sheet to solve the following three simultaneous equations using a 3×3 matrix inverse:

$$x + y + z = 2$$
$$2x - y + 3z = 9$$
$$3x - 2y - 2z = 1$$

WORKSHEET O – Data Analysis: Part 1   [DISC OPTIONAL]

Introduction
To use this sheet you need to have collected a set of data. As an example, it will be assumed that you have collected the heights and weights of the members of your form, but any two sets of values would do (Alternatively, the supplied file REACT24 contains data on reaction time and games ability for 24 pupils).

Starting
Load Excel.

Typing in the Data
Click the mouse in cell A1, type the heading: Height, then press Enter (↵) or Return. Similarly, enter in cell B1 the heading: Weight. Type the data values into the columns below these headings. Once you have typed the data in, save the spreadsheet by choosing **File Save As**. When a box appears asking you for a filename, type in the name DATA (be guided by your teacher as to an appropriate name if using a network computer).

Mean and Standard Deviation from Raw Data:
This section assumes you have the actual (raw) data values typed in. It assumes they occupy cells A2 to A25 and B2 to B25. Click the mouse in the first blank cell below the data in column A (A26 in this example). Type the following formula into this cell:
    =AVERAGE(A2:A25)

(If your data occupy a slightly different range of cells, modify the A numbers appropriately). When finished, press Enter (↵), and the average value should appear in the cell.

To get the standard deviation, click the mouse in the next blank cell down (A27 in this example) and enter the formula:
    =STDEVP(A2:A25)

(modifying the range of A's as necessary).

Click on A26, hold down and drag the mouse to A27; this should result in A26 and A27 being highlighted in black. Click on **Edit Copy**. Click the mouse on B26. Click on **Edit Paste**. This should result in the correct mean and standard deviation formulae being produced for column B.

At this stage you could print the data with **File Print**.

WORKSHEET P – Data Analysis: Part 2   [DISC NEEDED]

P1 Grouping Data, Histograms

Again, this section assumes you have the actual (raw) data values typed into the spreadsheet file called DATA.XLS (if using Nimbus/PC computers) or called DATA (using Apple Macintosh computers). Load it as follows:

    Select **File Load**, click on the name, and click on **OK**.

You must also load the file GROUPFRQ.XLM (if necessary, consult your teacher as to where to find this file).

    Select **File Load**, then click on the name GROUPFRQ.XLM and click on **OK**.

This loads in a 'macro' sheet that will count frequencies and draw a histogram for you.

Click on **Window**, DATA.XLS (or whatever else you called the sheet your data is on) to get back to your data sheet. Click on A2, then drag the mouse down to A25 so that the whole of your A column of data is highlighted (but not the mean and standard deviation). Then click on **Macro Run** and select 'groupf'. Several options will be presented to you, but just leave the settings at the values suggested and click **OK** on each. You should end up with a table of frequencies (appearing on 'Sheet 1' or a similar name) and a histogram (on 'Chart 1' or a similar name). You may have to use **Window** to switch to the frequency sheet or the histogram.

With the histogram window active, **File Print** should print the histogram.

P2 Median, Quartiles:

For this section you need to have already loaded GROUPFRQ.XLM. You either need the table of frequencies as produced on Sheet 1 when doing P1 above, with a column containing the lower boundary values of the classes alongside a column containing the frequencies, or you could type already grouped data like this directly into a spreadsheet.

To find the median, click in an empty cell below the data and choose **Formula Paste Function**. At the very bottom of the long list of functions you should find one called GROUPFRQ.XLM!percentile (a 'user defined function' provided by the macro sheet you loaded earlier). Click on this function name and click OK. Click between the brackets of the function and edit them to something like this:

    =GROUPFRQ.XLM!percentile(A2:B10,50)

The range of cells A2:B10 may need altering; it should be the rectangle of lower boundary values and frequencies. The 50 refers to 50%, and will give you the median value when you press Enter.

Type similar formulae into two more blank cells using values of 25 and 75 to give you the quartiles.

P3 Cumulative Frequencies and Cumulative Frequency Polygon:

You can build these up in column C, beside your table of frequencies. Assuming the first value and frequency are in cells A2 and B2 respectively, type a zero into cell C2. Then enter the formula: =B2+C2   into cell C3.

With C3 highlighted, click on **Edit Copy**. Then drag out a highlight down column C to the end of your data and click on **Edit Paste** – you should get the cumulative frequencies. You won't get the final value unless you **Paste** into the next cell down as well, and you should then type a value into the next cell down of column A so it has a boundary value to go with it.

To plot a cumulative frequency polygon from this data, click on **Macro Run** scatter. When asked for the range containing the x data, type in the range of cells containing the values: something like A2:A11, or drag over them with the mouse. The range of y data is the cells containing the cumulative frequencies, something like C2:C11. The scatter diagram should then be drawn. To link the points up with straight lines you will have to click on **Gallery** scatter and choose the joined up line option.

Again, **File Print** should print this.

P4 Mean and Standard Deviation from Frequencies:

You can set up the necessary columns for this working alongside the cumulative frequencies. Label cells D1, E1 and F1 as x, fx and fxx respectively. Then enter the following formulae into the cells specified:

    D2:   =0.5*(A2+A3)   class mid-value x

    E2:   =B2*D2   frequency times x

    F2:   =D2*E2   x times fx giving fx^2

Then highlight these three cells in black, **Edit Copy**. Highlight down columns D, E and F as far as the last frequency in column B and **Edit Paste**.

To work out the sums of the columns, type the formula:

    =SUM(E2:E10)

into a blank cell in column E (E12, say), and copy it into columns B and F also. This gives you the following sums:

    Σf in B12, Σfx in E12, and Σfx^2 in F12 (though they could be in a row other than 12).

Choose suitable cells to contain the formulae:

=E12/B12   (the mean – suppose it's in E14)

=F12/B12 - E14^2   (the variance – suppose it's in E16)

=SQRT(E16)   (the standard deviation)

Again, you will have to be sensible about adjusting cell numbers in the above formulae if your data go beyond row 10.

P5 Scatter Diagram

For this you need the original raw data, not the frequencies, and you need GROUPFRQ.XLM loaded. Click on **Macro Run** scatter. Type in the ranges that contain the data to be plotted on the x and y axes – they could well be something like A2:A25 and B2:B25. The scatter diagram should then appear.

WORKSHEET Q – Miscellaneous problems: Set 1

1 Interest
   (a) How many years will it take for £100 to increase to at least £200 when invested at 5% per annum? And to reach £300? And £400?
   Predict first (write it down !) and then find out using Excel.
   Have a cell for the Interest rate and one below it for the Capital and enter a formula below that and Fill Down. If it doesn't work and you can't fix it read the HINT at the bottom of this worksheet!
   (b) You can make the output better by using **Format Number**. Explore!

2 Iteration
   (a) Put 3 in A1. Put the formula (A1 + 99/A1)/2 in A2
   Copy down from A2 to A12 (using **Edit Fill Down**)
   Explore what happens if the number in A1 is changed.
   Explore what happens if 99 is changed in the formula.
   What is this doing? Why?
   (b) Rewrite (a) so the 99 is entered in a cell and not in the formula.

3 Random Numbers and Statistics
   (a) Put a random number in A1 using the function RAND(). Fill down to make 10 such numbers in all. Predict the mean and standard deviation of the column.
   Use Excel to calculate the mean and s.d., in A12 and A14 respectively.
   Use 5 d.p. number format throughout – achieved using **Format Number**.
   (b) Extend across the worksheet so you have 5 such columns.
   Calculate the grand mean in E16.
   (c) Find a pointer position such that <u>one or two mouse clicks</u> cause the whole table to be recalculated. Do this a few times.

4 Trigonometric tables
   Create a table for SIN, COS and TAN for 0° to 90° in steps of 5°. Use **Format Number** to get 2 d.p. output.

5 Matrices and Determinants
   (a) Calculate the determinant of a 2 x 2 matrix.
   (You can make the screen output bigger by using **Format Font** – try size 18).
   (b) Add together two 2×2 matrices.
   (c) For the same two matrices in (b) also calculate the product.
   (d) Show that $\det(AB) = \det(A) \times \det(B)$

[HINT for Qn 1: You will need to make both the Capital and Interest <u>fixed</u> so you will need absolute addresses which require $ signs before them. E.g. $A$1 keeps both the A and the 1 fixed.]

WORKSHEET R – Miscellaneous problems: Set 2

1 A fresh approach to Triangle Numbers

It is possible to generate Triangle Numbers starting from 1, 2, 3 ... in cells A1, A2, A3 ... and using SUM($A$1:A1) in cell B1 which is filled down. *Why does it work?*

2 Difference Tables

(a) Construct in column A the integers from 0 to 15 and in column B a table of values for $f(x) = x^4 + 2x^3 - x^2 + 3x - 2$ for $x = 0\,(1)\,15$.

(b) In column C place the differences between successive cells of column B. Repeat for D containing the differences of C and so on ...
What do you notice? Is it generalisable?

3 Simulation with random numbers

(a) Simulate throwing a die.

(b) Simulate throwing a coin.

4 Multiplication tables without multiplication

Build up a multiplication table without using any multiplications (or divisions).

5 Mysterious Squares

Enter the array

1	2	3
4	5	6
7	8	9

into a spreadsheet.

Calculate the two diagonal sums, the middle row sum and the middle column sum, placing the four sums in appropriate positions.
What do you notice? Is this generalisable?

6 Complex Numbers

Using four cells to store the real and imaginary parts of two complex numbers, and other cells to store the results, do complex arithmetic calculations for modulus, argument, sum, product and quotient.

7 Numerical Differentiation

Use the approximation $dy/dx \cong [f(x + h) - f(x)]/h$ with a small step size h to show that $d(\sin x)/dx \cong \cos x$, for various values of h and x.

WORKSHEET S: Optimisation problems

1 Minimum distance to sample water in a lake

A biologist must walk from his car to a lake, get a small sample of the water and walk to a hut to analyse the sample. (See the map below.) What route should he take to minimize the distance he must walk? Can you predict the point on the lakeside where the biologist should take the sample? See if your prediction is correct.

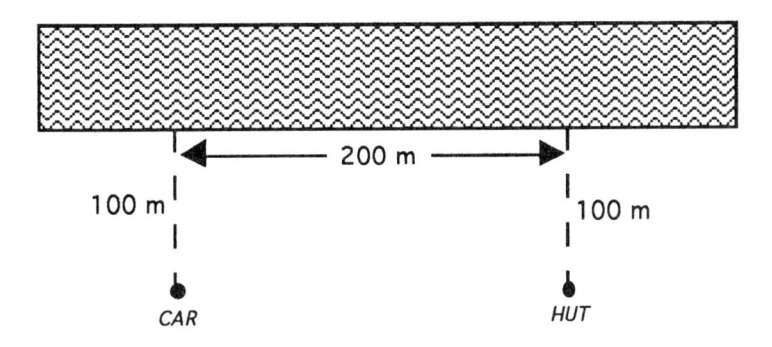

```
    ←——— 200 m ———→
100 m              100 m
  •                  •
 CAR                HUT
```

2 Minimum distance to sample water in a lake

Repeat C1 for the different map below. Can you predict the point on the lakeside where the biologist should take the sample? See if your prediction is correct.

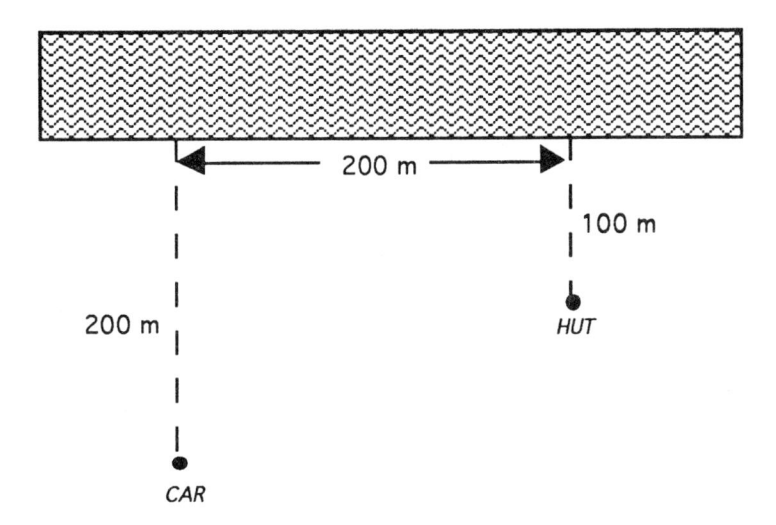

```
    ←——— 200 m ———→
                   100 m
                     •
                    HUT
200 m

  •
 CAR
```

3 Minimum time to sample water in a lake

Assuming that the biologist walks at a constant speed then the minimum time taken can be easily calculated from the minimum distance. What would be the minimum time for the problems in questions 1 and 2 if the biologist walks at a constant speed of 100m per minute?

4 Minimum time to fight a fire

One day when a different biologist arrives she sees that the hut is on fire. (See the map for question 1 at the top of the previous page.) She takes two large buckets from her car and walks to the lakeside. She then walks more slowly with the full buckets to put out the fire. Suppose that she can walk at her normal speed of 100m carrying the empty buckets but can only manage 50 m per minute with the full buckets. What route should she take to minimize the time? Can you predict the point on the lakeside where the biologist should fill the buckets? See if your prediction is correct. How far will she walk? How long will she take?

5 Minimum time crossing a marsh

The biologist must walk from her car to a lake and take a small sample of the water to a hut to analyse the sample. Near to the lake the land is marshy. (See the map below.) She walks at 100m per minute on dry land but can only manage half that speed when crossing marshy land. What route should she take to minimize the time he will take? Can you predict the points where the biologist should enter and leave the marsh and the point on the lakeside where she should take the sample? See if your predictions are correct.

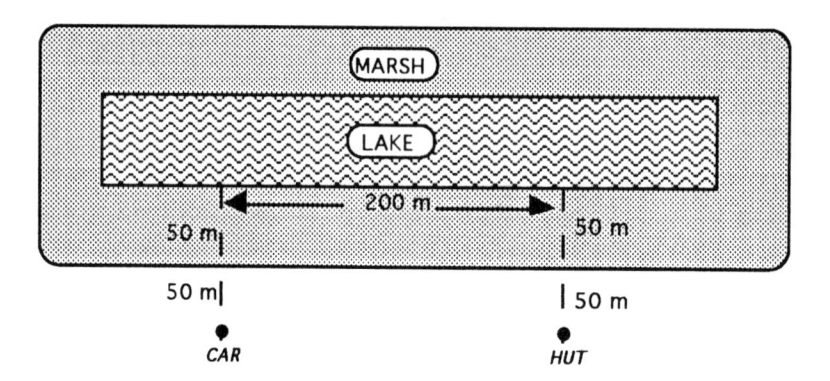

```
                    ┌──────────────────────────────────┐
                    │            (MARSH)               │
                    │ ≈≈≈≈≈≈≈≈≈≈≈≈≈≈≈≈≈≈≈≈≈≈≈≈≈≈≈≈≈≈≈≈ │
                    │ ≈≈≈≈≈≈≈≈≈≈≈≈(LAKE)≈≈≈≈≈≈≈≈≈≈≈≈≈≈ │
                    │ ≈≈≈≈≈≈≈≈≈≈≈≈≈≈≈≈≈≈≈≈≈≈≈≈≈≈≈≈≈≈≈≈ │
                    │       ◄──────200 m──────►        │
                    │    50 m│                │ 50 m   │
                    └──────────────────────────────────┘
                         50 m│                │ 50 m
                             ●                ●
                            CAR              HUT
```

6 Minimum time crossing a marsh and fight a fire

One day when the biologist arrives she sees that the hut is on fire. She takes two large buckets from her car and walks through the marsh to the lakeside. She then walks more slowly with the full buckets to put out the fire. The speed she can walk is shown in this table:

	Dry land	Marsh
Empty	100	50
Full	50	25

What route should she take to minimize the time she will take? Can you predict the points where the biologist should enter and leave the marsh and the point on the lakeside where the biologist should fill the buckets? See if you are correct.

WORKSHEET T – Excel Charts: Set 1

Place 1 in cell A1 and the formula = A1 + 1 in cell A2 and the formula =SUM($A$1:A1) in B1. Separately fill down each column to row 12. To plot a Chart of this data do as follows:

PLOTTING A CHART USING DATA IN ONE COLUMN
(1)   Highlight all the data in column B only.
(2)   Click on the Chart icon (fourth icon in from the right).

Now you must define the position of your Chart on the worksheet.

(3)   Move the cursor (a thin cross) to the required position for the Chart's top left corner and drag the cursor to the position for the Chart's bottom right hand corner and release. The Chart is then drawn automatically. The bars are automatically labelled 1 to 12.
(4)   Change the size and shape of the Chart by moving the cursor to a corner so that it changes to a thin cross, then drag.
(5)   Change the position of the whole Chart by moving the cursor inside the Chart (the cursor becomes an arrow) and drag.
(6)   Change B1 to 50 and watch the first bar of the Chart change size.
(7)   Restore the original Chart by placing 1 in B1.
(8)   Change A1 to 10 and watch the whole Chart change. Note that the bar labels remain 1 to 12.
(9)   Restore the original Chart by placing 1 in A1.

DELETING A CHART
We now want to delete the Chart

(10)   Click in the Chart so that six 'handles' appear round its edge then press the Delete key (a left pointing arrow) or use **Edit Clear**.

PLOTTING A CHART USING DATA IN TWO COLUMNS
We now repeat the previous exercise using both columns.

(11)   Highlight all the data in columns A and B. Click the Chart icon.
(12)   Position the Chart outline as in (3) and confirm that the First Column (i.e. column A) is to provide the Category (X) Axis Labels. The Chart appears.
(13)   Change A1 to 10 and watch the whole Chart change. Note that this time the bar labels also change. This time Excel is using the A column numbers as the X axis values rather than supplying its own numbers (which would be 1 to 12).

SEPARATING A CHART FROM A WORKSHEET

The Chart is currently just part of the Worksheet.
To alter it you need to establish it in its own window.

(14) Restore the Worksheet by putting 1 into A1 again. Then double-click on the Chart to produce a window for it.

(15) Click in the maximize box (top right in the Chart window) so the Chart enlarges and nearly fills the screen.

(16) Double click inside the chart <u>not over a bar</u> to get the border/area menu.

(17) Select **Border Custom**, Click on the Color box, Select blue, Click on the Weight box, Select a thick line, Click OK. This should give a blue border for the Chart.

(18) Again double click inside the chart <u>not over a bar</u> to get the border/area menu.

(19) Select **Area Custom**, Click on the Pattern box, Select a lightly dotted pattern, Click on the Background box, Select yellow, Click OK. This should give a yellow patterned background for the Chart. Lovely, isn't it!

(20) Minimize the Chart (click in the box at top right of the Chart window just below the Worksheet minimize box). Then click outside the Chart (i.e. over the Worksheet) to return to the Chart being just part of the Worksheet.

(21) Save the Worksheet, using **File Save** with the default name SHEET1.XLS.

CUSTOMISING A CHART

You can now alter the colour of the bars in the Chart to your own taste.

(22) Double click on the Chart once again to create a Chart window and then maximize it.

(23) Double click <u>over a bar</u> and then change the colour (plum is nice!) using the **Area** foreground option. Click OK.

Note that once a Chart is activated the menu bar includes a Chart menu.

(24) Open the **Chart** menu.

(25) Choose the **Attach Text** option, and select **Chart Title** and click OK. A dummy Title is displayed.

(26) Edit or type in the title for the Chart (a copy of the title will appear in the formula bar) and press Return or Enter.

(27) Use **Format Font** to alter the font, font size and style of the title (e.g. Roman, 24 pt, italic).

(28) NOW USE THE GALLERY MENU TO TRY OUT THE DIFFERENT TYPES OF CHART. Not all charts will be appropriate of course.

(29) Delete your Chart (or save it). Deleting is easy to achieve if you minimize the Chart window and click outside it and press the Delete key. Otherwise use **File Delete** whilst the Chart window still exists.

(30) Insert a new column of data: the square numbers in C1:C12.

(31) Highlight columns B and C only and click the Chart icon.

(32) Confirm that the First Column (i.e. column B) is to provide the First Data Series. A double column graph will appear.

(33) Double click to create a Chart window. Maximize the Chart if you wish. Try different graphs using the **Gallery** menu.

If you wish to add data to a Chart you can do it in two ways:
    EITHER *You can delete the Chart and draw a new one.*
                  (This we did in sections 28 to 31.)
    OR   *You can directly add in the extra data, as we shall now do:*

(34) Minimize the Chart and then change to Line chart type 2 using **Gallery**. Click outside the Chart to get back to the Worksheet.

(35) Add a new column of data to the worksheet: Fibonacci numbers (say) in D1:D12.

(36) Highlight all the new column only. Select **Edit Copy**.

(37) Open a window for the Chart by double clicking on it. (Repeat until it works!)

(38) Select **Edit Paste** (this gives total control to Excel over how the new data is treated).
OR Select **Edit Paste Special** (this gives you control, in this case "column" mode would be appropriate mode for the extra data).

ALTERING DATA IN A CHART
You can adjust bars which represent raw data in a Chart and thereby alter the raw data in the Worksheet!

(39) Highlight column 1 only in the worksheet. Create a column Chart for that.

(40) Activate the Chart by clicking inside it.

(41) Hold down CTRL and click on the first column of the Chart. Drag the black 'handle' which appears upwards to the position required. You can only adjust within the range specified on the y axis. When you let go the Chart is redrawn and the Worksheet updated.

If the bar height has been calculated from a formula this does not work. In this example only A1 contains raw data, the other cells contain fomulae.

(42) Delete the previous Chart before proceeding.
To draw a Chart using Column A and Column D only, highlight Column A and then hold down CTRL when highlighting column D. Then click the Chart icon .... Try it!

WORKSHEET U – Excel Charts: Set 2

1. (a) Create a graph for SIN for 0° to 180° in steps of 12°.
   (b) Create <u>one</u> graph showing both SIN and COS for 0° to 360° in steps of 5°.

2. Draw graphs to compare the growth of Capital (e.g. £1000) for two different rates of compound interest (e.g. 5% and 7%) over several years (e.g. 10 years).

3. Simulate tossing a coin n times and draw a graph showing the progressive ratio of Heads/Total as n increases. [You will need to use a random number generator.]

4. (a) Prepare a personal weekly or monthly budget and display it.
   (b) Use a Chart to compare your budget with that of a friend.

5. A box is made from the cut out cardboard shape below:

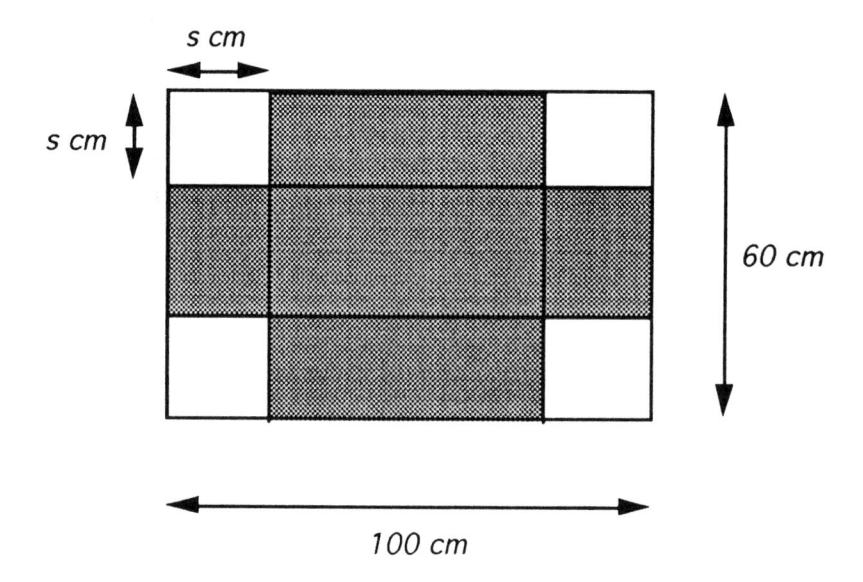

   [Diagram: rectangle 100 cm × 60 cm with squares of side s cm cut from each corner]

   Using Excel draw up a table and draw a graph to find the value of s to enclose the greatest volume, V. *Generalise.*

6. (a) Show graphically that a farmer making a rectangular pen using 400m of fencing can enclose most area if the rectangle is a square.
   (b) Find the rectangular shape to enclose most area if the farmer can use part of a 800m straight wall as one side of his enclosure instead of using some of his 400m of fencing.
   (c) What if two 800m long straight walls meeting at right-angles can be used for two sides?
   (d) Investigate cases when the walls in (b) and (c) are only short (e.g. 50m or 100m long).

CHAPTER 5

Iteration

Although this chapter refers to Microsoft *Excel*, earlier sections of the chapter use facilities which common to many spreadsheets. However, later sections refer to *Excel*'s **Goal Seek** and **Solver** facilities, only to be found on the most sophisticated spreadsheets.

5.1 Using Fill Down
A basic way to perform iterative calculations is simply to set up the initial condition(s) in row 1 and the equation(s) which use the initial condition(s) in row 2 and then **Fill Down** (Some spreadsheets use the term Copy Down.)

Example 1
To solve $x^3 - x^2 - 3x + 2 = 0$ we might use linear iteration on the re-arrangement
$$x_{r+1} = (x_r^2 + 3x_r - 2)^{1/3}$$ with initial condition $x_0 = 1$.

To do this put **1** into A1 and put the formula = **(A1^2 + 3*A1 – 2)^(1/3)** into A2, then **Fill Down** as far as is necessary. This puts each iterate into a new row (Fig. 1).

	A
1	1.000
2	1.260
3	1.499
4	1.680
5	1.803
6	1.882
7	1.930
8	1.959
9	1.976
10	1.986
11	1.992
12	1.995
13	1.997
14	1.998
15	1.999
16	1.999
17	2.000
18	2.000
19	2.000
20	2.000
21	2.000

Figure 1

It takes about 16 iterations to obtain the root 2.000 correct to 4 significant figures.

Filling down is a good approach. It provides insight, and from the resulting columns Charts are easily drawn and the behaviour of the iterative method can be readily examined. It is easy to add a column for a counter. There is, however, one difficulty: using fill down for iteration requires an indefinite extension of the spreadsheet and sometimes will need to be carried so far down that the screen scrolls and not all the relevant part of the spreadsheet can be seen all together. One way round this is to work with several columns, as the next example illustrates.

Example 2

To solve $x^4 - 5x^3 - 3x - 1 = 0$ we use linear iteration on the re-arrangement
$x_{r+1} = (5x_r^3 + 3x_r + 1)^{0.25}$ with arbitrary initial condition $x_0 = 1$.

In A10 place the initial condition x_0. (**1** say)

In B1 place the iterative formula to operate on x_0:

= (5*A10^3 +3*A10 + 1)^0.25

Fill Down the formula from B1 into B2 and amend it to refer to B1 (or type it in directly) as follows:

= (5*B1^3 +3*B1 + 1)^0.25

Then **Fill Down** from B2 to B10. That completes the first row of iterates (in row A).

To get further rows, highlight B1 to B10 and **Fill Right** as far as one wishes (Fig. 2).

	B1		=(5*A10^3+3*A10+1)^0.25			
	A	B	C	D	E	F
1		1.73205	4.88929	5.11048	5.12126	5.12178
2		2.38169	4.94936	5.11345	5.12140	5.12178
3		2.94963	4.99409	5.11564	5.12151	5.12179
4		3.42845	5.02731	5.11726	5.12159	5.12179
5		3.81929	5.05195	5.11845	5.12164	5.12180
6		4.13028	5.07019	5.11933	5.12168	5.12180
7		4.37298	5.08368	5.11998	5.12172	5.12180
8		4.55965	5.09365	5.12046	5.12174	5.12180
9		4.70167	5.10102	5.12081	5.12176	5.12180
10	1.00000	4.80887	5.10647	5.12107	5.12177	5.12180
11						

Figure 2

Example 3 – trouble with powers

To solve $x^5 + 2x^3 - 4x + 1 = 0$ we might try the re-arrangement $x^5 = -2x^3 + 4x - 1$ which naturally leads to $x_{r+1} = (-2x_r^3 + 4x_r - 1)^{1/5}$ with initial condition $x_0 = 1$.

First attempt

We put **1** into A1 and = (-2*A1^3 - 4*A1 + 1)^0.2 in A2 and **Fill Down** from A2, **but this does not work**. The error message #NUM! appears (Fig. 3) because the initial **1** in A1 leads to the expression (-5)^0.2 in A2 and *Excel* cannot find roots of negative numbers.

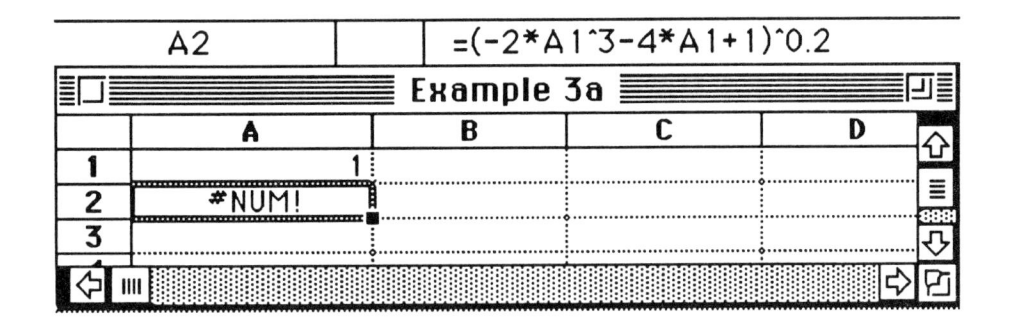

	A2	=(-2*A1^3-4*A1+1)^0.2		
	A	**B**	**C**	**D**
1	1			
2	#NUM!			
3				

Figure 3

Second attempt

A slightly different treatment of $x^5 = -2x^3 - 4x + 1$ is to note that since $(-1)^{1/5}$ is equal to -1 we can express $(-2x^3 - 4x + 1)^{1/5}$ as $-(2x^3 + 4x - 1)^{1/5}$.

This leads to the iterative formula $x_{r+1} = -(2x_r^3 + 4x_r - 1)^{1/5}$ with initial condition $x_0 = 1$.

We put **1** into A1 and = -(2*A1^3 + 4*A1 - 1)^0.2 into A2.

It may come as a surprise that we get exactly the same error again! This is because the negative operator (–) has higher precedence than the exponent operator (^). It must be remembered that there are two operators sharing the same symbol, negative and subtraction, but with different precedence levels!

Third attempt

We insert an extra pair of brackets in the formula, thus:

= -((2*A1^3 + 4*A1 - 1)^0.2).

We **Fill Down** from A2 as far as we wish. Having avoided the calculation of the cube root of the negative number so all should be well ... A2 displays the value –1.3797... but then fails again! The reason is that the formula in A3 has to evaluate $(-11.772...)^{1/5}$ which cannot be evaluated. Fig. 4 shows the outcome.

Fourth attempt

This is remedied by using the absolute value of (2*A1^3 – 4*A1 + 1) and adjusting the sign of the result to match the sign of (2*A1^3 – 4*A1 + 1) itself. To do this we need to

place in A2 the formula
$$= -\text{SIGN}(2*A1\wedge3 - 4*A1 + 1)*\text{ABS}(2*A1\wedge3 - 4*A1 + 1). \quad \text{(See Fig. 5.)}$$

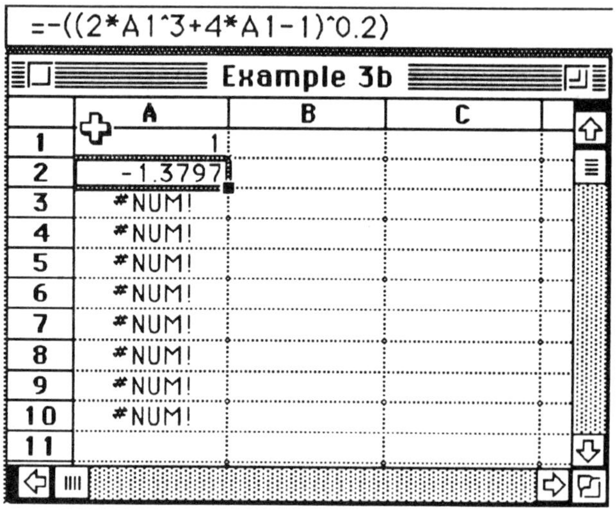

Figure 4

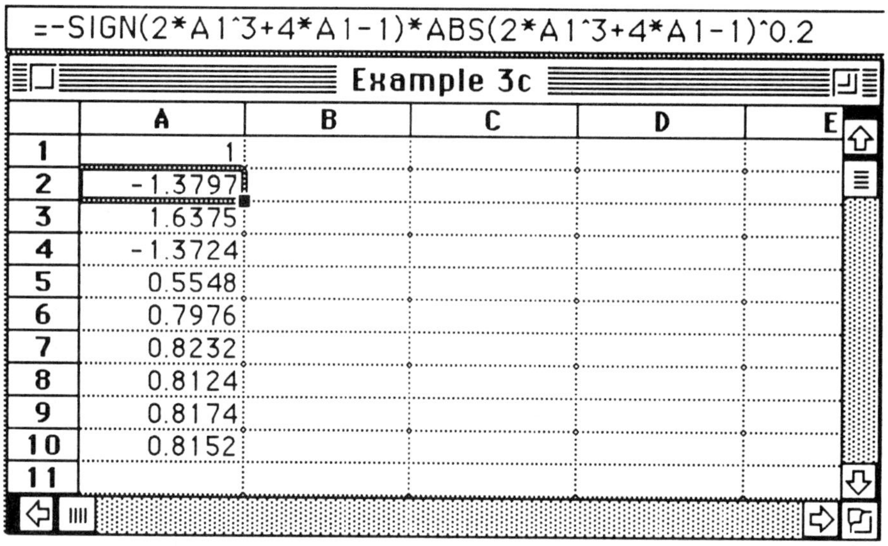

Figure 5

Note: Using *Excel*, evaluating A1^N is not a problem if N is a positive integer (or zero) even if A1 is negative. Some spreadsheets may not allow A1 to be negative in any circumstances. The evaluation of a polynomial expression may be safest expressed in nested multiplication form thereby avoiding the need for ^ completely. For example:
$x^4 + 2x^3 - 5x^2 + 3x - 1$ would be expressed as $(((x + 2)x - 5)x + 3)x - 1$.

The moral of this is that some knowledge or what is going on is needed and if negative values may arise ^ needs avoiding or used with care.

Other possible ways to avoid such problems include shifting the origin, and more subtle programming involving conditional tests (e.g. "IF"). These ideas are explored in later sections.

Another interesting and simple application of spreadsheets is to solving sets of simultaneous equations. The next example illustrates what is known as Jacobi's method.

Example 4
To solve a set of equations we use linear iteration in turn on the re-arranged set:

Initial equations	**Iterative re-arrangement**
$3x + y - z = 5$	$x_{r+1} = (-y_r + z_r + 5)/3$
$x - 3y + z = -5$	$y_{r+1} = (x_r + z_r + 5)/3$
$-2x + y + 6z = 3$	$z_{r+1} = (2x_r - y_r + 3)/6$

For this example we use the (arbitrary) initial conditions $x_0 = 1$, $y_0 = 1$, $z_0 = 1$.
(N.B. The re-arrangements should be chosen so as to ensure the largest possible divisors, or more precisely, the smallest coefficients for the right hand side variables x_r, y_r, z_r.)

Fig. 6 shows the application of this the Jacobi method. By studying this algorithm the reader may be able to devise a variant of the Jacobi method which has better convergence rate.

	A	B	C	D
1		JACOBI	METHOD	
2				
3	Iteration	x	y	z
4	0	1.00000	1.00000	1.00000
5	1	1.66667	2.33333	0.66667
6	2	1.11111	2.44444	0.66667
7	3	1.07407	2.25926	0.46296
8	4	1.06790	2.17901	0.48148
9	5	1.10082	2.18313	0.49280
10	6	1.10322	2.19787	0.50309
11	7	1.10174	2.20210	0.50143
12	8	1.09978	2.20106	0.50023
13	9	1.09972	2.20000	0.49975
14	10	1.09992	2.19982	0.49991
15	11	1.10003	2.19994	0.50000
16	12	1.10002	2.20001	0.50002
17	13	1.10000	2.20001	0.50001
18	14	1.10000	2.20000	0.50000
19	15	1.10000	2.20000	0.50000

Figure 6

Sometimes it would be nice to be able to use the *same* store for *successive* iterates, as normally happens when writing a BASIC program (say) or when using a calculator. For example to solve $x_{r+1} = \cos(x_r)$ one might use cell A1 and enter there the formula
=COS(A1).
However, a circular reference in a spreadsheet cannot normally be resolved i.e. a formula in a cell must not refer to its own cell, either directly or indirectly. This of course is exactly what we want! The next section explains how this self-referencing *can* be achieved.

5.2 Using the Calculation Iteration option

In *Excel* circular referencing is permissible by using the **Options** menu and selecting **Calculation** and turning **Iteration** on (see Fig. 7).

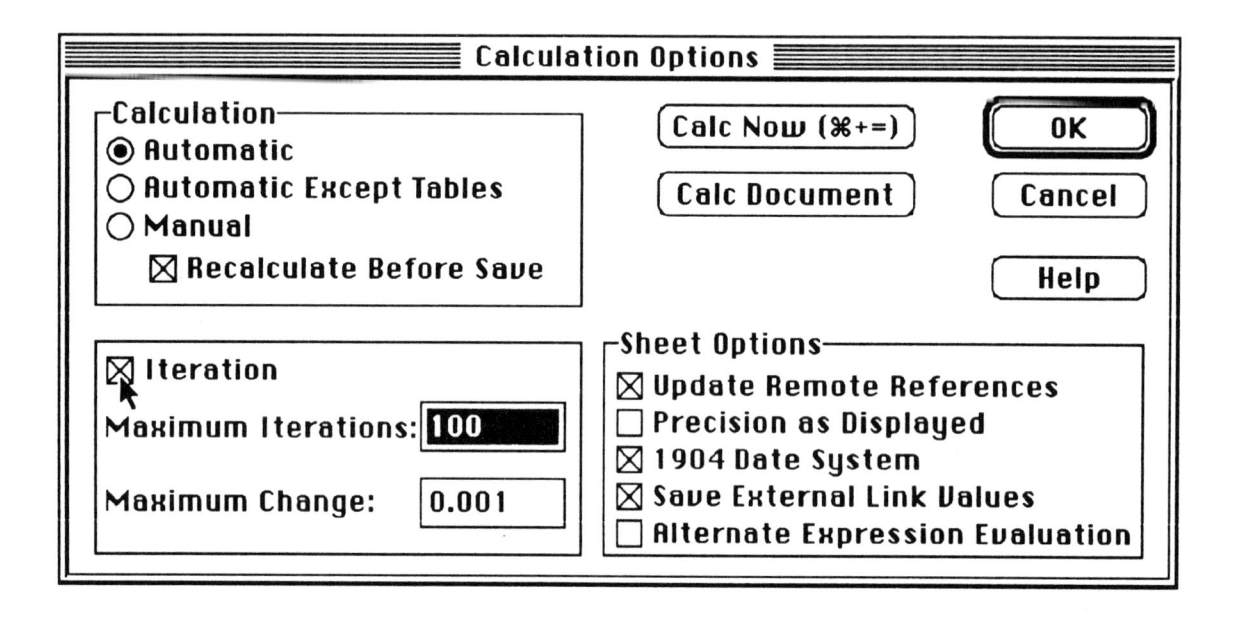

Figure 7

This allows up to 100 iterations (specified by **Maximum Iterations**) and an accuracy of 0.001 (specified by **Maximum Change**). These default values can be altered. It is useful for much numerical methods work to increase the accuracy (to 0.00001 perhaps); the 100 iterations maximum is usually more than sufficient.

Other spreadsheets are a little different from *Excel*. For example, with *Lotus 1-2-3* and *Quattro Pro 4* a circular reference is signalled by CIRC displayed near the bottom of the screen. By repeatedly pressing the Calc key (**F9** key on PC computers) the calculation will be repeated. Alternatively, by selecting **Recalculation Iteration** and entering the number of iterations wanted the whole spreadsheet can be recalculated the number of times specified by a single press of **F9**.

The following examples are *Excel* specific but results are similar with other spreadsheets.

Example 5

We wish to solve $x - 1 - \sin(x) = 0$ by simple iteration using $x_{r+1} = 1 + \sin(x_r)$.

Starting with an empty spreadsheet, place in A1 the formula **= 1 + sin(A1)**.

An error message "Cannot resolve circular references." appears. Click OK. Open **Options Calculation** and ensure that there is a cross in the **Iteration** box by clicking in it if necessary. Make the **Maximum Change** 0.000001. Then click OK while watching cell A1. Initially A1 will have numerical value 0 which will be the start value for the iteration process (there is no choice about that!). This will work well and the process will converge rapidly to 1.93456.....as indicated in Fig. 8. (N.B. Widening column A may reveal extra digits. This is done by placing the cursor on the border between A and B – it turns into a thick cross – and dragging it to the right.)

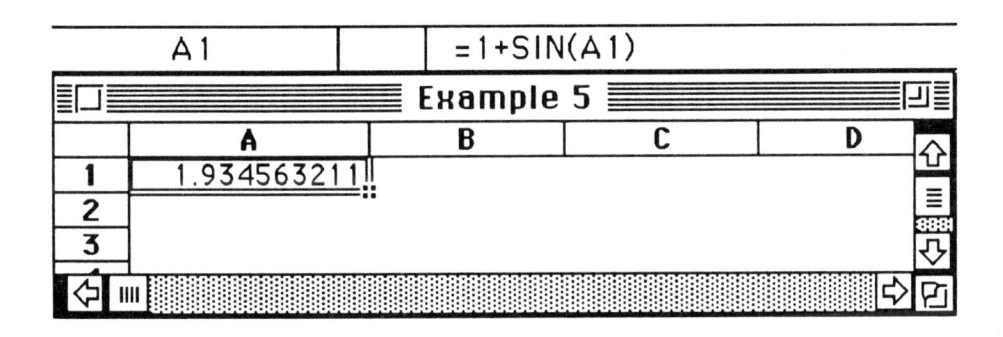

	A	B	C	D
	A1	=1+SIN(A1)		
	Example 5			
1	1.934563211			
2				
3				

Figure 8

Example 6

We now try finding square roots by Newton-Raphson iteration. To find $\sqrt{80}$ we would use: $x_{r+1} = (x_r + 80/x_r)/2$.

So, in A1 put the formula **= (A1 + 80/A1)/2**.

This does not work because we get #DIV/0! (or the less specific ERR with some spreadsheets) which indicates DIVISION BY ZERO, and the process terminates immediately (Fig. 9).

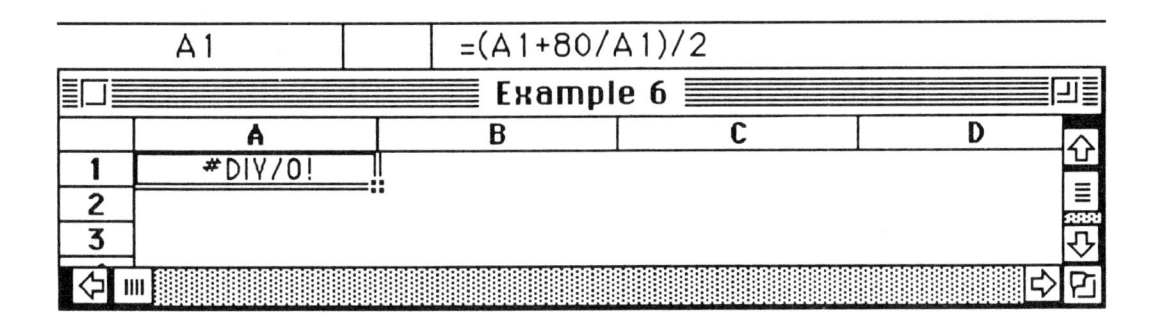

	A	B	C	D
	A1	=(A1+80/A1)/2		
	Example 6			
1	#DIV/0!			
2				
3				

Figure 9

Difficulty: A1 initially has 0 and we cannot avoid this!

Solution:

In A1 place the required initial value (**9**, say, since √80 ≅ 9).

In B1 place the formula

   =A1.

This will copy the value from A1 immediately.

In A1 replace the constant 9 by the required formula which in our case is

   =(B1 + 80/B1)/2.

This will iterate extremely rapidly to the solution 8.94427... provided that **Automatic Calculation** is selected, which is the default; if it is not selected **Calc Now** must be chosen to activate the process (on Apple Macintosh computers the key combination **Command =** has the same effect, as does **CTRL =** on PCs and Nimbus computers).

Updating the initial value to run the process again can be achieved by repeating the above steps, which is rather tedious. An alternative is to place a copy of the formula elsewhere for later use.

For example:

Place in cell D1 a copy of the formula which is in cell A1 (i.e. **=(B1 + 80/B1)/2**).

Then reset the initial value to 10 by typing **10** in A1 and copy the formula from D1 to A1.

(N.B. If **=(B1 + 80/B1)/2** is copied from A1 to D1 it will appear there as

=(E1 + 80/E1)/2). This will work when copied back but it is neater to use absolute column referencing i.e. use **=($B1 + 80/$B1)/2** in A1 which preserves the B reference throughout). This is shown in Fig. 10.

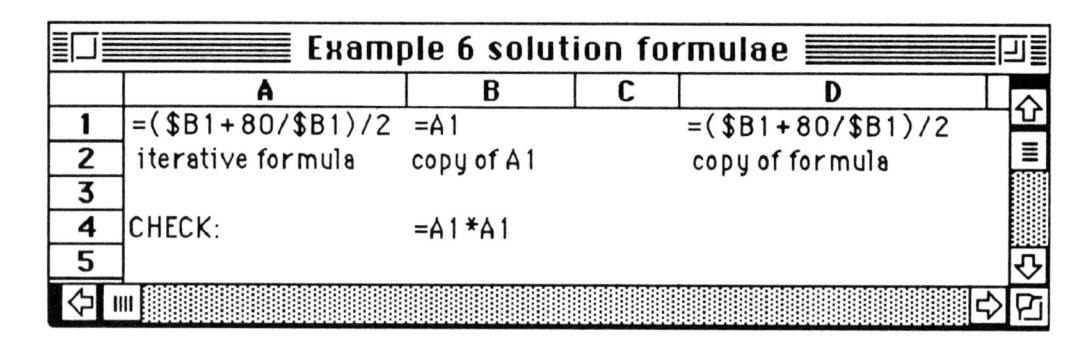

	A	B	C	D
1	=($B1+80/$B1)/2	=A1		=($B1+80/$B1)/2
2	iterative formula	copy of A1		copy of formula
3				
4	CHECK:	=A1*A1		
5				

Figure 10

Alternative solution:

Another approach is to 'shift the origin' so that a zero initial value does not cause division by zero. This is left to the interested reader to investigate, and discussed in Green (1993).

Example 7

It can be useful for many iterative problems to have a counter, to count the iterations. Can we achieve this? We explore this by considering a simple example.

We wish to solve $x^2 - 3x - 4 = 0$ by iterating the re-arrangement $x_{r+1} = \sqrt{(3x_r + 4)}$.
As a first attempt we might do this:
In A1 put **= A1 + 1**.
In B1 put **=SQRT(3*B1 + 4)**.
However, there are unexpected problems with this simplistic approach!

Difficulty 1: Since *Excel* normally recalculates the whole spreadsheet as soon as any value is changed, the opportunity to alter several cells simultaneously is denied! As soon as the counter formula (=A1+1) is placed in A1 recalculation takes place – before the function can be entered or amended. And if the function is entered or amended first, the counter starts off before we can reset it! Fortunately this comic turn of events can be averted in *Excel* by switching *off* the automatic calculation mode and using manual calculation. To do this use **Options Calculation** and click the **Manual** button. Then set up the spreadsheet as required, and finally select **Options Calc Now** to activate the calculation process.

Difficulty 2: Since A1 initially contains 0 it immediately takes on the value 1 when = **A1 + 1** is entered. This can be solved as follows:
In A5 (say) place **1**. In A1 place = **A1 + 1 – A5**. In A5 place **0**.

Difficulty 3: It is not straightforward to *reset* the counter to zero for a second run. Putting zero in A1 destroys the formula, which requires re-typing the formula (or copying from some other cell). Alternatively, an appropriate negative number can be put into A5 and then removed. This is rather unsatisfactory!

Difficulty 4: Having a counter prevents *Excel* stopping when the iteration process has achieved its required accuracy level because the counter values themselves don't converge!

The reader may feel that perhaps a counter isn't such a good idea after all, but there is a way round this ...

Final solution
Returning to our original problem, we wish to solve $x^2 - 3x - 4 = 0$ by iterating the re-arrangement $x_{r+1} = \sqrt{(3x_r + 4)}$ starting with $x_0 = 0$.
Choose **Options Calculation** and select **Manual**. This prevents the calculation going ahead automatically. Still in the **Options Calculation** menu, select **Iteration** and set the **Maximum Iterations** to **1**. This ensures that just one iterative step takes place (so that the process can be observed properly – some other small value could be used).

In A1 place the counter formula
   =**A1 + 1**.
It will immediately display 1.
In B1 place the iterative formula
   =**SQRT(3*B1 + 4)**.
It will immediately display 2.00000.

Ensure that the formats for cells A1 and B1 are appropriate, using the **Format Numbers** menu if necessary (highlight the cell(s) to which the formatting is to be applied.

Now select **Calc Now** (found in the **Options Calculation** menu, or achieved much more simply by pressing **Command =**). The spreadsheet is recalculated and one iteration is performed, giving 3.1622. Successive invocations of **Calc Now** update the spreadsheet and convergence to the root 4 is achieved (see Fig. 11).

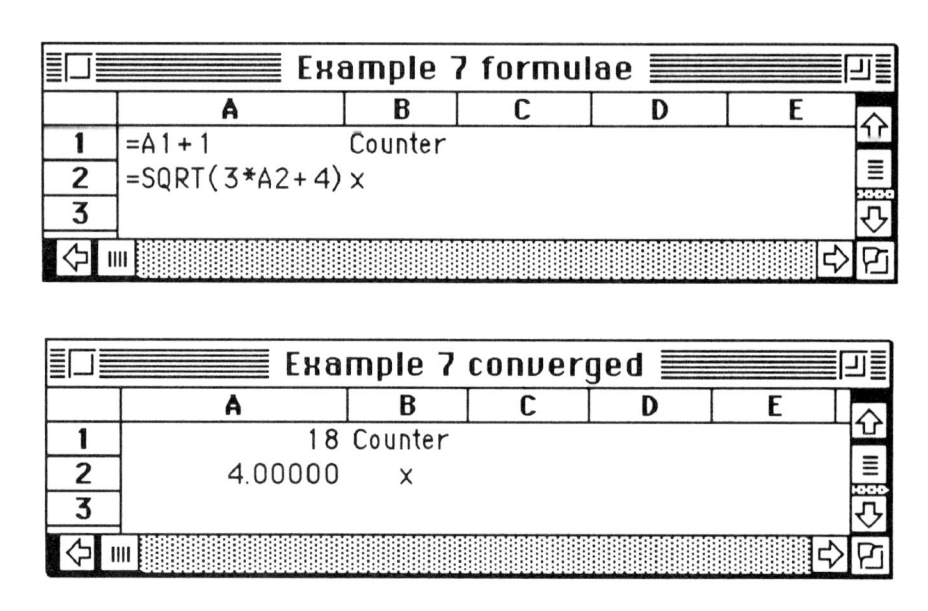

```
┌─────────── Example 7 formulae ───────────┐
│       A         B       C     D     E    │
│ 1  =A1+1     Counter                     │
│ 2  =SQRT(3*A2+4) x                       │
│ 3                                        │
└──────────────────────────────────────────┘

┌─────────── Example 7 converged ──────────┐
│       A         B       C     D     E    │
│ 1            18 Counter                  │
│ 2  4.00000      x                        │
│ 3                                        │
└──────────────────────────────────────────┘
```

Figure 11

To reset one could re-enter the formulae in the two cells, but there is an easier way:
Select A1 by clicking there. Then click in the formula edit bar near the top of the spreadsheet (where =A1 + 1 is displayed) and click the √ box. This re-enters the formula and treats A1 as effectively empty (i.e. containing zero) so the counter resets to 1. Similarly treat B1.

5.3 Using IF

Although the *Excel* 3.0 User's Guide only refers to IF in the context of 'macros' the Function Reference book reveals that IF can be used in an ordinary spreadsheet. (More correctly it is referred to as IF() to indicate its functional nature, but we will not be so pedantic here.) The equivalent to IF in *Lotus 1-2-3* is @IF.

IF has been met before in this book – it was described in Chapter 2 (page 20) and used in several examples in Chapter 3. It is such a useful function that it is worth devoting some more space here to its use.

Since IF can be used in an ordinary spreadsheet, it makes it possible, for example, to program the method of *False Position* for finding the root of a non-linear equation. This method, like the *Interval Halving* method described in the Numerical Methods section of Chapter 3, requires a decision to be made at each iteration as to which of two values to retain for the next iteration.

An essential feature of *False Position* is that that one must find two starting values, Xleft and Xright, which span a root of f(X)=0 in such a way that f(Xleft) and f(Xright) are of opposite sign. Given such a pair, the algorithm to determine the new iterate is:
$$Xnew = Xright - f(Xright) \times (Xright - Xleft)/(f(Xright) - f(Xleft)).$$

Once the new iterate is calculated a decision must be made as to whether to replace Xleft or Xright with Xnew. Whichever of f(Xleft) and f(Xright) has the same sign as f(Xnew) determines which is to be replaced. The following example indicates one way to implement this method.

Example 8

Solve $f(x) = x^3 - 4x + 2 = 0$ taking $x_0 = 1$ and $x_1 = 2$. The spreadsheet is set up as shown in Fig. 12.

	A	B	C	D	E	F
1	Xleft	FNleft	Xright	FNright	Xnew	FNnew
2	1	=A2^3-4*A2+2	2	=C2^3-4*C2+2	=C2-D2*(C2-A2)/(D2-B2)	=E2^3-4*E2+2
3						
4						
5						

Example 8 row 1-2 formulae

Figure 12

- ROW 1 contains headings.
- ROW 2 contains the initial values in cells A2 and C2. The function is entered into B2 and copy and paste are used to place copies into D2 and F2 also. The algorithm to calculate the new iterate is placed in E2.

It is necessary to replace either Xleft or Xright by Xnew depending on the signs of f(Xleft) and f(Xright); Xnew replaces Xleft if f(Xnew) and f(Xleft) have the same sign, otherwise Xnew replaces Xright. This is tested by seeing if Xleft*Xmean > 0 and if f(Xright)*f(Xmean) > 0. These tests are incorporated into ROW 3 described overleaf.

Cell	Contents	Description
A3	= IF(B2*$F2>0, $E2, A2)	Selects E2 if B2 and F2 have the same sign, otherwise A2.
B3	= A3^3 - 4*A3 + 2	Fill Down from B2 to get this formula for the function value.
C3	= IF(D2*$F2>0, $E2, C2)	Selects E2 if D2 and F2 have the same sign, otherwise C2.
D3	= C3^3 - 4*C3 + 2	Fill Down from D2 to get this formula for the function value.
E3	= C3 – D3*(C3 – A3)/(D3 – B3)	Fill Down from E2 to get this formula for the new iterate.
F3	= E3^3 - 4*E3 + 2	Fill Down from F2 to get this formula for the function value.

- ROW 3 contains the newly calculated values.

The test to determine whether Xleft is to be replaced by Xnew or not is placed in A3:
 = IF(B2*$F2>0, $E2, A2).
This is then copied from A3 into C3. (The $ signs signify absolute referencing to make it easy to copy this formula correctly. On copying, B changes to D but F and E remain fixed.)
The function evaluation formulae needed in cells B3, D3, F3 are copied down from cells B2, D2, F2. That completes the setting up. The implementation in *Excel* is shown below in Fig. 13.

Example 8 row 1-3 formulae

	A	B	C	D	E	F
1	Xleft	FXleft	Xright	FXright	Xnew	FXnew
2	1	=A2^3-4*A2+2	2	=C2^3-4*C2+2	=C2-D2*(C2-A2)/(D2-B2)	=E2^3-4*E2+2
3	=IF(B2*$F2>0,$E2,A2)	=A3^3-4*A3+2	=IF(D2*$F2>0,$E2,C2)	=C3^3-4*C3+2	=C3-D3*(C3-A3)/(D3-B3)	=E3^3-4*E3+2
4						
5						

Figure 13

Having established the basic spreadsheet, rows may be extended downwards from Row 3 as far as required using **Fill Down**. The numerical results are shown in Fig. 14 overleaf.

Different starting values may be tried just by altering A2 and C2. A different function may be entered in B2 and copied into D2 and F2 and **Fill Down** used to recreate Row 3. Then **Fill Down** could be used to extend the whole spreadsheet as before. Alternatively, a short macro could be written to allow easy replacement of the function. (This was done for the *Interval Halving* method in Chapter 4, which readers may consider a better approach.)

	A	B	C	D	E	F
1	Xleft	FNleft	Xright	FNright	Xnew	FNnew
2	1.000000	-1.000000	2	2	1.333333	-0.962963
3	1.333333	-0.962963	2	2	1.550000	-0.476125
4	1.550000	-0.476125	2	2	1.636529	-0.163120
5	1.636529	-0.163120	2	2	1.663938	-0.048824
6	1.663938	-0.048824	2	2	1.671946	-0.014018
7	1.671946	-0.014018	2	2	1.674230	-0.003977
8	1.674230	-0.003977	2	2	1.674876	-0.001124
9	1.674876	-0.001124	2	2	1.675059	-0.000318
10	1.675059	-0.000318	2	2	1.675111	-0.000090
11	1.675111	-0.000090	2	2	1.675125	-0.000025
12	1.675125	-0.000025	2	2	1.675129	-0.000007
13	1.675129	-0.000007	2	2	1.675130	-0.000002
14						
15						

Figure 14

5.4 Using relational operators

Using IF (or @IF) is not essential since the same effect can be achieved with relational operators such as > (e.g. A1 > 10). Relational operators yield TRUE and FALSE (or @TRUE and @FALSE), and since these are numerically coded 1 and 0 respectively they can be incorporated into calculation formulae. Before embarking on the details it is worthwhile studying some simple examples:

(a) Entering =2>1 in A1 yields TRUE.
(b) Entering =(2>1)*1 in A1 yields 1. Thus TRUE*1 gives 1.
(c) Entering =2>9 in A1 yields FALSE.
(d) Entering =(2>9)*1 in A1 yields 0. Thus FALSE*1 gives 0.
(e) Entering =A1>B1 in C1 yields TRUE or FALSE depending on the contents of A1, B1.
(f) Entering =(A1>B1)*1 in C1 yields 1 or 0 as appropriate.
(g) Entering =IF(A1>B1,1,0) in C1 yields 1 or 0 as appropriate.

We conclude that =(A1>B1)*1 and =IF(A1>B1,1,0) are *equivalent*; each gives 1 if A1>B1 and zero otherwise.

In Example 8 the IF function could be avoided by:
  placing in A3 the formula =(B2*$F2<0)*A2 + (B2*$F2>0)*$E2
  placing in C3 the formula =(D2*$F2<0)*C2 + (D2*$F2>0)*$E2.
This would achieve exactly the same effect **but using IF is neater and clearer** which are important considerations. For some problems there is little to choose, and with those spreadsheets which do not have the IF function this method might still work.

5.5 Using Formula Goal Seek

Using iteration as described previously assumes a certain level of sophistication in deciding on a formulation of the problem which is likely to converge. A quite different approach is to leave that to *Excel* and simply state the problem and use the **Goal Seek** option, available in *Excel 3.0* onwards and found in the **Formula** menu. A similar facility called **Solve For** is available in *Quattro Pro 4* in the **Tools** menu.

Example 9

I buy shares for £1000 and three years later sell them for £1500. What annual rate of compound interest, r%, is that?

We need to solve $1000(1 + r/100)^3 = 1500$.
(This particular problem can be done by 'taking logs' or using the nth root key on a calculator but it will do as an introduction and has the advantage of being easily checked.)

Formula and numeric views of a spreadsheet with estimate r = 10 are shown in Fig. 15.

	A	B
	Example 9 formulae	
1	Buying price	1000
2	Selling price	1500
3	Profit	=B2-B1
4	Whole years invested	3
5	Months invested	0
6	Time invested (years)	=B4+B5/12
7	Estimated interest rate, r	10
8	Forecast profit using r	=B1*(1+B7/100)^B6-B1
9		

	A	B	C
	Example 9 numeric values		
1	Buying price	1000	
2	Selling price	1500	
3	Profit	500	
4	Whole years invested	3	
5	Months invested	0	
6	Time invested (years)	3	
7	Estimated interest rate, r	10	
8	Forecast profit using r	331	
9			

Figure 15

What we want is to find r (i.e. B7) so that the profit (i.e. B8) comes to £500 (i.e. B3). We could do this by trial and error. Alternatively we can use **Formula Goal Seek**. This brings up a window and we enter the relevant data (see Fig. 16).

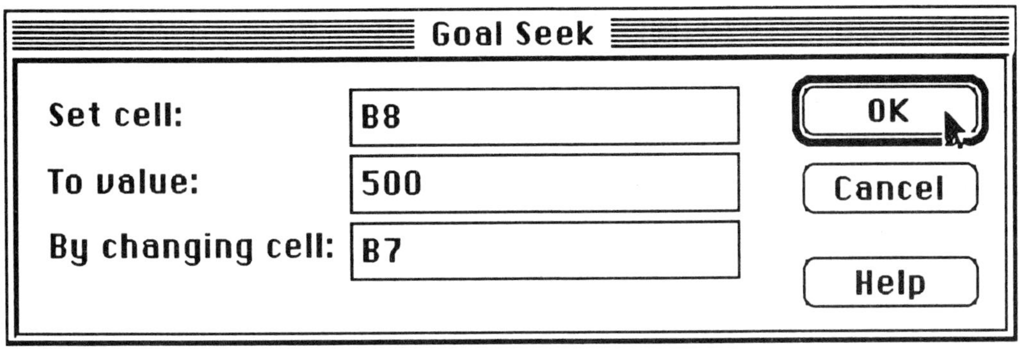

```
Goal Seek
Set cell:           B8
To value:           500
By changing cell:   B7

[OK]  [Cancel]  [Help]
```

Figure 16

When we click the **OK** button, **Goal Seek** finds the solution and reports the goal value obtained and the spreadsheet takes on the values found (Fig. 17 – compare with Fig. 15).

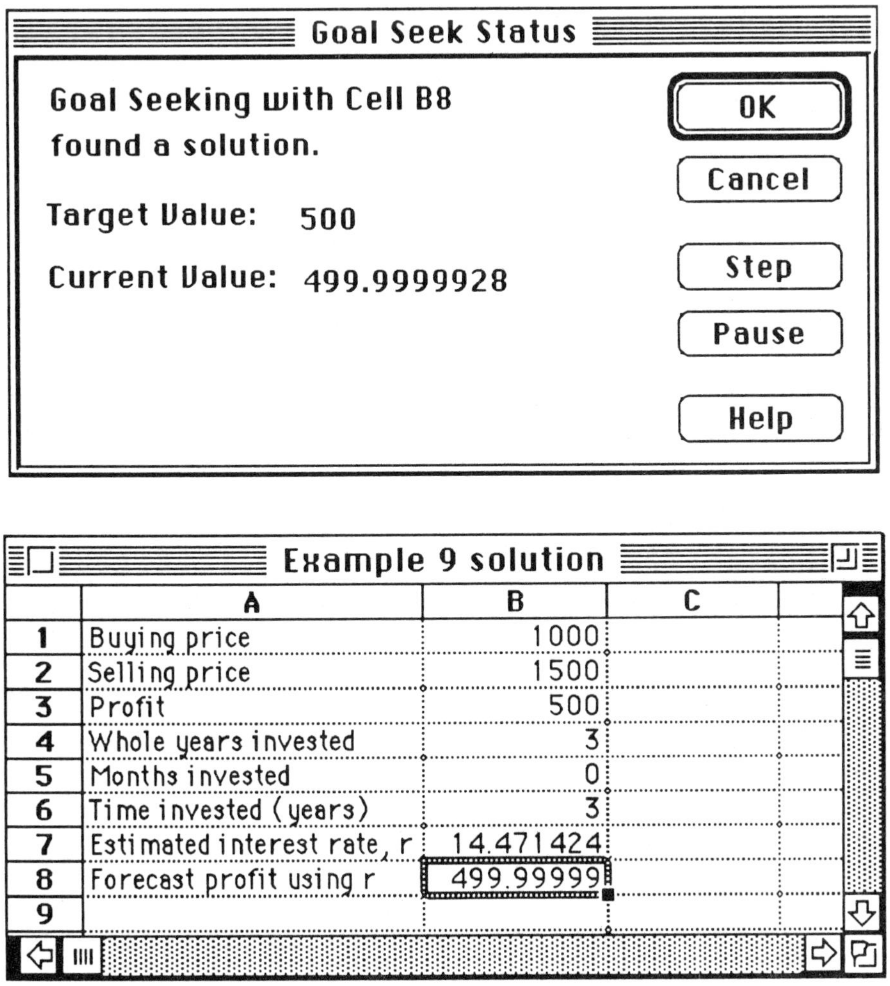

```
Goal Seek Status

Goal Seeking with Cell B8
found a solution.

Target Value:   500
Current Value:  499.9999928

[OK]  [Cancel]  [Step]  [Pause]  [Help]
```

```
Example 9 solution
     A                          B          C
1   Buying price              1000
2   Selling price             1500
3   Profit                     500
4   Whole years invested         3
5   Months invested              0
6   Time invested (years)        3
7   Estimated interest rate, r  14.471424
8   Forecast profit using r   499.99999
9
```

Figure 17

125

It is a pity that we cannot let *Excel* take the required profit from cell B3 itself (£500) but we must supply **Goal Seek** with an actual numeric value. A simple ploy to get round this is as follows. (We will use it on a numerically different problem, since having run **Goal Seek** once, *Excel* already has the solution!)

Enter the selling price £1357.90 in B2 (don't put in the £ sign). Then add an extra cell:

Cell	Contents	Description
B9	= B3 - B8	Difference to be made zero

For £1357.90 the interest rate is found to be 10.73...%.

This method works for many problems, including those discussed earlier in this chapter. A simple example of that type now follows.

Example 10
Solve $f(x) = x^3 - 6x^2 + 11x - 6 = 0$. (This has roots 1, 2, 3)
Place in A1 an initial estimate (say **0**). Place in A2 the formula:
   = A1^3 − 6*A1^2 + 11*A1 − 6
Then call **Formula Goal Seek** and enter the data (See Fig. 18).

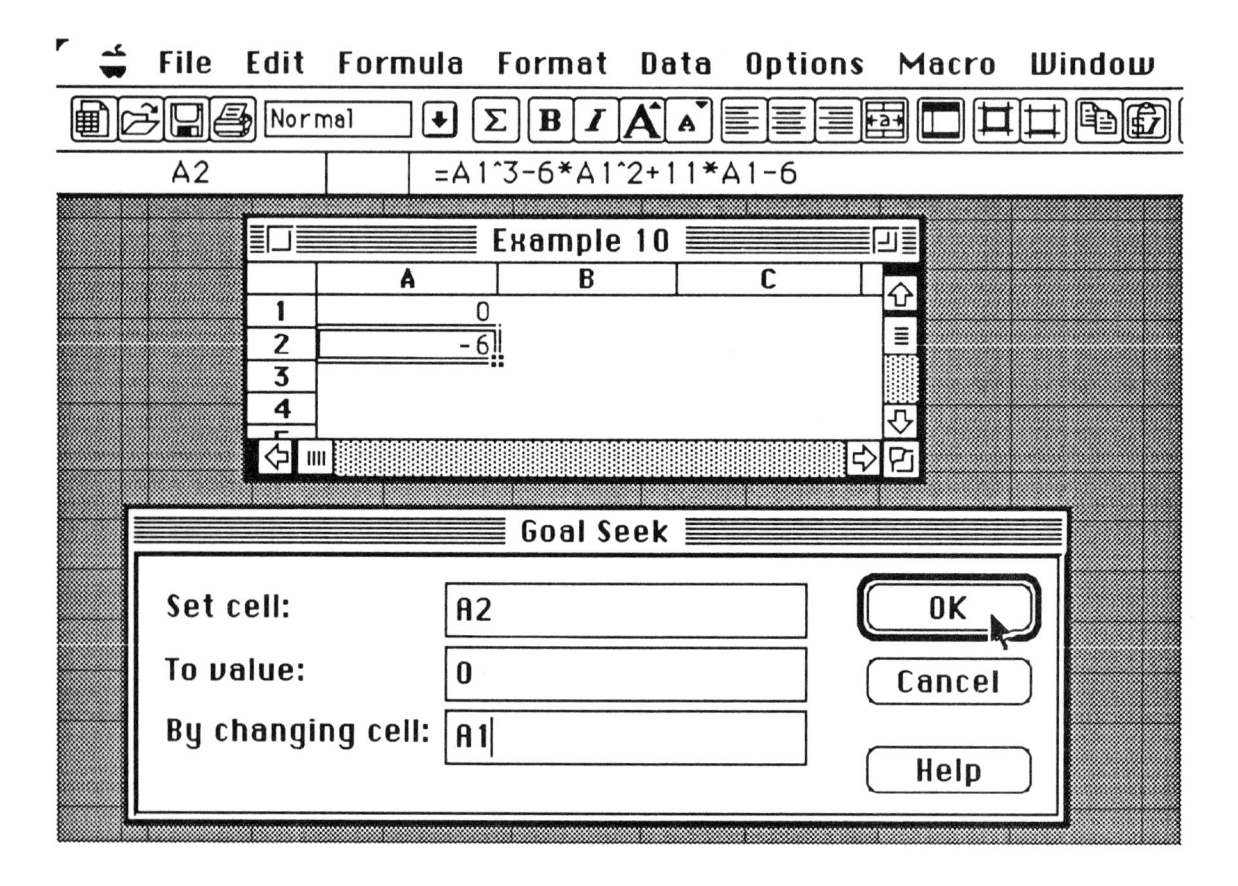

Figure 18

Goal Seek will try different values of A1 until A2 is zero to within some tolerance. The **Maximum Change** default is 0.001 and the **Maximum Iterations** default is 100. Spreadsheet recalculation will stop once every cell changes from one iteration to the next by less than 0.001 or if 100 iterations have taken place.

The reader is warned that the **Maximum Change** level does *not signify the accuracy level* of the answers obtained.
- The change of *every* cell is monitored and therefore the actual answer cell(s) may have *much greater accuracy*.
- On the other hand, answer cells may be changing by very small amounts but may be *very far from the accurate solution values (if they exist)*.

For the example under consideration, using **Goal Seek** with its default levels for **Maximum Change** (0.001) and **Maximum Iterations** (100) the results obtained were:

A1	root	|error|
0	0.999992	0.000008
2.5	1.999957	0.000043
5	3.000150	0.000150

5.6 Using Excel Solver

Excel Solver is a sophisticated add-in package available in *Excel* version 3.0 onwards and, when installed, appears as an option in the **Formula** menu. It is a generalization of **Goal Seek** and can vary more than one cell and can limit the variation of other cell values to within specified constraints. The goal it seeks need not be a particular value but can be a maximum or minimum. A similar facility called **Optimizer** is available in *Quattro Pro 4* in the **Tools** menu.

Example 11

We will consider an optimisation problem similar to those on Worksheet S found in Chapter 4 (page 105):

> An ecologist must walk from her car to a lake, get a small sample of the water, and then walk to a hut to analyse the sample (see Fig. 19). What is the minimum distance she must walk? One day the ecologist arrives to find that the hut is on fire. She takes two large buckets from her car and walks to the lakeside. She then walks more slowly with the full buckets to put out the fire. Suppose she can walk at speed of 1m per second carrying the empty buckets but can only manage 0.5 m per second with the full buckets. What route should she take to minimise the time to reach the fire and how long will this take her?

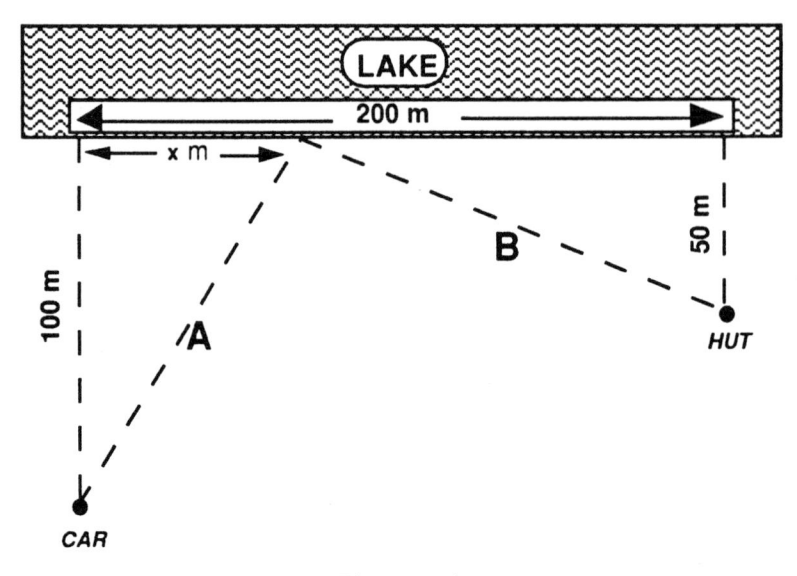

Figure 19

From Fig. 19 the following can be deduced:

Distance along A = $\sqrt{(100^2 + x^2)}$ metres.
Distance along B = $\sqrt{((200 - x)^2 + 50^2)}$ metres.
Time to travel along A = $1 \times \sqrt{(100^2 + x^2)}$ seconds.
Time to travel along B = $2 \times \sqrt{((200 - x)^2 + 50^2)}$ seconds.

We wish to minimise the total distance or the total time.

A spreadsheet is set up to represent this with an initial estimate for x of 100 (see Fig. 20).

B2	=SQRT(100^2+B1^2)			
	Example 11			
A	B	C	D	E
X	100.00			
DISTANCE A (m)	141.42	TIME A (s)	70.71	
DISTANCE B (m)	111.80	TIME B (s)	111.80	
TOTAL DISTANCE	253.22	TOTAL TIME	182.51	

Figure 20

Then **Formula Solver** is invoked and the data is entered as indicated in Fig. 21. The result when **Solver** has finished is shown in Fig. 22.

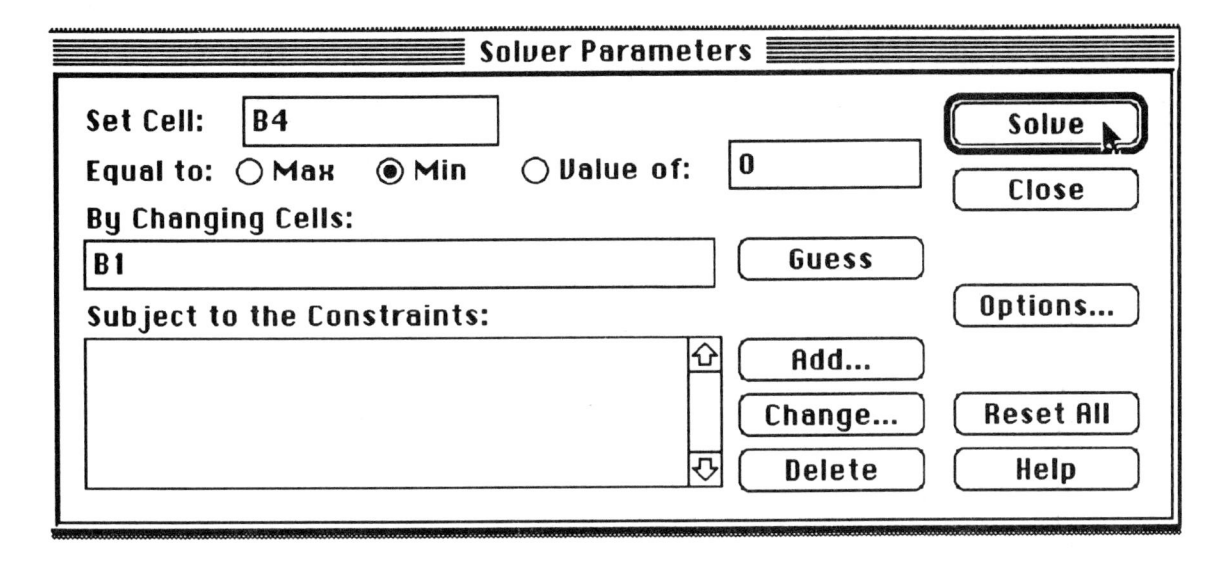

Figure 21

Figure 22

	A	B	C	D	E
1	X	133.33			
2	DISTANCE A (m)	166.67	TIME A (s)	83.33	
3	DISTANCE B (m)	83.33	TIME B (s)	83.33	
4	TOTAL DISTANCE	250.00	TOTAL TIME	166.67	
5					
6					

The minimum distance is found to be 250.00m when x = 133.33.
(Similarly the minimum time is found to be 156.67s when x = 175.87)

Example 12
This example is a variant of a familiar problem and introduces the idea of constraints which did not feature in Example 11 (although they might have).

> A rectangular enclosure is to be made from 200m of wire netting and incorporating sides of a farm building. What is the largest area which can be enclosed? A possible position is shown in Fig. 23. The fencing can join the building anywhere along the two ends so the distances p metres and q metres can each vary from 0m to 10m.

It is not clear which position will give most area.

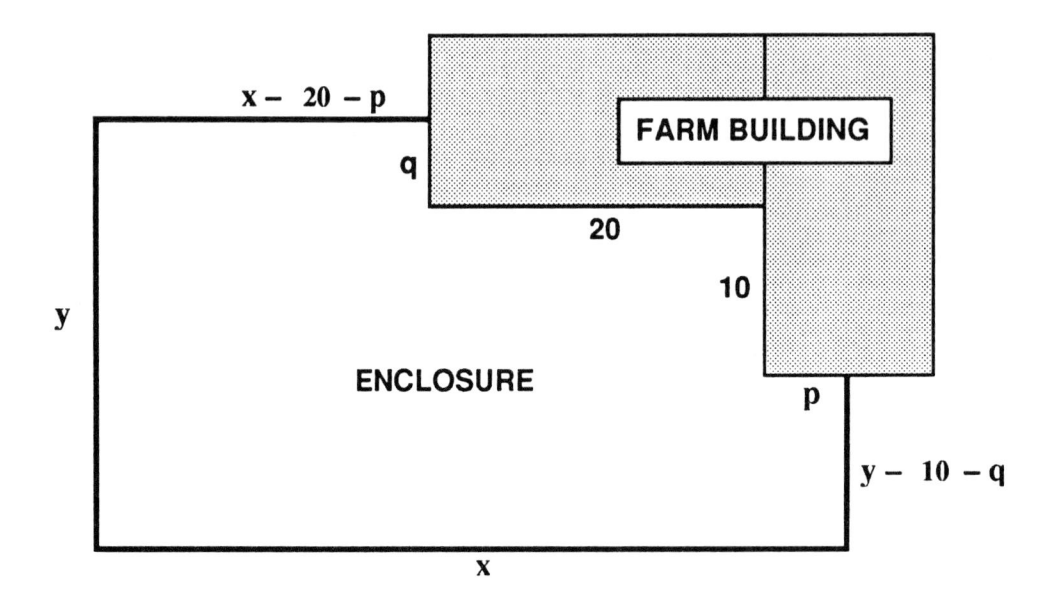

Figure 23 Enclosure – all distances in metres.

The situation can be modelled by:
Area = $xy - (20-p)q - 10p$
Length = $2x + 2y - 30 - p - q$.
Constraints are: $0 \leq p \leq 10$, $0 \leq q \leq 10$, Length ≤ 200

We wish to maximize the area subject to the above constraints. (Strictly speaking we must also have $20 \leq x$, $10 \leq y$. These need not be entered as they are bound to be satisfied in this particular case.) The spreadsheet is set up as shown in Fig 24.

	F2		=B2*C2-(20+D2)*E2				
	A	**B**	**C**	**D**	**E**	**F**	**G**
1	FENCE AVAILABLE (m)	x	y	p	q	AREA (m sq)	FENCE USED (m)
2	200	50.00	50.00	5.00	5.00	2375.00	160
3							

Figure 24

Then we invoke **Formula Solver**. This brings up a window and we enter the data as shown in Fig. 25. When we fill in the requisite information and click **OK**, **Solver** gets to work and quickly reports that it has found a solution (Fig. 26). When we click on **OK** the result is displayed in the spreadsheet (Fig. 27).

Solver Parameters

Set Cell: $F$2
Equal to: ● Max ○ Min ○ Value of: 0
By Changing Cells:
$B$2:$E$2
Subject to the Constraints:
$A$2 >= $G$2
$D$2 <= 10
$D$2 >= 0
$E$2 <= 10

Buttons: Solve, Close, Guess, Options..., Add..., Change..., Reset All, Delete, Help

Figure 25

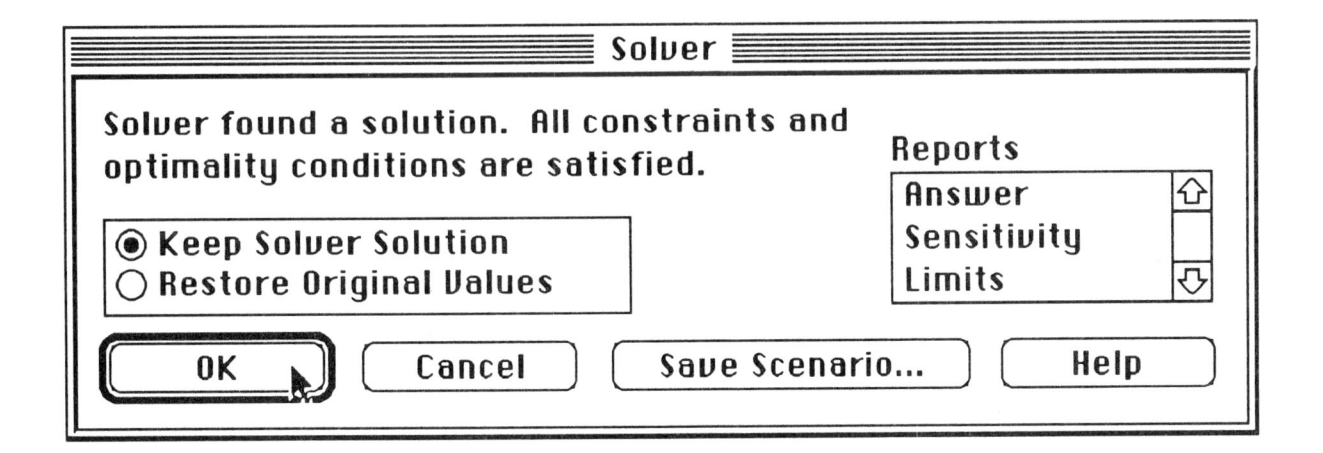

Solver

Solver found a solution. All constraints and optimality conditions are satisfied.

● Keep Solver Solution
○ Restore Original Values

Reports: Answer, Sensitivity, Limits

Buttons: OK, Cancel, Save Scenario..., Help

Figure 26

Example 12

	A	B	C	D	E	F	G
1	FENCE AVAILABLE (m)	x	y	p	q	AREA (m sq)	FENCE USED (m)
2	200	62.50	62.50	10.00	10.00	3606.25	199.9999989
3							

Figure 27

The only non-trivial part when using **Solver** is entering the constraint(s). For the above problem the solution 3606.25 m² is obtained within the accuracy level set.

Solver has been found to be an extremely useful tool in varying several parameters in fitting a complex function to a set of data by the method of least squares. For instance, in linear regression the least squares straight line of best fit to a set of data points (x_i, y_i) is obtained by varying the parameters a and b in the function $y = a + bx$ to minimise the sum of the squares of the residuals $(y_i - a - bx_i)$. A spreadsheet can be laid out with the parameters a and b to be varied at the top (any guessed values will do initially), the x and y data in adjacent columns, together with a column of squared residuals which is summed (the references to the parameters a and b being absolute). **Solver** is then called up and asked to minimise the value in the cell containing the sum of the squares of the residuals by varying the contents of the cells holding the a and b values. As this is a linear problem, the a and b values solving it are found extremely quickly.

In this case **Solver** is not really required as closed formulae for the regression coefficients are well known, and are in fact already implemented in *Excel* with the LINEST function. Even so, the approach using **Solver** may be more understandable to students meeting the idea of regression for the first time.

Solver really comes into its own on non-linear problems. To round off this chapter, three case studies from physics are sketched out.

Example 13

Our first case study involved fitting a quadratic function in t of the form $y = a + bt + ct^2$ to a set of (t, y) values where y represented the height at time t of a bouncing ball, as measured from a strobe photograph.

The equations for the coefficients of such a quadratic regression are linear and could have been solved by inverting a 3×3 matrix (using *Excel*'s MINVERSE function of course!), but *Excel*'s **Solver** did the job equally well, minimizing the sum of the squares of the residuals $(y_i - a - bt_i - ct_i^2)$ by varying a, b and c.

Example 14

Our second case study involved finding the 'dead time' T of a Geiger Müller tube. It was required to vary the parameter T in the function $y = x/(1 + xT)$ to obtain the best fit to a set of (x_i, y_i) values.

The minimization could have been done by trial and error, but **Solver** provided an easier way to minimise the sum of the squares of the residuals $(y_i - x_i/(1 + x_iT))$ by varying T.

Example 15
Our third case study involved finding the orbital parameters r, T and α to best fit a set of observations (t_i, x_i) of Jupiter's moons to the function $x = r \cos(2\pi t/T - \alpha)$,

Excel's **Solver** was successfully employed to minimize the sum of the squares of the residuals $(x_i - r \cos(2\pi t_i/T - \alpha))$ by varying r, T and α. This highly non-linear problem took **Solver** rather more steps than usual to find the optimum solution, but it was far more efficient than the writer's efforts!

Clearly, *Excel*'s **Solver** – and similar facilities in other spreadsheets – can be applied to many similar problems.

5.7 Conclusion

If the user is not concerned with the actual algorithm for solving a problem, the advanced 'solver' features may be appropriate, although mathematics teachers may see these as pushing us one further step down the slippery road to oblivion. More optimistically, trying to find out how such facilities work could provide a welcome stimulus.

Even experienced users may be surprised to discover what what their spreadsheets can do; consulting the manual is highly recommended!

References

Bridges, R. (1990). The dead time of a Geiger-Müller tube.
Physics Education Vol 25 pp 60-65.

Bridges, R. (1991). The spin of a bouncing 'superball'.
Physics Education Vol 26 pp 350-354.

Green, D.R. (1993) Solving iteration problems using a spreadsheet.
Teaching Mathematics and its Applications Vol 12 No 1.

CHAPTER 6

Dynamic Modelling and Simulation with a Spreadsheet

Introduction

Despite the work which has been done to champion computer based modelling in the curriculum it is evident that, for many teachers, the mathematical model continues to be a rather distant concept. This is a great pity, since the mathematical model should contribute significantly to any debate about a changing mathematics curriculum and, in particular, to any review of sixth form mathematics. For example: (i) the introduction of more numerical methods into the sixth form curriculum would be enhanced if these methods were associated with modelling and simulation techniques, (ii) differential and difference equations might be more accessible to sixth formers, if they were constructed as modelling exercises rather than being presented as ready-made problems.

Consider how spreadsheets might be used as as an alternative to specifically designed modelling packages such as *STELLA* (Richmond, 1987) and *Dynamic Modelling System* (Ogborn, 1987). Such modelling packages are rarely to be discovered in mathematics classrooms and certainly not as often as spreadsheets. This is only to be expected since spreadsheets have much wider utility than software designed for limited and specific purposes. Given that spreadsheets are becoming increasingly available it would be a shame if they were not used to maximum advantage.

From Model to Simulation

There are many 'real world' situations and problems which are suitable as modelling exercises for mathematics classrooms, particularly if a cross-curricular approach is adopted. The natural sciences and social sciences are rich sources. It should not be too difficult to devise a simple introduction to the nature of mathematical models and modelling processes, if cross-curricular references are used.

In many cases suitable situations could be modelled by constructing a mathematical equation (or a set of equations) as the basic model. These situations could then be simulated by transferring the basic model onto a spreadsheet. The resulting simulation would usually consist of predicted values in the form of a table or a graph, although the *Iteration* and *Macro* facilities available in spreadsheets such as Microsoft *Excel* have the potential to make simulations even more dynamic.

The easiest situations to model and simulate with a spreadsheet are, perhaps, those in which the basic model could be a simple difference equation. In many cases these equations are readily deduced and they are sometimes suggested by the problem itself. For example, the manner in which an investment grows with time under compound interest may be modelled by the equation:

$$P_{n+1} = P_n + (r/100)P_n \qquad \text{I}$$

where £P_n is the sum invested at the start of year n and r% is the annual rate of interest.

The growth of a population may also be easily modelled by a similar equation, if it is assumed that the change in the population in one year is proportional to the population size at the start of the year:

$$P_{n+1} = P_n + bP_n \qquad \text{II.}$$

Now, taking equation II as the basic model, a spreadsheet simulation may be constructed easily, using the cells of a spreadsheet and, if available, graphics facilities (Fig. 1, Fig. 2).

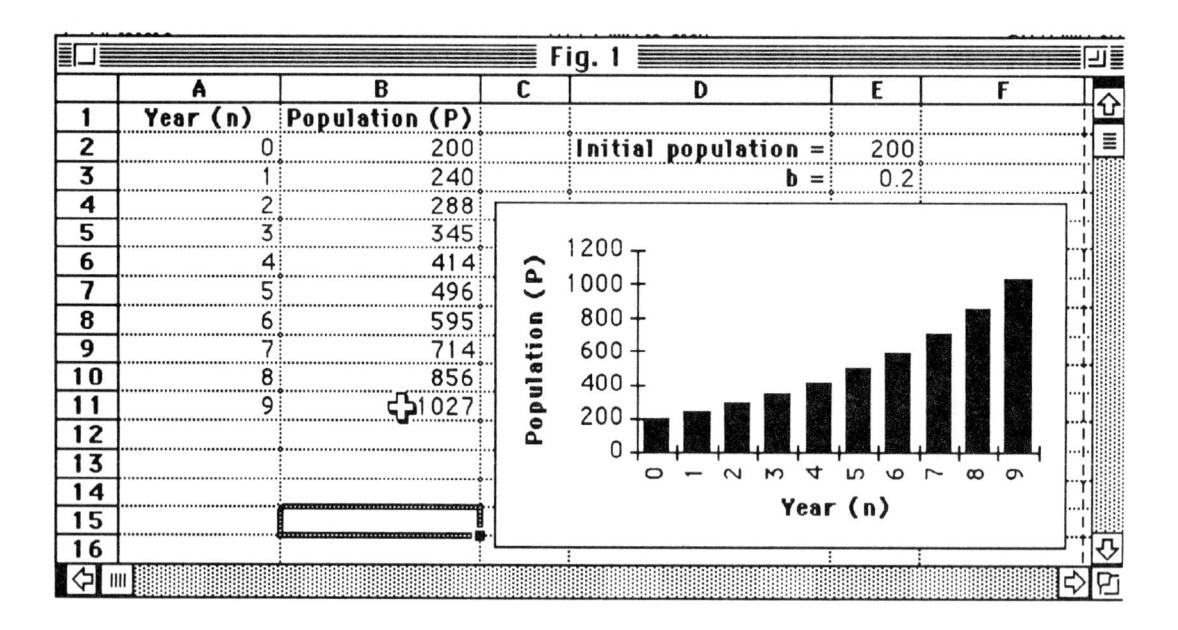

	A	B	C	D	E	F
1	Year (n)	Population (P)				
2	0	200		Initial population =	200	
3	1	240		b =	0.2	
4	2	288				
5	3	345				
6	4	414				
7	5	496				
8	6	595				
9	7	714				
10	8	856				
11	9	1027				

Figure 1

	A	B	C	D	E
1	Year (n)	Population (P)			
2	0	=$E$2		Initial population =	200
3	=A2+1	=INT(B2+$E$3*B2)		b =	0.2
4	=A3+1	=INT(B3+$E$3*B3)			
5	=A4+1	=INT(B4+$E$3*B4)			
6	=A5+1	=INT(B5+$E$3*B5)			
7	=A6+1	=INT(B6+$E$3*B6)			
8	=A7+1	=INT(B7+$E$3*B7)			
9	=A8+1	=INT(B8+$E$3*B8)			
10	=A9+1	=INT(B9+$E$3*B9)			
11	=A10+1	=INT(B10+$E$3*B10)			

Figure 2

In equation **II** 'b' is sometimes described as the *rate of change*. This is, perhaps, understandable since one refers to 'annual rate of interest' in equation **I**. It is, however, not a practice to be recommended since b is a 'constant of proportionality' not a *rate of change*. Such a careless description may promote learning difficulties when models based on continuous functions are constructed. At that stage it is extremely important that students understand what is meant by *rate of change*.

Rates of Change

Many real world situations may be modelled and simulated in a similar fashion to the population growth above. These include growth and decay problems related to radioactivity, charge on capacitors, drug concentration in the bloodstream, spread of epidemics, and cooling bodies (Armstrong and Bajpai, 1988). Many of these situations are first encountered in science classrooms where, perhaps unwittingly, they are usually modelled by continuous functions (despite the fact that they are all discrete physical phenomena). This is usually done because, by assuming continuity, situations can easily be modelled graphically. Unfortunately, if it is not realised that the continuous functions are being used as models of discrete events, students and teacher may be tempted to make some very strange predictions; such as suggesting that a cup of coffee never quite reaches room temperature or that a capacitor never completely discharges.

The second aim is to introduce the notion of *rate of change* and in particular the notion of *instantaneous rate of change*. Continuous graphs and tangents to these graphs are invaluable in achieving this aim. It is common for A level physics classes to introduce calculus notation when discussing *rate of change* and mathematics teachers should recognise this. For example, physics classes are really modelling mathematically when, in discussing radioactivity, they argue that "at any given time, the rate of change of nuclides in a radioactive sample is directly proportional to the number of nuclides remaining unchanged":

that is   rate of change $\propto N$

so   rate of change $= \lambda N$ **III**

This is usually translated directly into the following differential equation:

$$\frac{dN}{dt} = \lambda N \qquad \text{IV}$$

Of course, in physics classes, this is not often called a differential equation and it usually contains a negative sign, since it is assumed that λ (the radioactive decay constant) is a positive real number. Nevertheless, it is pleasing to see that, in physics classes, this differential equation does not simply 'come out of the blue' as it often does in mathematics classes.

A Simple Modelling Metaphor

Equation **IV** is not too difficult to construct using the notion of *rate of change*. However, more complex situations do not yield models quite so easily. Fortunately, many of the difficulties encountered in modelling more complex situations may be eased by using a suitable metaphor which might help students to construct their own models. This should be preferable to the teacher producing ready-made differential equations for students to solve. We must all have heard students ask "Where does this equation come from, what use is it and what does it mean?".

Consider the metaphor of a 'water supply' which consists of 'storage tanks', 'reservoirs', 'pipes', 'pumps', 'connectors' and 'control boxes'. If we assume that these 'water supply' components behave conventionally this metaphor should not prove to be counter-intuitive to learners. To illustrate how the metaphor might be used let us try to model radioactive decay.

At some time (say t seconds) assume that the number of unchanged nuclides in a sample of the radioactive substance is N. This number (N) may be represented pictorially by the height of water in a 'storage tank' labelled N. Using the analogy of water being pumped through a pipe from the storage tank into a reservoir we can simulate a decay. Assume that the rate at which water is pumped along the pipe depends partly on the level of water in the tank. In other words, the number of unchanged nuclides (N) controls the pump. We might imagine that the pump is also controlled by a 'numerical-control' (a little like an electronic calculator) which stores a constant (λ). A pictorial model may now be drawn in which 'connectors', which look something like wires, are drawn to indicate which items control the pump. Although the picture in Fig. 3 is drafted by a computer package, less sophisticated but equally effective pictorial models may be drawn quite easily, and quickly, using pencil and paper.

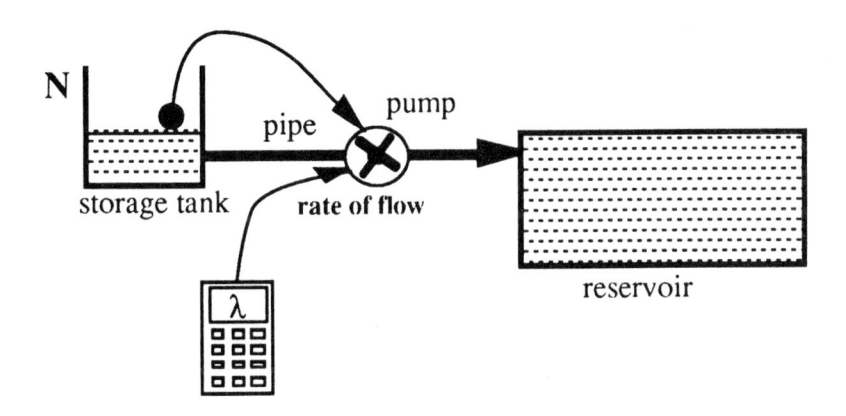

Figure 3

By considering which things control the rate of flow along the pipe simple modelling assumptions should emerge. These might be :

rate of flow $\propto$ N,   where the constant of proportionality is λ,
so   rate of flow = λN
or   rate of decay = λN
or   rate of change = λN.

For those students familiar with calculus notation this should lead quite readily to equation **IV** (i.e., $dN/dt = \lambda N$) and, for those familiar with the Euler computational method, to the finite-difference approximation

$$N_{n+1} = N_n + dt\,(\lambda N_n) \qquad \textbf{V}$$

Note that, when first introducing the Euler method, it may be difficult to justify the use of dt as the time increment but to do so may produce some valuable discussion concerning the differentials dN and dt (see Tall, 1985). Using dt certainly helps in more complex modelling and simulation (see later Fig. 6, Fig. 9 and Fig. 12).

If we wished to avoid numerical methods and differential equations altogether, however, the pictorial water supply metaphor could be presented in a different manner by imagining that the pump is switched on only once during each time interval. The length of time for which the pump is switched on and the rate at which it pumps water along the pipe depend partly on the level of water in the tank at the start of the interval and partly on the number (λ) stored in the 'numerical-control'. This analogy would enable the difference equation **V** to be constructed without specific reference to differential coefficients or differentials.

Another approach would be to use the notion of *rate of change* directly. For example, if the time interval was taken to be τ we might argue that "the number of unchanged nuclides at time $(t+\tau)$ is equal to the number of unchanged nuclides at time t plus the rate of change (or decay) multiplied by τ to produce the equation

$$N(t+\tau) = N(t) + (\text{rate of change}) \times \tau \qquad \textbf{VI}$$

Of course, the basic model described by equation **V** or by equation **VI** may be readily converted to a spreadsheet simulation as shown in Fig. 4 and Fig. 5.

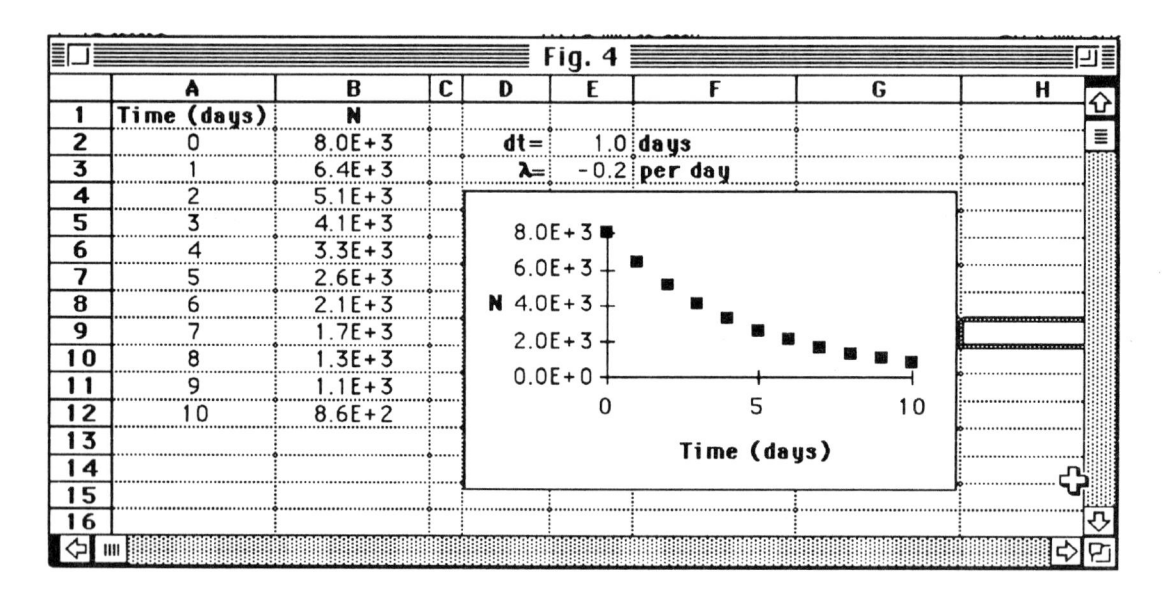

Figure 4

	A	B	C	D	E	F	G
1	Time (days)	N					
2	0	8000		dt=	1	days	
3	=A2+$E$2	=B2+$E$2*$E$3*B2		λ=	-0.2	per day	
4	=A3+$E$2	=B3+$E$2*$E$3*B3					
5	=A4+$E$2	=B4+$E$2*$E$3*B4					
6	=A5+$E$2	=B5+$E$2*$E$3*B5					
7	=A6+$E$2	=B6+$E$2*$E$3*B6					
8	=A7+$E$2	=B7+$E$2*$E$3*B7					
9	=A8+$E$2	=B8+$E$2*$E$3*B8					
10	=A9+$E$2	=B9+$E$2*$E$3*B9					
11	=A10+$E$2	=B10+$E$2*$E$3*B10					
12	=A11+$E$2	=B11+$E$2*$E$3*B11					
13							
14							
15							
16							

Figure 5

Extending the Metaphor

For simple growth and decay situations the water supply metaphor is helpful but not essential. In more complicated situations the metaphor has much greater potential as both a modelling tool and a learning aid. Consider, for instance, the spread of an infection through a population. At a given time suppose that I people are infectious, R people have recovered from illness and have become immune, S people are still susceptible to the infection (they may not have been infected yet, or they may have recovered from illness, but they have not become immune). How do the sizes of the separate groups in the population change? A pictorial water supply model might be constructed as in Fig. 6.

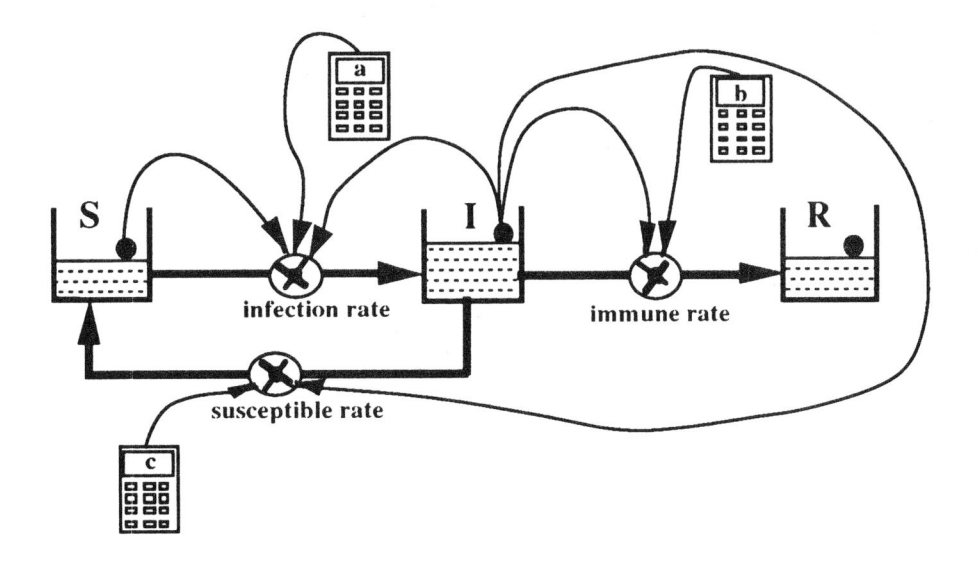

Figure 6

Now, prompted by the picture (Fig. 6), make the following modelling assumptions:

$$\text{infection rate} = aSI$$
$$\text{immune rate} = bI$$
$$\text{susceptible rate} = cI$$

So we have

rate of change of size of susceptible group = $cI - aSI$
rate of change of size of infected group = $aSI - bI - cI$
rate of change of size of immune group = bI

These lead to the basic modelling equations

$$S_{n+1} = S_n + dt\,(cI_n - aS_nI_n)$$
$$I_{n+1} = I_n + dt\,(aS_nI_n - bI_n - cI_n)$$
$$R_{n+1} = R_n + dt\,(bI_n)$$

and, hence, to a spreadsheet simulation (Fig. 7).

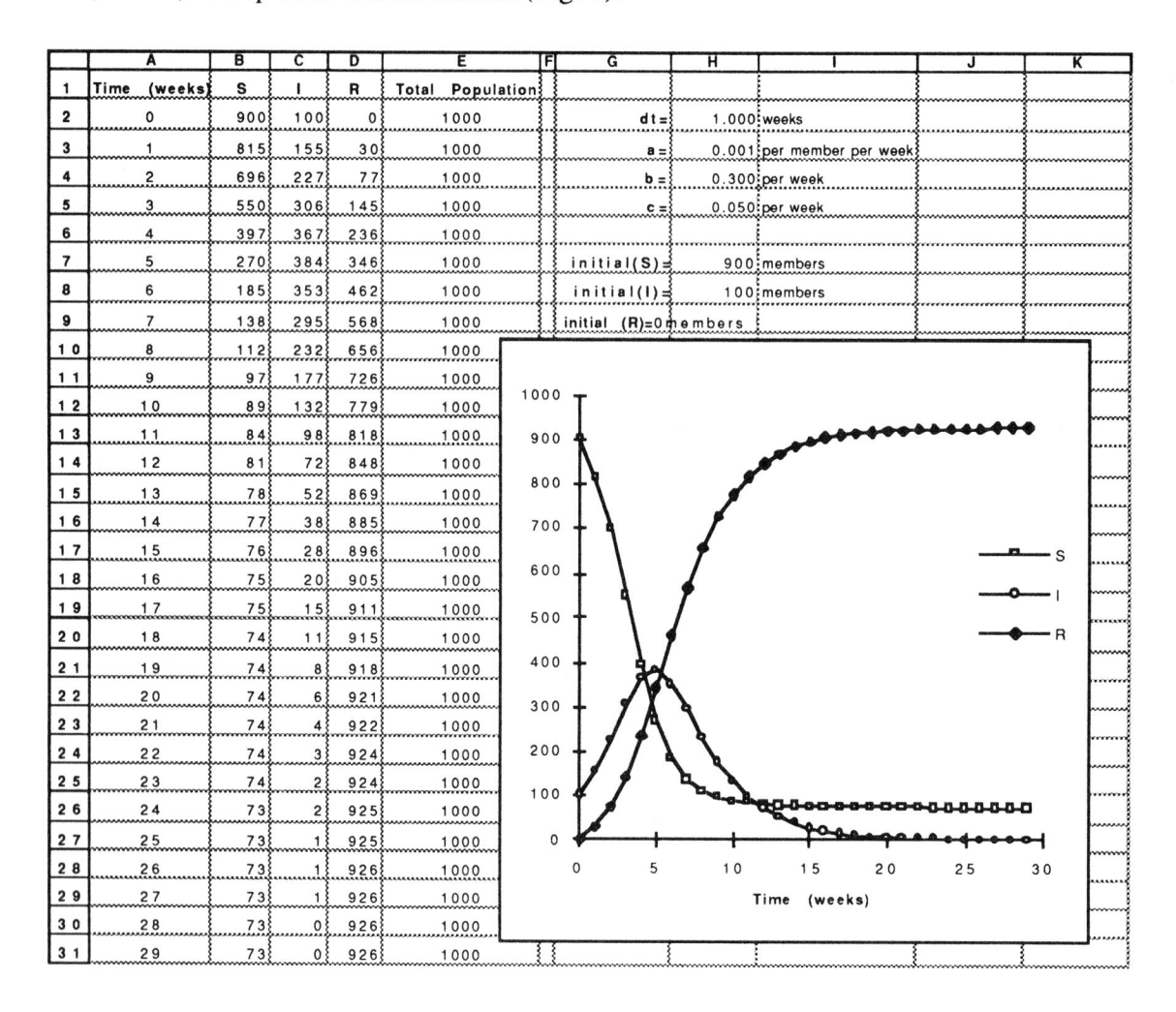

	A	B	C	D	E	F	G	H	I	J	K
1	Time (weeks)	S	I	R	Total Population						
2	0	900	100	0	1000		dt =	1.000	weeks		
3	1	815	155	30	1000		a =	0.001	per member per week		
4	2	696	227	77	1000		b =	0.300	per week		
5	3	550	306	145	1000		c =	0.050	per week		
6	4	397	367	236	1000						
7	5	270	384	346	1000		initial(S) =	900	members		
8	6	185	353	462	1000		initial(I) =	100	members		
9	7	138	295	568	1000		initial(R) =	0	members		
10	8	112	232	656	1000						
11	9	97	177	726	1000						
12	10	89	132	779	1000						
13	11	84	98	818	1000						
14	12	81	72	848	1000						
15	13	78	52	869	1000						
16	14	77	38	885	1000						
17	15	76	28	896	1000						
18	16	75	20	905	1000						
19	17	75	15	911	1000						
20	18	74	11	915	1000						
21	19	74	8	918	1000						
22	20	74	6	921	1000						
23	21	74	4	922	1000						
24	22	74	3	924	1000						
25	23	74	2	924	1000						
26	24	73	2	925	1000						
27	25	73	1	925	1000						
28	26	73	1	926	1000						
29	27	73	1	926	1000						
30	28	73	0	926	1000						
31	29	73	0	926	1000						

Figure 7

The Advantages of a Pictorial Modelling Metaphor: A Summary

Although the pictorial metaphor should match the intuition of learners (particularly if it is based on a water supply which behaves conventionally) it is likely that students in a secondary school mathematics classroom would need some time to assimilate its concepts. This time would be well spent if the students were allowed to design their own systems, to predict how they would behave and to discuss this behaviour with other students and with the teacher. These discussions might help students to understand what is meant by *rate of change* and how this is related to the *differential coefficient*.

Perhaps the most important advantage of the metaphor as a learning aid is that it helps students to construct their own models. Where these models involve differential coefficients the metaphor can assist, and encourage, students to construct differential equations so that they do not have to rely on equations presented by the teacher, or by a text book (i.e. 'out of the blue'). By building their own equations students should come to understand what the differential equations represent and, indeed, what equations and solutions might mean.

One of the essential skills of mathematical modelling is to select variables and to state assumptions about relationships between them. The metaphor is invaluable in encouraging students to do this in a structured manner. In the process of drawing storage tanks, reservoirs, pipes, pumps and connectors and labelling these, the student is, in many ways, paralleling good, structured programming practice (e.g. by selecting, declaring and relating variables). Indeed, the pictorial metaphor acts rather like a structured program since it enables the modeller and others to see how the model is constructed and to isolate any elements which may be faulty or which might be modified to advantage. In addition, the metaphor facilitates the process of adding or eliminating variables (and tightening or relaxing assumptions) as the cyclic process of modelling progresses. Without a metaphor this may become a somewhat haphazard process under which structure rapidly disappears. If a student is able to construct simple pictorial models, such as that in Fig. 3, the metaphor opens the way for more complex situations to be modelled. The simple pictures act as building blocks in this process. For instance, Fig. 6 is constructed from such simple building blocks so that the equivalent of three interrelated differential equations are produced. This may prove to be a rather daunting task if tackled without the aid of a metaphor.

By encouraging discussion of *rate of change*, the metaphor should help those students who are familiar with the calculus not only to distinguish, but also to relate, differential equations and difference equations. This should provide an extremely useful introduction to the applications of, and need for, numerical methods such as Euler. Spreadsheets (e.g. Fig. 7) have a natural role to play, as a learning aid, in any school mathematics curriculum which aims to reflect the importance of numerical methods and computers. The simulations which can be developed by transferring modelling equations onto a spreadsheet should make such a curriculum a feasible proposition.

Those students who are not familiar with calculus may also be provided with opportunities to experience modelling and simulation, since the metaphor would allow them to use the notion of *rate of change* to construct simple finite-difference approximations without resorting to the notation of differential coefficients and differentials. This would also provide a different and more applicable introduction to iterative processes than is often the case in mathematics classrooms.

Cautionary Note

In order to construct the simulation illustrated in Fig. 7 a student would need to develop important skills and techniques of modelling. An inexperienced modeller could well choose initial starting values and parameters which would produce some very strange results (e.g. the total population may appear to decrease although no deaths are predicted). These results may alarm and panic the beginner but, with practice, a modeller will learn to look out for strangely behaving simulations and to consider if the predictions are acceptable or if the underlying model needs to be modified. The advantage of using a spreadsheet to produce simulations is that its speed and size should help the tyro modeller to change variables, constants, or the model itself, in order to eliminate unacceptable predictions. At first this might be done by by trial and error and, as experience in modelling increases, by foresight and analysis.

One essential technique of successful modelling is to compare modelling predictions with observational results. Consider, for example, a simulation of the decay of charge on a capacitor. It should not be a very difficult task, particularly for students of physics and mathematics, to build a pictorial metaphor which would lead to a very useful simulation of damping in electric circuits (Fig. 8). In addition, through cross-curricular cooperation, it should be possible for these students to test some of their predictions in a science laboratory.

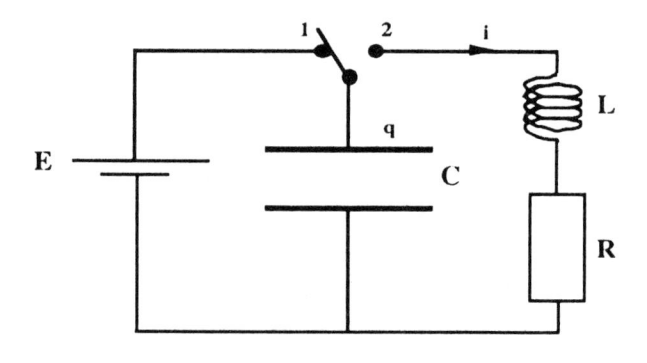

Figure 8

Suppose the switch was in position 1 for a sufficiently long time to charge the capacitor fully. If the switch was then moved to position 2 current would flow in the right-hand circuit. Applying Kirchhoff's Laws we have:

$$L\frac{di}{dt} + iR - \frac{q}{C} = 0$$

so

$$\frac{di}{dt} = \frac{q}{CL} - \frac{iR}{L}$$

and

$$\frac{dq}{dt} = i$$

The pictorial metaphor then becomes (Fig. 9):

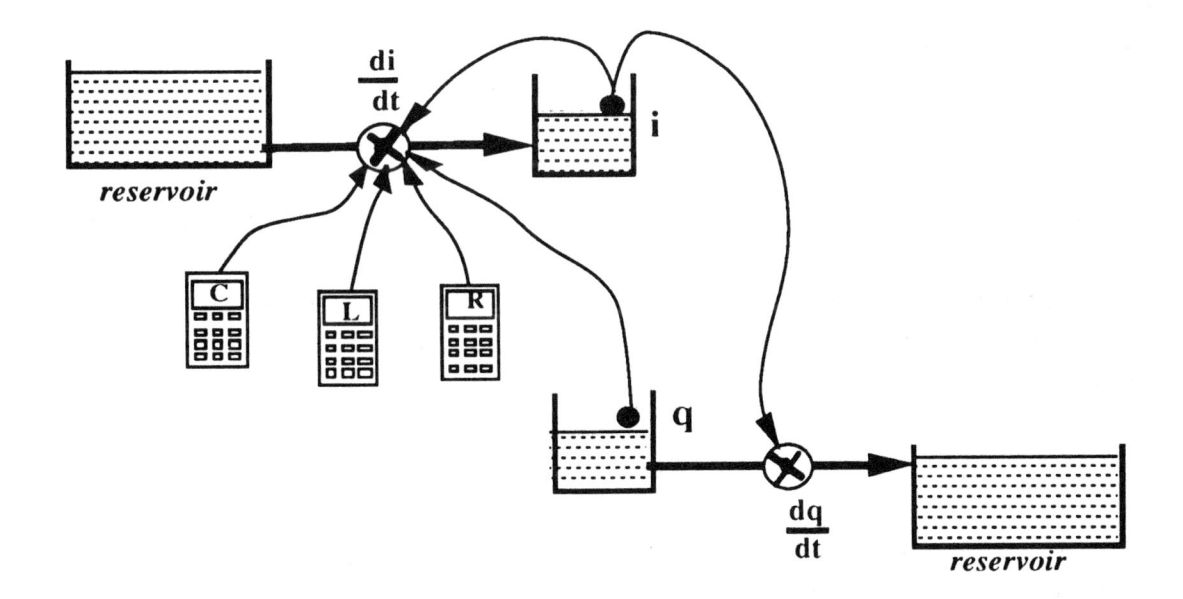

Figure 9

From the picture the following basic modelling equations may be constructed:

$$i_{n+1} = i_n + dt \, (q_n/(CL) - i_n R/L)$$

$$q_{n+1} = q_n - dt \, (i_n).$$

Now, by choosing typical values for the components of the circuit (i.e. for R, C, L and E), initial values for the charge and the current and a value for dt the spreadsheet simulation shown in Fig. 10 might be constructed.

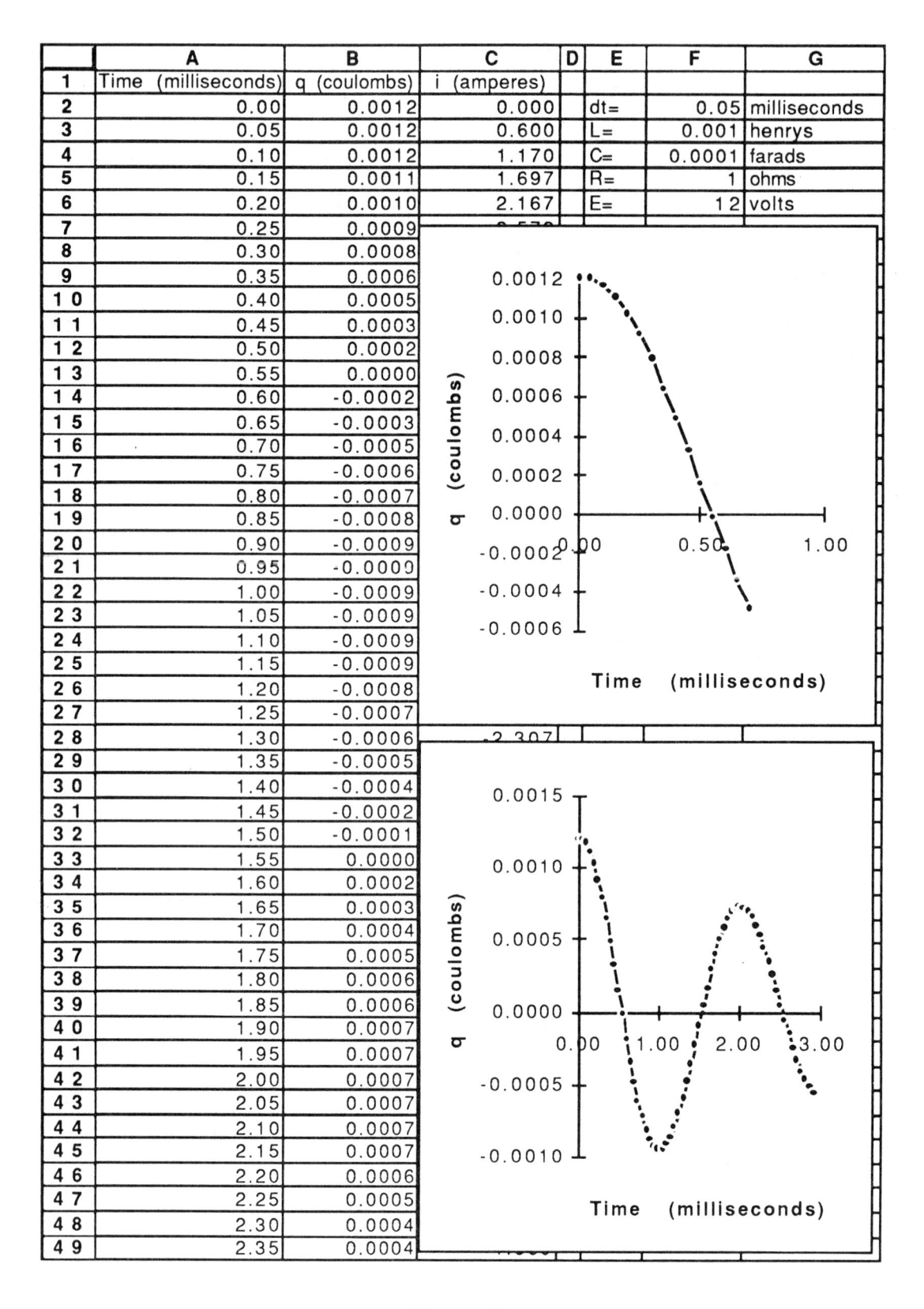

	A	B	C	D	E	F	G
1	Time (milliseconds)	q (coulombs)	i (amperes)				
2	0.00	0.0012	0.000		dt=	0.05	milliseconds
3	0.05	0.0012	0.600		L=	0.001	henrys
4	0.10	0.0012	1.170		C=	0.0001	farads
5	0.15	0.0011	1.697		R=	1	ohms
6	0.20	0.0010	2.167		E=	12	volts
7	0.25	0.0009					
8	0.30	0.0008					
9	0.35	0.0006					
10	0.40	0.0005					
11	0.45	0.0003					
12	0.50	0.0002					
13	0.55	0.0000					
14	0.60	-0.0002					
15	0.65	-0.0003					
16	0.70	-0.0005					
17	0.75	-0.0006					
18	0.80	-0.0007					
19	0.85	-0.0008					
20	0.90	-0.0009					
21	0.95	-0.0009					
22	1.00	-0.0009					
23	1.05	-0.0009					
24	1.10	-0.0009					
25	1.15	-0.0009					
26	1.20	-0.0008					
27	1.25	-0.0007					
28	1.30	-0.0006					
29	1.35	-0.0005					
30	1.40	-0.0004					
31	1.45	-0.0002					
32	1.50	-0.0001					
33	1.55	0.0000					
34	1.60	0.0002					
35	1.65	0.0003					
36	1.70	0.0004					
37	1.75	0.0005					
38	1.80	0.0006					
39	1.85	0.0006					
40	1.90	0.0007					
41	1.95	0.0007					
42	2.00	0.0007					
43	2.05	0.0007					
44	2.10	0.0007					
45	2.15	0.0007					
46	2.20	0.0006					
47	2.25	0.0005					
48	2.30	0.0004					
49	2.35	0.0004					

Figure 10

The predictions of the simulation in Fig. 10 appear to match laboratory observations fairly well but observe what has happened in Fig. 11 where the value of the resistor has been changed.

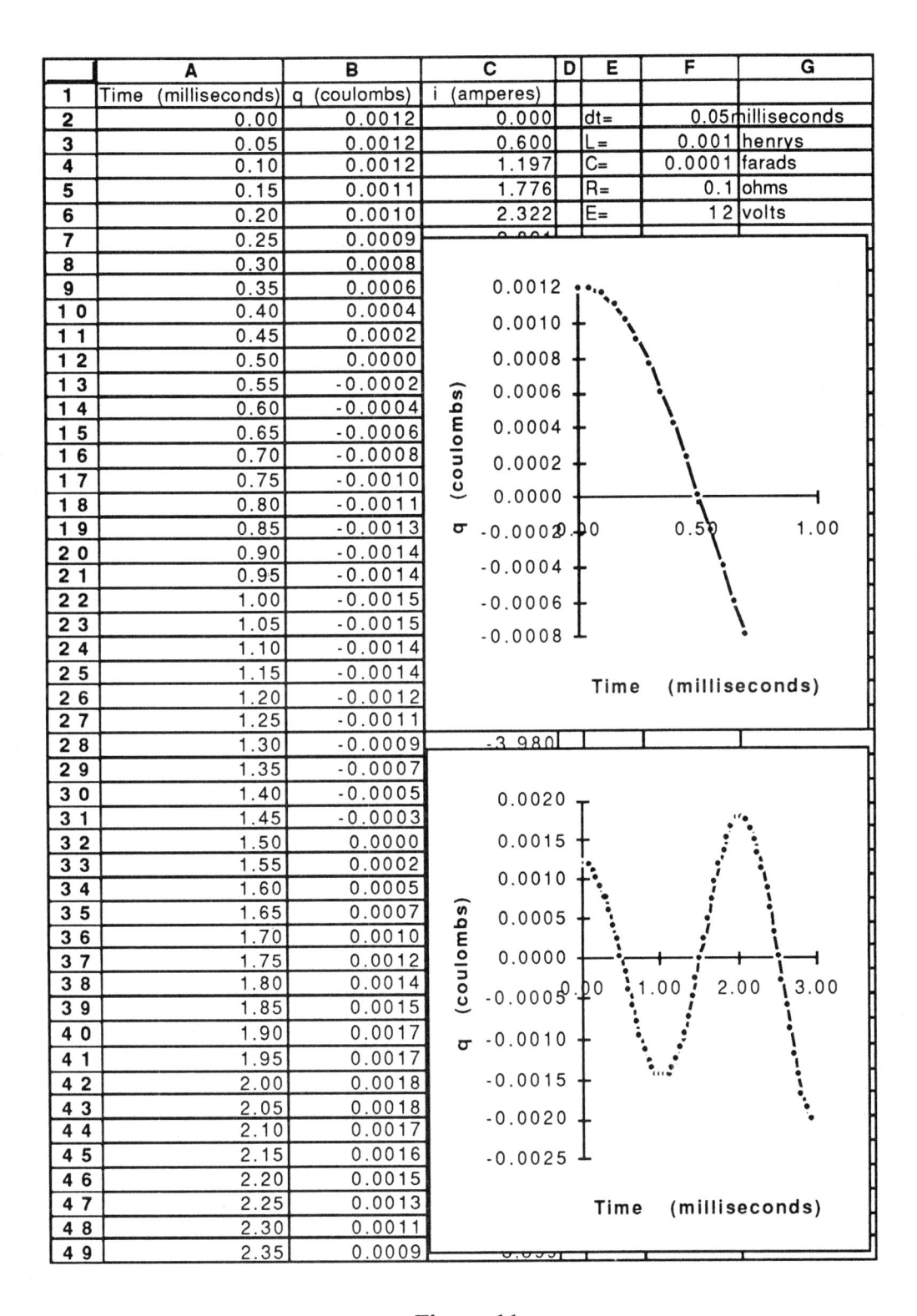

	A	B	C	D	E	F	G
1	Time (milliseconds)	q (coulombs)	i (amperes)				
2	0.00	0.0012	0.000		dt=	0.05	milliseconds
3	0.05	0.0012	0.600		L=	0.001	henrys
4	0.10	0.0012	1.197		C=	0.0001	farads
5	0.15	0.0011	1.776		R=	0.1	ohms
6	0.20	0.0010	2.322		E=	12	volts
7	0.25	0.0009					
8	0.30	0.0008					
9	0.35	0.0006					
10	0.40	0.0004					
11	0.45	0.0002					
12	0.50	0.0000					
13	0.55	-0.0002					
14	0.60	-0.0004					
15	0.65	-0.0006					
16	0.70	-0.0008					
17	0.75	-0.0010					
18	0.80	-0.0011					
19	0.85	-0.0013					
20	0.90	-0.0014					
21	0.95	-0.0014					
22	1.00	-0.0015					
23	1.05	-0.0015					
24	1.10	-0.0014					
25	1.15	-0.0014					
26	1.20	-0.0012					
27	1.25	-0.0011					
28	1.30	-0.0009	-3.980				
29	1.35	-0.0007					
30	1.40	-0.0005					
31	1.45	-0.0003					
32	1.50	0.0000					
33	1.55	0.0002					
34	1.60	0.0005					
35	1.65	0.0007					
36	1.70	0.0010					
37	1.75	0.0012					
38	1.80	0.0014					
39	1.85	0.0015					
40	1.90	0.0017					
41	1.95	0.0017					
42	2.00	0.0018					
43	2.05	0.0018					
44	2.10	0.0017					
45	2.15	0.0016					
46	2.20	0.0015					
47	2.25	0.0013					
48	2.30	0.0011					
49	2.35	0.0009					

Figure 11

The erroneous prediction in Fig. 11 that the amplitude of the charge oscillation would increase with time, rather than decay, is a result of the computational method used (which is really the Euler Method). This problem can be overcome by using a smaller time increment or, better still, by using a better computational method such as 4th order Runge-Kutta.

Looking Ahead

Under current GCE A level requirements, it is unlikely that students would be familiar with improved computational methods such as Runge-Kutta. However, with an eye to the future development of sixth form mathematics (and certainly to first year undergraduate mathematics courses) the reader might care to consider the learning advantages to be gained by allowing students to construct a spreadsheet simulation which uses the computational model known as the Improved (or Modified) Euler Method. Such a constructive approach may enhance student learning of the computational method itself. In any event, spreadsheet simulation and modelling may make the student aware of the need for numerical methods and should illustrate their usefulness. This potential is illustrated in the following model and simulation, which is based on the well-known situation of rabbits (prey) and foxes (predators) co-existing on an island. The rabbits have an unlimited supply of food but the foxes' staple diet consists of rabbits (Fig. 12).

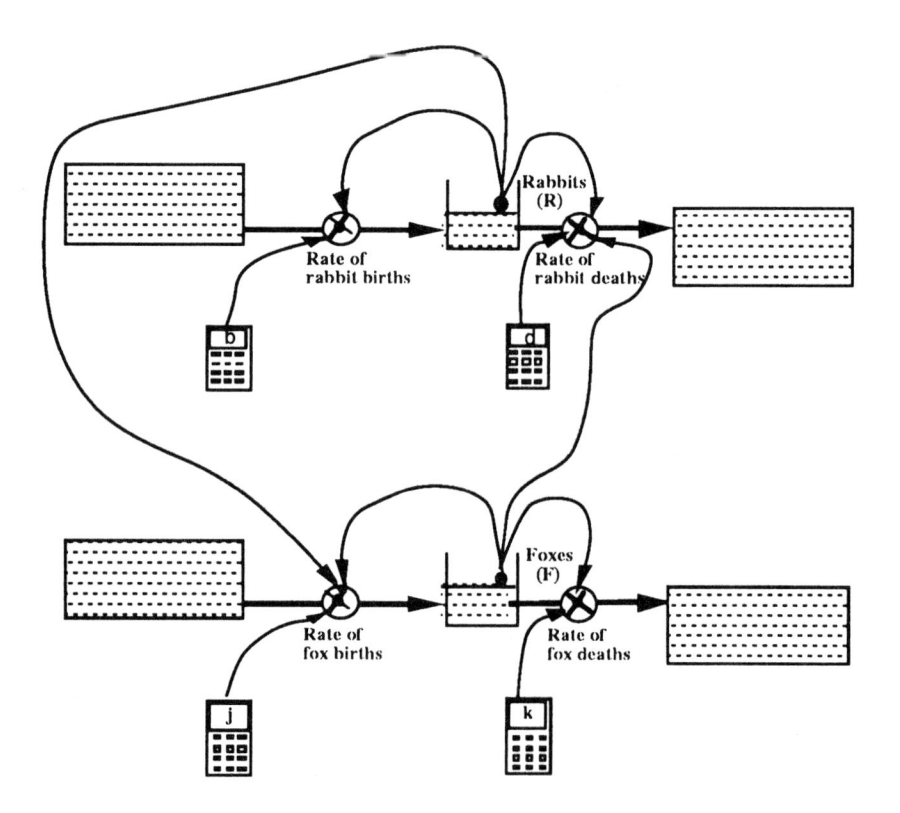

Figure 12

The pictorial metaphor suggests that the rate of rabbit births depends on the number of rabbits (R) and some constant of proportionality (b), the rate of rabbit deaths depends on the number of rabbits (R), the number of foxes (F) and some constant of proportionality (d), the rate of fox births depends on F, R and some constant of proportionality (j) while the rate of fox deaths depends on F and some constant of proportionality (k). So we might assume that:

$$\text{rate of rabbit births} = bR$$
$$\text{rate of rabbit deaths} = dRF$$
$$\text{rate of fox births} = jFR$$
$$\text{rate of fox deaths} = kF$$

so
$$\text{rate of change of rabbits} = bR - dRF$$
$$\text{rate of change of foxes} = jFR - kF$$

and
$$R_{n+1} = R_n + dt\,(bR_n - dR_nF_n)$$
$$F_{n+1} = F_n + dt\,(jF_nR_n - kF_n).$$

A spreadsheet simulation (Fig. 13) based on these equations agrees fairly well with the predictions which would be obtained if a simulation based on differential equations were used. However, we need to note that the graph in Fig. 13 shows an open trajectory, whereas a differential equations model predicts a closed trajectory.

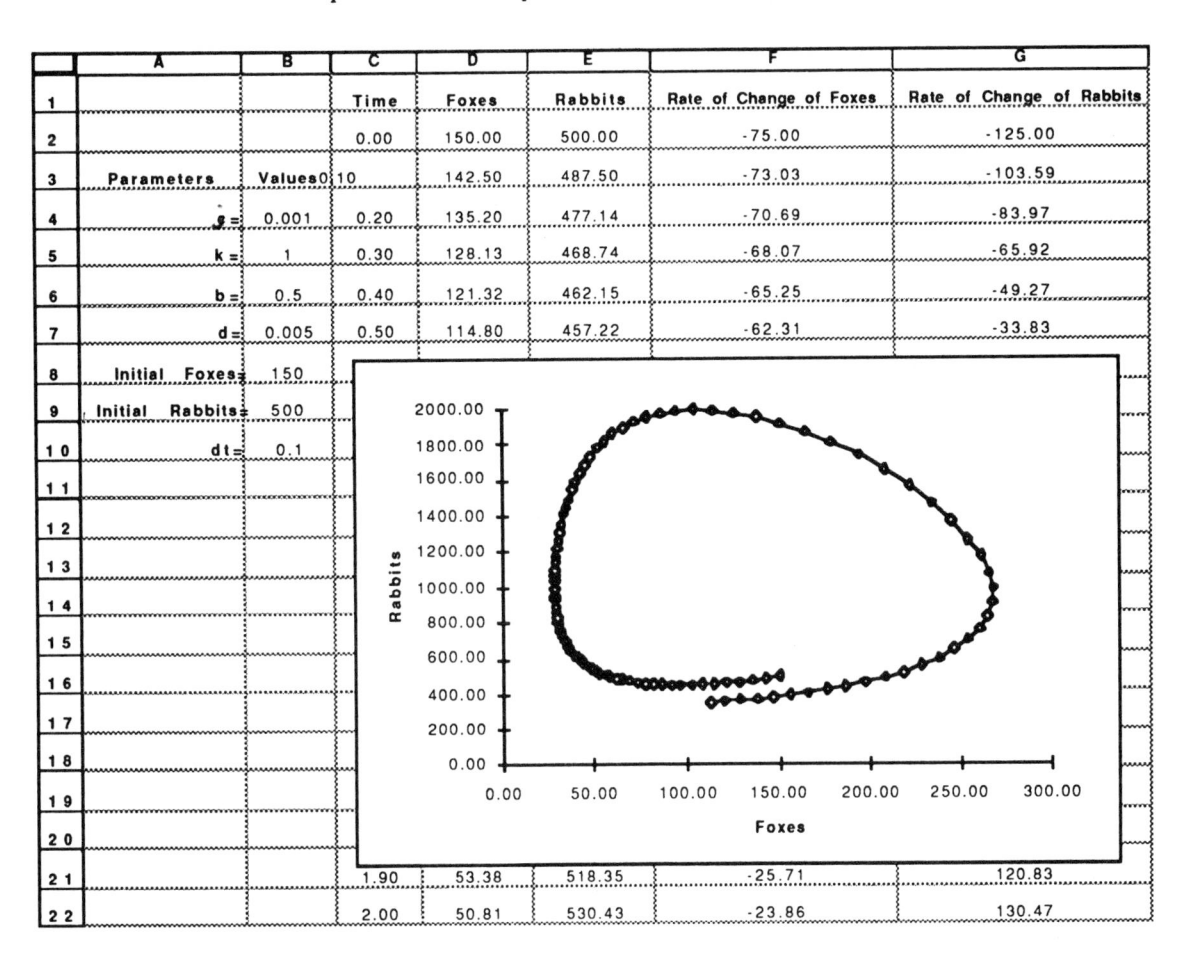

	A	B	C	D	E	F	G
1			Time	Foxes	Rabbits	Rate of Change of Foxes	Rate of Change of Rabbits
2			0.00	150.00	500.00	-75.00	-125.00
3	Parameters	Values	0.10	142.50	487.50	-73.03	-103.59
4	j =	0.001	0.20	135.20	477.14	-70.69	-83.97
5	k =	1	0.30	128.13	468.74	-68.07	-65.92
6	b =	0.5	0.40	121.32	462.15	-65.25	-49.27
7	d =	0.005	0.50	114.80	457.22	-62.31	-33.83
8	Initial Foxes=	150					
9	Initial Rabbits=	500					
10	dt =	0.1					
21			1.90	53.38	518.35	-25.71	120.83
22			2.00	50.81	530.43	-23.86	130.47

Figure 13

Fig. 14 illustrates how the simulation could be constructed. The formulae in cells are shown and certain cells are referred to by *names* rather than by their column and row coordinates.

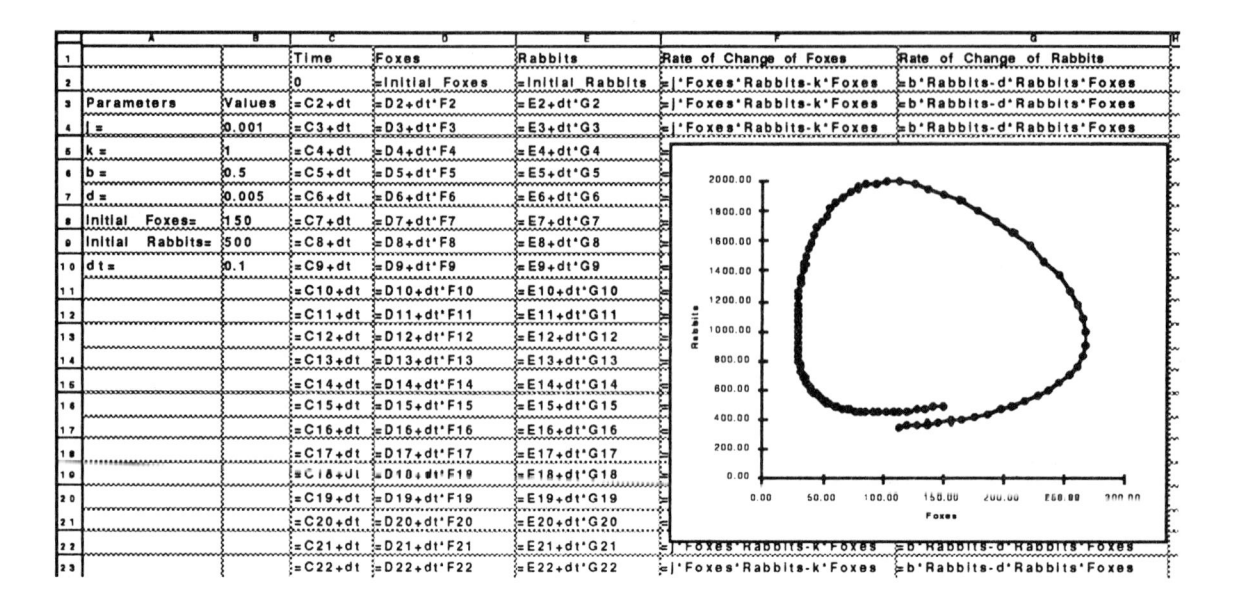

	A	B	C	D	E	F	G
1			Time	Foxes	Rabbits	Rate of Change of Foxes	Rate of Change of Rabbits
2			0	=Initial_Foxes	=Initial_Rabbits	=l*Foxes*Rabbits-k*Foxes	=b*Rabbits-d*Rabbits*Foxes
3	Parameters	Values	=C2+dt	=D2+dt*F2	=E2+dt*G2	=l*Foxes*Rabbits-k*Foxes	=b*Rabbits-d*Rabbits*Foxes
4	l =	0.001	=C3+dt	=D3+dt*F3	=E3+dt*G3	=l*Foxes*Rabbits-k*Foxes	=b*Rabbits-d*Rabbits*Foxes
5	k =	1	=C4+dt	=D4+dt*F4	=E4+dt*G4		
6	b =	0.5	=C5+dt	=D5+dt*F5	=E5+dt*G5		
7	d =	0.005	=C6+dt	=D6+dt*F6	=E6+dt*G6		
8	Initial_Foxes=	150	=C7+dt	=D7+dt*F7	=E7+dt*G7		
9	Initial_Rabbits=	500	=C8+dt	=D8+dt*F8	=E8+dt*G8		
10	dt =	0.1	=C9+dt	=D9+dt*F9	=E9+dt*G9		
11			=C10+dt	=D10+dt*F10	=E10+dt*G10		
12			=C11+dt	=D11+dt*F11	=E11+dt*G11		
13			=C12+dt	=D12+dt*F12	=E12+dt*G12		
14			=C13+dt	=D13+dt*F13	=E13+dt*G13		
15			=C14+dt	=D14+dt*F14	=E14+dt*G14		
16			=C15+dt	=D15+dt*F15	=E15+dt*G15		
17			=C16+dt	=D16+dt*F16	=E16+dt*G16		
18			=C17+dt	=D17+dt*F17	=E17+dt*G17		
19			=C18+dt	=D18+dt*F18	=E18+dt*G18		
20			=C19+dt	=D19+dt*F19	=E19+dt*G19		
21			=C20+dt	=D20+dt*F20	=E20+dt*G20		
22			=C21+dt	=D21+dt*F21	=E21+dt*G21	=l*Foxes*Rabbits-k*Foxes	=b*Rabbits-d*Rabbits*Foxes
23			=C22+dt	=D22+dt*F22	=E22+dt*G22	=l*Foxes*Rabbits-k*Foxes	=b*Rabbits-d*Rabbits*Foxes

Figure 14

The simulation may be modified so that it agrees more closely with one based on differential equations by using the Improved (or Modified) Euler Method (see Fig. 15 and Fig. 16). Notice the closed trajectory.

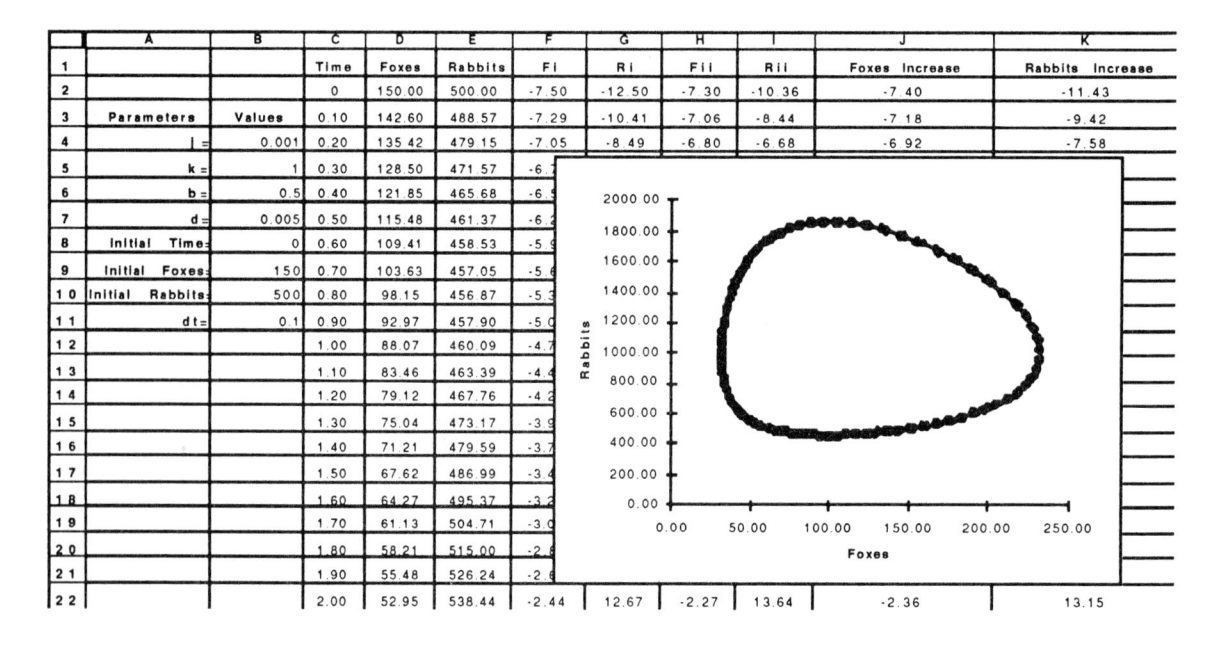

	A	B	C	D	E	F	G	H	I	J	K
1			Time	Foxes	Rabbits	Fi	Ri	Fii	Rii	Foxes Increase	Rabbits Increase
2			0	150.00	500.00	-7.50	-12.50	-7.30	-10.36	-7.40	-11.43
3	Parameters	Values	0.10	142.60	488.57	-7.29	-10.41	-7.06	-8.44	-7.18	-9.42
4	l =	0.001	0.20	135.42	479.15	-7.05	-8.49	-6.80	-6.68	-6.92	-7.58
5	k =	1	0.30	128.50	471.57	-6.					
6	b =	0.5	0.40	121.85	465.68	-6.					
7	d =	0.005	0.50	115.48	461.37	-6.					
8	Initial Time=	0	0.60	109.41	458.53	-5.					
9	Initial Foxes=	150	0.70	103.63	457.05	-5.					
10	Initial Rabbits=	500	0.80	98.15	456.87	-5.					
11	dt =	0.1	0.90	92.97	457.90	-5.					
12			1.00	88.07	460.09	-4.					
13			1.10	83.46	463.39	-4.					
14			1.20	79.12	467.76	-4.					
15			1.30	75.04	473.17	-3.					
16			1.40	71.21	479.59	-3.					
17			1.50	67.62	486.99	-3.					
18			1.60	64.27	495.37	-3.					
19			1.70	61.13	504.71	-3.					
20			1.80	58.21	515.00	-2.					
21			1.90	55.48	526.24	-2.					
22			2.00	52.95	538.44	-2.44	12.67	-2.27	13.64	-2.36	13.15

Figure 15

Conclusion

It is hoped that the examples described in this chapter demonstrate the exciting potential that spreadsheets have for generating dynamic modelling in the mathematics classroom and for introducing new mathematical techniques and concepts into the curriculum of the future. Nevertheless, it is realised that facility with spreadsheets and with modelling techniques does not develop without practice and the expenditure of time. As is the case with many innovations in teaching and learning, both teachers and students may be reluctant to devote the necessary time and effort to this development but they should find that, in the long run, this would be extremely worthwhile. A changing school mathematics curriculum should reflect changes in the development and use of technology in the world at large and in the nature of mathematics itself. Spreadsheets are already helping to effect curriculum change at all levels of the secondary school. It is suggested here that dynamic modelling and simulation may complement and enhance the growing use of spreadsheets in the mathematics classroom and in other subject areas. The examples above are necessarily selective but models from a wide variety of curriculum interests lend themselves to spreadsheet simulations. These may range from the very simple to the complex so they should be available to a wide variety of ages and abilities (see for example, Armstrong and Bajpai, 1988; Edwards and Hamson, 1989; Hassell, 1991; Huntley and James, 1990; and Ogborn, 1987).

References

Armstrong, P.K. and Bajpai, A.C. (1988). Modelling in GCSE Mathematics. *Teaching Mathematics And Its Applications,* Vol. 7, No. 3, 121-131.

Hassell, D. (1991). *Getting to Grips with EXCEL.* Institute of Education, University of London: Computer Based Modelling across the Curriculum Project.

Huntley, I.D. and James, D.J.G. (1990). *Mathematical Modelling: A Source Book of Case Studies.* Oxford: OUP.

Edwards, D. and Hamson, M. (1989). *Guide to Mathematical Modelling.* London: Macmillan Education.

Ogborn, J. (1987). *Dynamic Modelling System.* York: Longman Microsoftware.

Richmonds, R., Peterson, S. and Vescuso, P. (1987). *An Academic User's Guide to STELLA.* New Hampshire, USA: High Performance Systems Inc.

Tall, D. (1985). Tangents and the Leibniz Notation. *Mathematics Teaching,* 113, December 1985, 48-51.

Paterson, A. (1991). *SMP Further Mathematics Series: Differential Equations and Numerical Analysis.* Cambridge: CUP.

Index of Mathematical Topics

Note: The symbol (w) denotes a worksheet.

accuracy 127
Annual Percentage Rate (APR) 31
arithmetic - domestic 30-3
Arithmetic Progression (AP) 17, 39, 83(w), 86(w)

base arithmetic 34-5
binary 35
binomial expansion 12, 52
binomial distribution 59

Carroll diagram 70(w)
chart (see graph)
Central Limit Theorem 12
cobweb diagram 51
coin tossing simulation 59, 110(w)
complex number 104(w)
compound interest 33
correlation 55, 70(w), 76(w), 79(w), 81(w)
cosine 54, 103(w), 110(w)
covariance 55
cube numbers 39
cumulative frequency 56, 101(w)

Data Analysis - see Statistics
decimal expansion 34, 89-90(w)
determinant 12, 97(w), 103(w)
dice rolling simulation 59
differences 38-9, 84(w), 104(w)
difference equation (see sequence)
differential equation 147-8
domestic arithmetic 30-3

e (constant) 33, 53
electric circuit 144-7
equations - quadratic 12, 25, 45
 - simultaneous 41-2, 115
 - solution of (see also iteration and other pages throughout)
Euclid's algorithm 37
Euler method 147-8

False Position method 121-3
Fibonacci sequence 17, 23, 39, 84-5(w)
finite difference - see difference
frequency distribution 55, 101(w)

Geometric Progression (GP) 17, 18, 27, 39, 83(w), 87(w)
geometric transformation 40-4, 93-6(w)
geometry 40-4, 46
goal seeking 124-7
Golden Ratio 39
graph 13, 26, 86-88(w) (and throughout)
growth and decay 137-142

Highest Common Factor (HCF) 37
histogram 100(w)

interest 31-3, 103(w), 110(w), 124-6
Interval Halving method 49
iteration 25, 49, 103(w), 111-133 (and throughout)
Iteration method 51, 111-4

Jacobi method 115

limit 33, 52-4
line - straight 46
Lowest Common Multiple (LCM) 37

Magic Square etc. 91-2(w)
matrix 40-3, 93-8(w), 103(w)
maxima and minima 110(w) (see also optimisation)
mean 55, 70(w), 73(w), 78(w), 99(w)
median 70-3(w), 78(w), 100-1(w)
mileage recording 30
mode 70(w), 78(w)
modelling 135-51
mortgage 32
moving average 30

natural numbers 84(w)
Newton-Raphson method 50, 117
normal distribution 60
number patterns 38-9, 64-8(w)
number properties 34-7
numerical differentiation 104(w)
numerical integration 47-8
numerical methods 47-51, 104(w), 111-133

optimisation 105-6(w), 110(w), 127-33

Pascal's Triangle nos 39, 67-8
percentile 56
population growth 136-7, 148-50
prime factors 36

quadratic equation 12, 25, 45
quartile 100(w)

random numbers 59, 103(w), 110(w)
random variable 59-60
range 70(w), 73(w), 78(w)
rate of change 138-144
recurrence relation (see sequence)
recurring decimal 34-5
Retail Price Index (RPI) 30
Runge-Kutta 147-8

scatter diagram 76(w), 102(w)
sequence 25, 38-9, 41-2, 83-8(w), 97-8(w), 115
series 52-4
significance test 60
simulation 59, 104(w), 110(w), 135-151
sine 54, 103(w), 110(w)
Simpson's rule 20, 47-8
simultaneous equations 12, 41-2, 97-8(w), 115
skew lines 44
smoothing 30
solution of equations (see equations, simultaneous equations, iteration)
square numbers 39
standard derivation 55, 99(w), 101(w)
Statistics 55-60, 69-81(w), 99(w)

tangent 103(w)
time series 30
transformation 40-4, 93-6(w)
Triangle numbers 39, 84(w), 104(w)
trigonometric table 103(w), 110(w)

variance 55 (see also standard deviation)

Index of Spreadsheet Terms

Note: The symbol (w) denotes a worksheet.

active cell 4

calculation iteration 116
cell 1
    - names 9, 36, 77(w), 150
    - protection 17, 34
chart 5, 19, 26, 86-8(w),
    107-10(w)
circular referencing 17, 116
conditional 20, 24
copying 17, 83(w)
copy down 17
copy right 17
customisation 2, 3

enter box 4
Eureka! 21
Excel 2, 21

FALSE 123
fill down 6, 8, 9, 17, 111-6
filling 6
fill right 6, 17
formula 4, 6, 16
formula bar 4
function macro 20
function plotting 24, 46
functions 18

Goal Seek 124-7
graph - see chart
Grasshopper 2, 21
grid 2

highlighting 4

IF 20, 27, 45, 47, 49, 115,
    120-123
iteration 116

Logistix 21
loop 23
Lotus 1-2-3 21

macro 20, 25, 30, 46, 48, 50-1,
    58-60, 100
MS/DOS 21

naming cells 9, 36, 77(w), 150

Oriel 23

pane 32, 37
pasting 17, 83(w)
Pipedream 21
plotters - function 24, 46
printing 84(w)
programming 14, 20, 22-5
    (see also macro)
protection 17, 34
PSS 2

Quattro 21
Quest 23
Quickcalc 21

reference box 4
referencing 4, 16
    - absolute 8, 18, 25, 83(w)
    - circular 17, 116
    - relative 6-8, 25
relational operator 123
    (also see IF)
repetition - see iteration
replication (see copying
    and filling)
sheet - (see worksheet
    and spreadsheet)
Solver 127-133
sorting 78-80(w), 82(w)
Spread 2, 21
spreadsheet 2
Supercalc 21

TRUE 123

Windows 21
workbook 33
Works 21
workspace 33
worksheet 2, 33

.XLC 29
.XLM 30
.XLS 29
.XLW 29

Index of Worksheets

Worksheet	Title	Software needed	Pages
A	Number Patterns (not using a computer)	no	64
B	Number Patterns (using a computer)	no	65
C	Number Patterns	no	66
D	Number Patterns (Pascal's Triangle)	no	67
E	Number Patterns (extension)	no	68
F	Statistics: Reaction Time Database	optional	69-73
G	Statistics: Reaction Time Further Analysis	yes	74-82
H	Sequences	no	83-85
I	Further Work with Sequences	no	86-88
J	Decimal Expansions	yes	89-90
K	Mystic Square	no	91
L	Magic Square	no	92
M	Matrices and Geometrical Transformations	yes	93-96
N	Matrices and Simultaneous Equations	yes	97-98
O	Data Analysis: Part 1	optional	99
P	Data Analysis: Part 2	yes	100-102
Q	Miscellaneous Problems: Set 1	no	103
R	Miscellaneous Problems: Set 2	no	104
S	Optimisation Problems	no	105-106
T	Excel Charts: Set 1	no	107-109
U	Excel Charts: Set 2	no	110